THE COMPLETE BOOK OF DEVILS AND DEMONS

Other books by Leonard R.N. Ashley
published by Robson Books

The Complete Book of Magic and Witchcraft
The Complete Book of Superstition, Prophecy and Luck

The Complete Book of
DEVILS and
DEMONS

Leonard R.N. Ashley

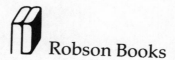

Robson Books

First published in the United States of America in 1996 by
Barncade Books Inc.
First published in Great Britain in 1997 by Robson Books Ltd,
Bolsover House, 5-6 Clipstone Street, London W1P 8LE

British Library Cataloguing in Publication Data
A catalogue record for this title is available from the British
Library

ISBN 1 86105 041 0

Printed and bound in Great Britain by WBC Book
Manufacturers Ltd., Bridgend, Mid-Glamorgan

FOR MARK

The Antiquities of the Common People
cannot be studied without acquiring
some useful Knowledge of Mankind. By
the chemical Process of Philosophy, even
Wisdom may be extracted from the Follies
and Superstitions of our Forefathers.

—JOHN BRAND
Observation on Popular Antiquities (1777)

Woodcut from Jacobus de Teramo's *Das Buch Belial*. The demon Belial dances before the magician King Solomon.

Table of Contents

A church mural in Schleswig c. 1300.

Read This First

Because people seldom bother with anything called "Introduction" and would be baffled by *"Prolegomenon"* (though I tried that once as an attention-grabber), I have asked you to "Read This First." I hope you will. I want to tell you why the book exists and why and how I think you ought to read it.

Encouraged by the readers of my books entitled *The Complete Book of Superstition, Prophecy and Luck* and *The Complete Book of Magic and Witchcraft*, I now offer *The Complete Book of Devils and Demons*. I believe that with the current vogue for angels in the United States (which is spreading to Canada, Britain, Australia, and elsewhere) the Bad Angels deserve some attention as well as the Good Ones.

I cast this book in the same engaging format of short entries as characterized in the two other books I have mentioned. There is in fact an esoteric reason for the arrangement of the bits of this mosaic but never mind that: Simply regard the book as adapted to the sound-byte, short-attention-span habits of many modern readers. Dip into the book, read a little, pause, and think about what you have read. This is a serious book on a serious subject and, to make the myriad materials contained herein available to the modern public, I have made the book very modern: reader-friendly, entertaining as well as educational, less dreary in tone than most books on demonology and the delusions of crowds. Once again, as Dr. Samuel Johnson would say, I have turned over whole libraries to make a single book. I direct my readers to many of my sources and I am, like all scholars, indebted to all those who have been over this territory before.

The results of this research and my commentaries are addressed to the three classes of readers mentioned by G.B. Harrison, another expert on Shakespeare and the Renaissance who, like myself, strayed into the field of witchcraft. In his history of the subject, Harrison mentioned "believers who admit the evidence and, in part at least, its diabolical explanation; skeptics who deny both and regard the whole business of witchcraft as the products of hysteria and gross credulity; rationalists who accept the evidence but deny the supernatural explanation." For myself, put me down as what Harrison would call a rationalist but one having, in my opinion, no firm basis for a decision either way about whether devils and demons are supernatural reality or human folly, pure and simple.

The truth in this case, as in so many other cases, may be neither pure nor simple. "It is the nature of all greatness," as Edmund Burke observed, "not to be exact." The preponderance of material in the question of good and bad is on the side of those who consider they have a monopoly on the good. God's side we are said to have heard from Him Himself, at least in part, and we are promised that what we view in life "as in a glass, darkly" we shall later see more clearly and understand. It is not in the nature of The Devil, if indeed there is a devil, to tip his hand. The side of The Devil is more difficult to determine. The position of those who believe in neither God nor The Devil, or are agnostic rather than atheist, is also less documented than the arguments of the theologians, the demonologists, the diabolists, and the rest. But even if you do not believe a word ever written about devils and demons, there is no reason at all why you should not be captivated by the oddities of those who do believe. You do not have to be interested in God or The Devil or anything at all supernatural to be fascinated by the subject of this book. You only have to be interested in people and their histories and hopes and fears.

Whether you are inclined toward the psychic or the psychological, *The Complete Book of Devils and Demons* can intrigue and inform you.

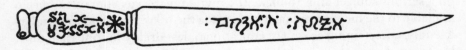

A thame, the magic knife for drawing the circle. The handle (shown white here to make the inscription clear) is black, the blade steel and inscribed or damascened.

Despite the title, no book on such a subject can be utterly complete, not even one that starts with some of the earliest personifications of evil and comes down to teenage Satanism in the current era. I have had to make major decisions about the art of this assemblage—what to put in, what to leave out. I have, to the best of my ability, tried to omit the boring and to stress the important even at the risk of repetition (people allege that university professors never say anything just once). I have attempted to give the collection an attractive originality in both style and content.

This book, *The Complete Book of Devils and Demons*, will be followed very shortly by another in the series, *The Complete Book of The Devil's Disciples*. Each book is complete in itself; however, readers who like one will want to look at the other. After you have learned about devils and demons, read in the companion volume about witchcraft in Britain and Ireland, the United States, France, Germany, the Northern Countries, and the rest of Europe and the rest of the World (Africa, Asia, etc.), and about how devils and demons and witches and wizards are featured in world literature and folklore and how they fare in everyday life in the modern world, among the fortune-tellers, the spiritualists and others who call up the dead in necromancy, the devotees of voodoo and others involved in occult rites and practices.

To those who think that in one book or another something important has been scanted or omitted, I apologize. I invite them to bring errors of omission or commission to my attention by writing to me in care of my publisher. Then, if reprinting is in the cards, as it has been lately for some other books from my pen (or computer), I may have the opportunity to revise and correct and expand. I know from experience that I cannot undertake to respond to all letters but you have my assurance that I always welcome any comments from my readers and that I read all the letters I receive and give full and fair consideration to corrections and criticisms (and compliments) when people are kind enough to take the trouble to express them. As a teacher for some forty years, I learned eventually to listen, and I have learned by listening. I have listened to my patient editor, Eileen Brand, and learned from her, too.

God bless you. Blessed be.

The Feast of Saint Oswald

The Devil from an old Tarot.

1

His Satanic Majesty

THE DEVIL AND DEVILS AND DEMONS

In common usage, there is only one entity called The Devil. He is Satan, contending with God. All the angels who fell with him and come from hell to torment mankind are referred to interchangeably as devils and demons, and we shall use "devils and demons" also for all the *shedim* or foreign, evil gods of *Deuteronomy* and elsewhere.

MAIL IN YOUR MIND AND BELIEVE IN THE OCCULT

Immanuel Kant, *Dreams of a Spirit-Seer* (1766, translated by E.F. Goerwitz):
If we balance against each other the advantages and disadvantages which might accrue to a person organized not only for the visible world, but also, to a certain degree, for the invisible (if ever there was such a person), such a gift would seem to be like that with which Juno honoured Tiresias, making him blind so that she might impart to him the gift of prophesying. For...the knowledge of the other world can be obtained here only by losing some of that intelligence which is necessary for this present one.

FROM ANIMISM TO THE ADVERSARY

The famous 11th edition of the *Encyclopædia Britannica* may have the very best concise description of how The Devil came to be:

The primitive philosophy of animism involves the ascription of all phenomena to personal agencies. As phenomena are good or evil, produce pleasure or pain, cause weal or woe, a distinction in the character of these agencies is gradually recognized; the agents of good become gods, those of evil, demons. A tendency towards the simplification and organization of the evil as of the good forces, leads towards belief in outstanding leaders among the forces of evil. When the divine is most completely conceived as unity, the demonic is also so conceived; and over against God stands Satan, or the devil.

HOW AN IDEA BECAME A PERSON

Jeffrey Burton Russell has a notable trilogy (Cornell University Press) on how the concept of Satan originated and continually changed over the centuries. "Paul Carus" even before Russell completed this survey wrote *The History of the Devil and the Idea of Evil* (1974) and more recently Elaine Pagels has closely examined *The Origin of Satan* (1994), following up on her studies of *The Gnostic Gospels* (startling documents were discovered in the desert of the Holy Land in 1945) and *Adam, Eve, and the Serpent* (The Devil in *Genesis*). As our notions of evil have changed, so has The Devil.

Pagels's "social history" of The Devil starts with the fact that the "fallen angel" as adversary (Satan) is not in the Hebrew Bible. It is an invention of the first century of Christianity—but not of Christians. Dissident Jewish groups thought it up. In the New Testament Satan appears first in *Mark*. Following His baptism in the Jordan, Christ goes into the desert and is tempted by Satan. It's Christ and the angels against Satan and the demons. Those who are against Christ are identified as of The Devil's party. Certain Jewish groups are beginning to be demonized. This gets stronger in the three subsequent gospels. Professor Pagels sees this anti-Semitism and the demonization of all sorts of enemies, real and imagined, the tendency to identify The Other with the work of The Devil, as still virulent in the world today. The evil may be not in The Other but inside ourselves, as the Gnostic gospel of *Philip* suggests. We may be projecting our own evil on the figure of The Devil.

Voltaire is often quoted as saying that if God did not exist we would be forced to invent Him. The modern argument is that to a great extent The Devil as we know him is our invention. We made him up because we don't quite understand God.

The Chronicle of Higher Education (14 July 1995) interviewed Professor Pagels at Princeton on her disturbing and debated scholarly findings and concluded with a mention that she had dismissed the movies *Reservoir Dogs* and *The Bad Lieutenant* as simplistic, "straight good and evil, black and white; you can't get much more blatant." Professor Pagels thinks that The Devil is not a simplistic concept, not a black and white one, and she has sought the origins of the ambiguities.

How an idea can "change its complexion" is noted in *Witchcraft and Black Magic* by Montague Summers, reprinted often since 1946. He's worth quoting at length on this:

> Satanist, as is plain, means a devotee of Satan, a person who is regarded as an adherent and follower of Satan. It is significant however, and worth remembering that when first employed the word Satanist was equivalent to an atheist, and it is used in this sense by John Aylmer [1521-1594], who was Bishop of London under Queen Elizabeth. In his political pamphlet, *An Harbour for Faithful and True Subjects*, published in 1559 at Strassburg, where he was then living [because of Queen Mary's Catholicism], he speaks of Satanists, implying infidels and unbelievers generally. Later the word became more restricted and changed its complexion, since, whatever else, the witch is certainly no atheist. In *The Life of Mr. Lynn Linton*, published in 1901, the following passage occurs: "There are two sects, the Satanists and the Luciferists—and they pray to these names as Gods."

Actually, there was a sect called Luciferians against whom Gregory IX loosed his anger, writing in 1233:

> Each year at Easter [time for the "Easter duty" of taking Holy Communion to retain one's membership in the Church] the sect members receive the host consecrated by a priest, hold it in their mouths, and returning home spit it into the latrines. Finally, these blasphemers dare to assert that the God of Heaven condemned Lucifer out of jealousy, violence, and against all justice. These poor unfortunates believe that some day Lucifer will be restored to his place of glory. It is with him and not before him that they look to be granted eternal blessedness. They believe that they must take care to do nothing which would please God and contrariwise they behave in ways they know God will detest.

To return to Summers and the two "sects":

> This is a distinction without a difference, Satan and Lucifer being
> identically the same entity and power. Dr. Charles H. H. Wright,
> sometime Grinfield lecturer on the Septuagint, Oxford, may say
> of Lucifer, "the word in Scripture has nothing to do with the devil,"
> but he is wrong. In English, all accepted understanding and ordi-
> nary use are against him, and we parallel the words of Isaiah (XIV,
> 12), "How art thou fallen from heaven, O Lucifer, son of the morn-
> ing!" with the gospel (*St. Luke* X, 18): "I beheld Satan as lightning
> fall from heaven."

Now, Isaiah may in fact be calling a defeated earthly king "Lucifer" in
that gloating over a fall, but let that pass. The point is made by Russell's three
books, with which we started here, that *Satan*, *Lucifer*, and *Mephistopheles* are
three different names for the three very different ways we have personified
the same evil over the centuries, reflecting shifts or modifications of "complexion" in the way we structure our personification of evil and anthropo-
morphize a force of which we are aware, reifying it with a name.

In the Bible story of Dives and Lazarus we prefer what look like real
names to the vagueness of "The Rich Man" and "The Leper." When we are
not given names of historical characters (the Roman soldier whose lance
pierced the side of the crucified Christ), we invent one (Longinus). When
we do not know the names of characters who may or may not be historical,
like the Three Magi, we create names: Caspar, Balthazar, Melchior. (We made
one of them black, for political reasons, not because the Bible said so.) Chal-
lenged to understand inhuman forces, we humanize them, name them, and
start attributing to them such human characteristics as anger and jealousy
and malice. We make them into nasty people. That we can understand.

Evil is real. The man with horns or bat wings is the creation of words.
But "in the beginning was The Word" and out of that came God. Out of
words The Devil came, too.

ALCIMIUS AVITUS ON THE DEVIL

Avitus was a sixth-century poet and author of *De Originale Peccato* (On Original Sin). He wrote of the fall of Satan:

> He had long been an angel, but after he became inflamed by his
> own wickednesses and exploded into haughty acts of arrogance,
> thinking that he had created himself—that he was his own creator,
> then in his mad heart he grew enraged and, denying his creator,

he said, "I shall adopt the divine title, and set my throne above the heavens and be like the Most High, his equal in awesome strength." Even as he boasted thus, the Supreme Power cast him down out of heaven and stripped the outcast of his old distinctions. He who shone forth as first in the order of creation will pay the principal penalty by verdict of the Judge who is to come.

GOD AND THE ADVERSARY

Jules Michelet, author of *La Sorcière* (1862), wrote:
When Colbert (1672) gave Satan short shrift by urging the judges to abandon trials for sorcery, the dogged Norman Parliament, with fine Norman logic, pointed out the dangerous implications of such a decision. The Devil, it argued, is more than a dogma to be minimized in importance or altogether discounted. For does not meddling with the eternally conquered involve meddling with the conqueror? To question the power of the first leads to questioning the power of the second, and the miracles He worked to combat The Devil. The pillars of heaven have their base in the abyss. The heedless person who denies this base could shatter paradise....

THE USEFULNESS OF THE CONCEPT OF THE DEVIL

From Charles Harris's *A Text-Book of Apologetics* (1905):
The hypothesis of a personal Devil has many advantages. It explains the whole of the facts; it avoids the postulation of two first causes; it vindicates the moral perfection of the Deity; and it allows the optimistic hope to be entertained that in the end good will triumph over evil.

Without belief in the Antichrist, we cannot look forward to everything turning out all right in the end.

DOUBTING THE EXISTENCE OF THE DEVIL

From Cotton Mather's *Wonders of the Invisible World* (1692):
That there is a Devil is a thing doubted by none but such as are under the influences of the Devil. For any to deny the being of a Devil must be from an ignorance or profaneness worse than diabolical.

GOD AND THE DEVIL BEFORE THE DIASPORA

In the original Jewish conception, evil came from God. It was God who permitted the Serpent to tempt Eve (knowing also, of course, what the outcome would be). It was God who sent the "evil spirit" to possess Saul. It was God who bet with the Evil One on the loyalty of Job. It was God who created the enmity between Abimelech and the Shechemites. "A lying spirit in the mouth of all His prophets" drives Ahab to destruction. Watchers sent to earth turned out to be bad angels (some of them) who mated with the sons of men for no good result, but it was God who sent them and permitted what occurred. The two books of *Samuel*, especially, make it clear that evil is under the control of God and The Evil One reports to God. The Devil is a tempter and accuser but it is God who takes action.

The god of the witches.

It is only after the Exile that the Jews begin to pick up on Zoroastrian dualism and to build up Satan as an opponent rather than as a servant of God. By the *Book of Enoch*, Satan has his own evil kingdom. By the time of the New Testament, Satan is The Adversary, acting out of his own evil motives. Satan's best work in the New Testament, of course, is inspiring Judas. Without Judas there would have been no Crucifixion, no Redemption. The Devil has been tricked by God into contributing to God's great plan. Nonetheless, in the long run Satan will be cast into a lake of fire and brimstone (II *Peter* II:4) and will be totally, finally defeated by Christ (*John* XVI:33). Christ's First Coming delivered mankind from Satan's control of the dead. His Second Coming will complete the defeat of Satan. To say that the goodness of God will eventually pardon His tool Satan is heresy in Christianity.

Those who believe in the inerrancy of the Scripture have the problem of the evolution of The Evil One, a change in his role and even basic nature. The 11th edition of the *Encyclopædia Britannica* again: having discussed various views about the evolution of Satan the author (Reverend Alfred Ernest Garvie) writes that:

> the possibility of the existence of evil spirits, organized under one leader Satan to tempt man and oppose God, cannot be denied; the sufficiency of the evidence for such evil agency may, however, be doubted; the necessity for any such belief for Christian thought and life cannot, therefore, be affirmed.

Briefly, you do not have to believe what the ancient Jews believed, what the Gospels taught, what the early doctors of the church believed, what the Middle Ages were so sure about, or what others say about The Devil active in the world today. Unless your religion insists.

GOD AND THE DEVIL, GODS AND DEMONS AND DEVILS, AND THE GODDESS

In Homer, the Greeks are seen to equate *theos* (god) with *dæmon* (demon), the first stressing personality and the second activity. Later came the concept of a personal *dæmon*, along with one's fate. Later, when the Jews turned the gods of their enemies into evil forces, the pagan gods became demons and the personal spirit was usually called *genius*. From the Jews we also got the idea of angels fallen from heaven by the sin of pride under the leadership of Satan (The Adversary). This chief Evil One we call The Devil, and all the angels who fell with him (and presumably all the pagan gods) are devils and demons. In this book, devils and demons are regarded as the same thing. Where the devils and demons of other religions fit into the Judeo-Christian idea is a vexed question. We made, for instance, the chief evil god (Ahriman) of the Persians into our Devil and the occult practices of their Magi into our black magic, alternatively feared or dismissed as charlatanism. If the Magi who followed the star to Bethlehem were among the first to honor Christ, the early Christians believed, then there must be some power in their astrology, and if The Devil is active in the world, there must be some ways of taking his side against God and obtaining power from The Devil by a pact bartering the soul.

Those whom the church regarded as heretics were of The Devil's party in the eyes of the church and were to be put down. Students of cabalistic and other hermetic lore were suspect. Witches were thought to be practicing the religion of The Devil, often with ceremonies parodying those of the church. Alchemy and astrology and other pseudo-sciences became entangled with demonology and witchcraft. Magic potions and medicine existed side by side.

The superstitious medieval mind was much infected by all of this. It was not really until after the medieval witchcraft scare that the great witch persecutions began in earnest. The Renaissance and Reformation were the darkest periods of superstition and violence as regards to The Devil and his devils and demons. Hundreds of thousands of persons were accused of witchcraft and their bodies destroyed, presumably for the good of their souls—or those of the faithful.

In the twentieth century, witches tend to be involved not with The Devil but with The Goddess, whose religion (claimed Margaret Murray in much-debated books) was the Old Religion that Christianity could not quite destroy and which was the base of magic and witchcraft. Most modern witchcraft pays little or no attention to devils and demons and is not to be equated with Satanism.

Where the religion of The Devil was one of anarchy and destruction of God's great plan, the religion of The Goddess is one of harmony and living in accord with nature.

MANICHEANISM

It is often assumed that the Hebrew scriptures are the beginning of religion, but of course they are built upon much earlier foundations. A number of their details are clearly reminiscent, intentionally or not, of such features as The Devil, called "the king or prince of darkness" in the religion of the Persian, Mani. The Jews copied angels with wings and the demon Lilith from the Babylonians. The Jews took other points of religion, if contrariwise, from other peoples such as the Chaldean magicians and the Assyrian astrologers. The Jewish identification of The Evil One with pigs, or their abhorrence of pork, is a tiny detail that has obscure, pre-Jewish explanations. In the Middle Ages some Christian depictions of The Devil involve pigs. Albrecht Dürer depicted The Devil as a pig following the figure of Death. Pig and The Devil were equated as unclean.

Manicheanism truly enters the Judeo-Christian mythos, however, with Saint Augustine and other early writers forming the Christian theology. Manicheanism had to be fought as a heresy among early Christians and in one form or another a thousand years later in the heretical sects of the Middle Ages.

The Luciferians and other Satanists, however, were not following Mani when they worshiped this adversary of God. It is an error to think so. Mani believed The Devil to be the equal of God in power, and in fact to have preceded Him in existence as Chaos came before Creation, but Mani did not say The Devil was to be worshiped. Rather, The Devil and all his ministers were to be assiduously avoided.

CAST-OUT DEMONS

Jesus cast out demons and conferred the power on his disciples. In *Matthew* X:8 we find a commandment to "Heal the sick, raise the dead, cleanse lepers, cast out demons." Today physicians have taken over most of the work of dealing with the sick, even lepers, and those sick in the soul are more likely to be sent to psychiatrists than to exorcists.

In casting out demons, Jesus was following the traditions of the Three Magi who came to Bethlehem at His birth and others who combined astronomy and astrology, magic and necromancy. The silver cup that *Genesis* says Joseph in Egypt used to cause trouble for his own brother Benjamin was, in fact, a magical chalice with which Joseph practiced the Egyptian magic also known to an even more famous character in the Books of Moses, Moses himself. Saint Stephen recounted how adept Moses was in Egyptian magic, and that magic involved dealing with devils and demons and the dead as well as tricks with magic wands that the Bible describes. Moses calls the magic wand, however, "the Rod of God."

THE REVELATION OF SAINT JOHN THE DIVINE

Maybe a Revelation, certainly not by the beloved apostle. It deals in prophecy: the Fall of Rome, described as "The Whore of Babylon," the Second Coming of Christ, the great battle at the end of the world ("Armageddon"), and the chaining of Satan and the final triumph of good over evil.

If Satan is scheduled to lose, it may be unwise to take that side, even though he seems to be doing well at this present stage of history.

WHAT GOD PERMITS

Unless you subscribe to the Manichean heresy, you have to admit that God permitted the Serpent to tempt Eve and that he made a bet with The Devil about the faithfulness of Job. (That was unworthy of Him. All-knowing, He was acting despicably, rather like Arnold Rothstein, the gambler who fixed the World Series, the man who said he would gamble on anything except the weather because "You can't fix the weather." God can even fix the weather. The Devil was cheated by Old Nobbodaddy.) God sent trials and tribulations not only to His Enemies—think of the dreadful plagues visited upon the Egyptians—but also demons to assault King Saul and the prophets of Achab and His Own Son, to cite but a few instances.

Some people say God has already selected the Elect and the Damned and, in carrying out His plans, the devils and demons are just following orders.

What do you think?

In the Old Testament, Satan (The Adversary) is not the opponent of God but His servant. The Satan that encourages God to tempt Job is a messenger of The Lord who wanders the earth finding out evil and reporting on it: He is therefore the adversary of sinful man, not of God. G. Papini's book on *The Devil* (1954) points out that Satan works for God.

If there is chaos, it is because God has not for His reasons undertaken to replace it with order; if there is darkness, it is where His light does not shine; and, most striking, if there is evil it is from Him, for God is the source of everything. It is God who for His reasons has put evil into mankind (I *Samuel* XVI:14) and somehow even those who seem to be working against God are part of His plan. Even in creating the archangel who refused to obey Him and was cast out of heaven into the fires of damnation, even in creating mankind whom His angel with a fiery sword cast out of Paradise, God, Who knows all, knew what would happen to them.

NO NEED FOR THE DEVIL

Joseph Conrad in *Under Western Eyes* (1911): "The belief in a supernatural source of evil is not necessary; men alone are quite capable of every wickedness."

SAINT AUGUSTINE ON THE DEVIL

"Do you seek to know the origin of The Devil? It is the same as that of the other angels. But the other angels persevered in their obedience, whereas he, by disobeying and being proud, fell and became The Devil."

"The Devil is not evil insofar as he is an angel but insofar as he is, of his own volition, perverse. Loving himself more than God, he was unwilling to be subject to God, and he grew swollen with pride and forsook the divine essence."

"Deceived by himself, he longs to deceive another. He has become an enemy of our human race, the inventor of death, the teacher of pride, the origin of malice, the chief of criminals, the prince of all vice, the promoter of base passions. Because of this, when he beheld the first man God made, Adam, the father of us all, and saw man made from the muck of the earth in the image of God, and adorned with modesty, gifted with temperance, surrounded with love, robed in immortality, he grew jealous and envious that man had received the great blessing which he himself had as an angel, as he realized, and lost through pride. Instantly he became envious and, insatiable killer of men that he was, he stole the blessings from our first parent and brought us all to destruction."

DEVILS AND DEMONS WERE CREATED NATURALLY GOOD

It is hardly to be expected that Christian theology would say that God created both good and evil. Saint Thomas Aquinas got Him off that hook when he cleverly defined evil as "the absence of a due and necessary good," which is to say that evil exists where God did *not* create, not where He did.

The Decrees of the Fourth Lateran made official for Roman Catholics in the first chapter of stated belief, *Firmiter credimus*, that *Diabolus enim et alii dæmones a Deo quidem natura creati sunt boni, sed ipsi per se facti sunt mali*, "The Devil and the other demons were created by God naturally good; but they of themselves became evil." The Devil was among the highest of angels. His original name ended in -*el* (like archangels Michael, Gabriel, Raphael) and he was one of the gods, therefore, before the One God triumphed over all.

In pride, this archangel would not serve and he stood up against God before man and woman were ever created, and those angelic spirits who sided with The Adversary (he is called The Dragon in *The Apocalypse*) in that ridiculous rebellion were cast into Hell with him. In revenge, The Devil tempted both man and woman, and those who die in mortal sin will join him in Hell and suffer the tortures of the damned. Over the failure and suffering of The Devil, *Isaiah* XIV: 12-15 gloats. The Gospel of John calls the fallen angel The Dragon and says he fell "with Satan." *Isaiah* may address him as Lucifer: "How art thou fallen from heaven, O Lucifer, who didst rise in the morning." Lucifer, the bearer of light, the morning star, The Prince of Darkness. The Gospel of Luke says, "I saw Satan like lightning falling from heaven." *Ephesians* recognizes The Devil as "Prince of the power of the air" and having an army of "the sons of disobedience."

Among the fallen angels and human "sons of disobedience," The Devil is god. He is worshiped and sacrificed to and prayed to, makes miracles and utters prophecies (being as an archangel a much superior creation to mere mortals), though nothing whatever about his miracles and prophecies is other than false and nothing should be trusted. To serve The Devil is to deny God. Not to believe in The Devil is heresy. To choose to follow The Devil makes one like a fallen angel, a "son of disobedience."

"The Devil made me do it" whines many a modern psychopath. But Christian orthodoxy demands adherence to the belief that The Devil and his minions are at all times and all places "seeking the ruin of souls." Without the grace of God, any human will fall prey to this terrible and puissant lord of lies. And if one tries to sell one's soul to The Devil, even if he does not come or send to collect it, the sin is done and damnation is certain, as it would be if there were no Devil at all but someone wished there were and was prepared to begin or join an opposition to The Most High. Evil existed even before The Devil was created good, even before he went bad. Evil exists in all chaos, in everything that God does not, for whatever reason, touch. The Devil merely exploits it. It is shocking to say so but orthodoxy has to say The Devil works if not for God then with the full knowledge and toleration of God. Everything, even The Devil, is part of God's plan. The Devil's fall was part of it; the fall of Man was part of it.

That The Devil was once an archangel, given great spiritual and supernatural powers, and despite his intelligence made an unforgivable mistake, ought to give pause to sinners who are only human. Created good and powerful, it was much harder for The Devil to sin than a human being born into Original Sin and surrounded by the temptations of the world, the flesh, *and* The Devil.

"The Devil," writes Richard Cavendish in *The Black Arts,* "is a legacy of the widespread tendency to attribute the origin of evil to non-human influences. In primitive societies evil and misfortune are usually thought to come from the gods. The powers which created the universe and rule it are the ultimate authors of all things and they are given responsibility for the presence of evil as well as credit for the existence of good," and that is the case with the Judeo-Christian view and The Enemy of Man as well.

Cavendish continues: "In matters which are too trivial to be the concern of the gods primitive people put harm and suffering down to the malice of evil spirits, which are less powerful than the gods but more numerous." In the Judeo-Christian system all beings, no matter how "trivial," are under the rule of the omnipotent God. In practice we separate the big evils and big devils from the smaller ones (mostly borrowed from non Judeo-Christian sources) so that with Lucifer we also have leprechauns, with demons we have banshees, and with all the trouble we inherit from the fall of The Devil and the fall of man we have trolls and such creatures to worry about.

If in our danger we can have any compassion for others, we ought to try to find what a pop song once called "Sympathy for The Devil." What a hard time *he* and his friends have doing the work they have chosen, which God knew they would choose when He made them as He did.

Like the *ying* and the *yang* elements fitting together to fill the circle in Asian thought—a symbol Europeans found in Mexico and Peru when they first reached the New World—evil combines with good to form the whole. You and I and Old Nick are all part of the big scheme of things. That must be good.

THE DEVIL IS A FALLEN ANGEL

In the seventeenth century, Sir George Etheredge (who modeled Dorimant in his play *The Man of Mode* on the notorious John Wilmot, Earl of Rochester, whose debauched life ended in his thirties in 1680) said of Wilmot, "I know he is a Devil, but he has something of the Angel yet undefac'd in him."

Satan was an archangel once. Do you perceive in his character as known to us any aspects of "the Angel undefac'd" at all? How justifiable do you think Satan's anger was when God favored a later and inferior creation,

The Devil tempting St. Patrick, *Le purgatoire Sainct Patrice* (1530).

Adam? In that jealousy, seen in other places in the Bible where one son is favored over another, lies the seed of a far from motiveless malignity.

THE DEVIL COMES AND IS SEEN

Eliphas Lévi wrote a great deal about magic but says he attended magical ceremonies only three times in his life. He may possibly have had my objections to them. So many drugs are in the air that they are dangerous to the body, let alone the soul. The psychedelic substances burned at many such rites alone are sufficient to cause hallucinations.

"When anyone invokes the devil with intentional ceremonies," Lévi wrote, "the Devil comes." Where Christian thought holds that the intention to commit evil is tantamount to actual sin, this is true. "Wishing will make it so" is another, perhaps even stronger, belief of modern man. When you want to see devils and demons, if you want it enough, you will convince yourself you see them even if you have to break down the barriers of your sanity.

In one of Shakespeare's plays a magician says that he can call spirits from the deep and another character snidely asks if they will *come* when called. If desire is strong enough, you can delude yourself into seeing them, whether they are there or not. Whether The Devil is real or not, evil is real and as such it can be experienced or imagined by anyone foolhardy enough to do so.

Even if the devils and demons or The Devil himself should appear, it may be that they come not from Hell but from within yourself. That's something to worry about.

THE DEVIL IS AN ASS

Outwitting The Devil by tricks or quibbles occurs in the self-congratulatory folk tales of many peasantries, but long life and experience are supposed to have given great shrewdness to vampires and of course to The Devil himself, which makes any congress with evil perilous. Whether in *Jack and the Beanstalk* or with the giants in Muslim folklore, large evil creatures (ogres, demons, etc.) are often supposed to be stupid on the principle that "the bigger they are, the harder they fall." Telling such stories makes little or very threatened people feel better, as do protective charms, beliefs that The Devil is limited (demons or vampires cannot cross water or appear in daylight), etc.

In fact, theology says that The Devil started much superior to mankind, being an archangel, and that he has had time to accumulate a great deal of knowledge of human behavior. *Ephesians* VI: 12 suggests that, although Christ's sacrifice has redeemed mankind, we still have a powerful enemy against whom to struggle, and a sly one.

CHRIST AND THE DEVIL'S TEMPTATIONS

Joseph Campbell, who taught mythology for almost forty years at Sarah Lawrence College and wrote *The Masks of God* and much more, is probably best known today for the television interviews on "The Power of Myth" conducted by Bill Moyers with Campbell just before his death. In the book that records those conversations of 1985–1986, *The Power of Myth*, Campbell is quoted as discussing the hero, who is a model for all of us as we struggle to overcome the savage passions within us and reach spirituality, in the case of Jesus Christ.

Campbell said that:

There's a universally valid hero deed represented in the story of Jesus. First he goes to the edge of the consciousness of his time when he goes to John the Baptist to be baptized. Then he goes past the threshold into the desert for forty days. In the Jewish tradition the number forty is mythologically significant. The children of Israel spent forty years in the wilderness, Jesus spent forty days in the desert. In the desert, Jesus underwent three temptations. First there was the economic temptation, where the Devil comes to him and says, "You look hungry, young man! Why not change these stones to bread?" And Jesus replies, "Man lives not by bread alone, but by every word out of the mouth of God." And then next we have the political temptation. Jesus is taken to the top of a mountain and shown the nations of the world, and the Devil says to him, "You can control all these if you will bow down to me," which is a lesson, not well enough made known today, of what it takes to be a successful politician. Jesus refuses. Finally the Devil says, "And so now, you're so spiritual, let's go up to the top of Herod's Temple and let me see you cast yourself down. God will bear you up, and you won't even be bruised...." This is what is known as spiritual inflation. I'm so spiritual, I'm above the concerns of the flesh and this earth. But Jesus is incarnate, is he not? So he says, "You shall not tempt the Lord, your God." Those are the three temptations of Christ, and they are as relevant today as they were in the year 30 A.D.

The same temptations are offered to us all and some unwise souls are drawn into black magic for selfish, power-hungry, and wrongly conceived spiritual motives. Christian or not, anyone should attempt what Saint Thomas à Kempis called *The Imitation of Christ*. Campbell was the nearest thing to a saint of any man I ever met, with all the enthusiasm and erudition and occasionally kooky ideas of (say) Saint Augustine—and a more gentle and loving person than the Bishop of Hippo, too. If I couldn't meet Saint Thomas Aquinas or The Buddha, I am grateful to have had the opportunity to meet Joseph Campbell. In his conversations with Moyers you yourself can have something like the pleasure of his company. He can explain the uses of ritual—and the perils of black magic's rituals—as we seek our "bliss."

THE ANTICHRIST

The end of a century brings to people's minds the end of the world and, inevitably, the arrival of the Antichrist promised in *Revelation*. Call it apocalyptic eschatology, if you like long words, and read, if you like long stories, *Antichrist: Two Thousand Years of the Human Fascination with Evil* by Bernard McGinn, the authority on millenarianism. McGinn demonstrates that in one form or another the Antichrist legend of the final clash of good and evil and the separating of the sheep from the goats, The Last Judgment following chaos and cataclysm, has been powerful since the third century before Christ. It remains powerful and polyvalent, especially strong among the growing ranks of Christian Fundamentalists who say that the present world is so full of lies and falsehoods (the Antichrist is false, sly, and deceptive) and lechery and dismay that the Antichrist's time is certainly here, or near. War, destruction, despair, apostasy, a false Messiah, the conclusive triumph of good over evil that has been coming since good began, that was before the Jews, before the Bible, when the *Eneuma elish* of the Akkadians, in the late second millennium before Christ, pitted the male champion of the gods (Marduk) against Tiamat (the female Dragon of the older and evil gods). Marduk won, and out of Tiamat's blood and that of her consort, the evil Kingu, Marduk constructed the cosmos and the race of mankind.

Things are shaping up for more horror films along the lines of *Rosemary's Baby* or the trilogy of *The Omen*, *Damien*, and *The Final Conflict*. Our literature is turning more and more toward thoughts of final combat and destruction rather than faith and hope. The time draws near, some fear, some almost rejoice, when the last pope (who will take the name Peter II) will appear in white linen to attempt to reform the Roman Catholic

Church, and when the Antichrist will arise to great popular acclaim in a time of worldwide terror and confusion and begin his foreordained reign of forty-two months, after which comes The End. The fire this time.

It used to be said that those whom the gods wish to destroy they first make mad. People are certainly acting nuttier all the time, or so you hear people saying. It's a mad world, my masters!

Someone has pointed out that the oddballs who roam the streets with placards proclaiming "The End Is Nigh!" are not being laughed at as they used to be.

Bousset, Wilhelm. *The Antichrist Legend* (reprinted 1982).
Emerson, Richard. *Antichrist in the Middle Ages* (1981).

DETESTED GROUPS OF ALLEGED DEVIL WORSHIPERS

Of course anyone accused of heresy might be tarred by the orthodox with the brush of devil worship, but history tells us of a number of groups that suffered particular persecution, fairly or unfairly, because of such allegations. Among them are some interesting ones, each worth a book of its own, such as these:

ASTRUM ARGENTUM. Aleister Crowley, whom even his mother called "The Beast," founded this secret society, which was notorious for its deviant orgies at the Abbey of Theleme in Sicily. It was a fake Satanist group even though at his funeral the "Hymn to Satan" was sung over Crowley's corpse. Sex and drugs were a large part of the appeal of *A.A.* to its perverse followers.

BOGOMILS. These Bulgarians were heretics and their espousal of free love and rejection of marriage gained them a reputation for buggery, which is what English made of their name. Alexis of Byzantium tried to extirpate the sect but some escaped to France and Italy, where they also were anathema and said to be in league with The Devil (whom they saw as battling God on equal terms). Innocent III launched a crusade against them (1209).

CATHARS. Also believing in a Manichean battle between good and evil in the world and heretical on many other matters (including, like the Bogomils, the Resurrection of Christ), the Cathars fought against the Roman Catholics for a long time. Theirs was the famous Albigensian Heresy. For them, The Prince of Darkness was the god of this world.

DRUIDS. Supposed to have secret knowledge of nature, Druids (it was said) once served pagan gods and by astrological calculations foretold the future and by spells and incantations controlled the elements. Most of what is "known" about them is pure fabrication. Stonehenge predates them in Britain; it is not of their construction. They were never devil worshipers, but all non-Christians were once so called. That's demonizing.

ILLUMINATI. Several "enlightened" organizations had this name in the eighteenth century. In France there was a theosophical sect under Dom Pernety at Avignon, and in Germany a quasi-magical group under Professor Weishaupt at Ingoldstadt, but neither of these were devil worshipers, despite public opinion.

LUCIFERIANS. Sexual perversions and violence went along with the heretical ideas of this and other medieval groups of Satanists. They were equated with the worshipers of Baphomet but did not resemble the Knights Templar, similarly accused. There seem to have been real Satan worshipers in Europe in the Middle Ages. They differed from witches, wizards, *magi*, and other occultists.

PALLADINISM. Alleged Satanism in some Masonic orders of the last century recalling the charges made against the Knights Templar. All secret societies are suspected by the ignorant of being up to no good. A Roman Catholic libel against the Freemasons.

TEMPLARS. One of the orders of knights serving crusades and crusaders in the Holy Land, the Knights Templar (defenders of the Holy Sepulcher in Jerusalem, whence their name) were accused of adopting perversions of the infidels and worshiping Baphomet. A synod at Paris condemned fifty-one knights to a horrible death by fire (1311), the order was dissolved by command of Clement V (1312), and the grand master was burned to death (1314). Their main crime seems to have been accumulating so much wealth as to create jealousy. None of the more recent Orders of the Temple, Templars, etc., are in any way the inheritors of the Knights Templar. Templars under torture confessed to being devil worshipers but the Grand Master Molay urged them to recant those confessions.

WALDENSIANS. Founded in the twelfth century by the Frenchman Pierre Waldo, the Waldensian heretics were soon accused of everything from cannibalism to Satanism. Eugene IV and Innocent VIII (especially) urged their annihilation. They are related to all the witches seen in art worshiping The Devil in the form of a goat, which seems to combine memories of The Horned God of the pagans with the satyr reputation of the goat still evident in our phrase "you old goat" for a "dirty old man." The charges of devil worship have never been proved.

You can add here as current various Churches of Satan those which proclaim or are accused of devil worshiping. None that I know of contain genuine Satanists. If they did, I would be compelled to call the police on them rather than write about them, for true Satanist activities would involve heinous sacrifices, whether The Devil received the sacrifices or not.

EVIL AND KNOWLEDGE

You will recall that it was The Devil, in the guise of a serpent, that tempted Eve and Adam with the knowledge of good and evil. You may not know that the son of Adam and Eve, called Cain, the one who slew his brother Abel in jealousy, was said in the early occult writings to be the son not of Adam but of The Devil. (Adam had an earlier wife than Eve, a demon called Lilith, but presumably they had no children.) The Devil was said to have instructed Cain in evil ways as well as his descendants. (Whom did Cain marry? A good question.) The Cainites are said to have been the first to serve The Devil as their god. Of course The Devil and his bad angels were still angels, possessed of superior powers of intelligence, privy to great secrets of the universe. These they could use at any time to work evil, with the help of instructed and enslaved mankind.

The evil ways of mankind were, according to the fathers of the church, the reason God decided to destroy almost all of mankind in The Flood. The Flood spared Noah and his wife and their three sons (Shem, Japhet, and Ham). Ham was cursed, like Cain, and instructed his son (Mizraim, patriarch of the Egyptians) in evil. From Ham came Canaan and Sidon and those who worshiped idols that the Jews condemned as demons. Ham's descendants were cursed, diabolically clever, deprived of the true knowledge, the knowledge of God. To the evil ones came knowledge of metals (and of weapons of war), of magic (sorcery, necromancy, astrology), and more. The old stories include one about Ham going to Persia and becoming the sun-god magician Zoroaster, inventor of a religion that averred that good and evil are equally matched and in a battle for the universe, the forces of light against the forces of darkness. This reduced God from The Power to A Player.

The knowledge attained by the magicians of the Egyptians, the Assyrians, the Babylonians, the Chaldeans, the Phoenicians, and many others corrupted mankind, according to the Judeo-Christian tradition, and put many in the power of The Evil One, damning to Hell all those mere mortals who wanted (like Marlowe's Dr. Faustus) "to practice more than heavenly power permits."

Still today black magicians speak of having learned The Craft and boast of occult knowledge and the power that comes with knowledge. Some claim to worship the sun as did the Mayans and Heliogabalus. Some claim to be fire-worshipers, a perversion which old accounts say Nimrod introduced into the Jewish world. Some say they have *wicca* of the earth. Those who could read the stars, or the runes, or the signs in nature which directed us (for instance) to choose a heart-shaped leaf to treat diseases of the heart, or otherwise attain any kind of superior knowledge, have always been both respected and feared.

The black arts have always exerted a baleful attraction on the perilously curious and the ambitious who want to know more, perhaps even being willing to risk their immortal souls for knowledge. Whereas some persons fall through stupidity and carelessness, more, it seems, fall because of mis-directed intelligence and recklessness, or so say the guardians of the faith-ful who repeat, "What you don't know can't hurt you."

NAMES OF THE DEVIL

From Ernest Weekley's *Words and Names* (1932):
> It is said that our dialects are provided with some forty names for the Enemy of Mankind....circumlocutions, sometimes half propi-tiatory, which aim at avoiding a dreaded name. One of his more pic-turesque titles is the *Earl of Hell*, and it is refreshing to find that "as black as the Earl of Hell's waistcoat," describing a dark night, is still used by the imaginative. [Robert] Burns' *Address to the Devil* begins:
>
> O thou! whatever title suit thee,
> *Auld Hornie, Satan, Nick* or *Clootie.*

Edgar, in his character of *Tom o'Bedlam* [pretended madman in Shake-speare's *King Lear*], proclaims that:
> The prince of darkness is a gentleman,
> *Modo*, he's called, and *Mahu.*

MORE NAMES OF THE DEVIL AND OF HELL

Satan, Lucifer, The Prince of Darkness, The Prince of Devils, The Prince of This World, The Prince of the Air, His Satanic Majesty, The Prince of Hell, The Prince of Pandemonium, The (Arch-) Fiend, The Evil One, The Wicked One, The Tempter, The Author of Evil, The (Common) Enemy (of Mankind), Old Harry, Old Nick, The Angel of the Bottomless Pit, Old Horny, Old Gooseberry, Mr. Scratch, The Old Gentleman, etc.

Gehenna, Hades, The Bottomless Pit, The Place of Torment, Everlasting Fire, Acheron, Avernus, Cocytus, The Inferno, The Infernal Regions, The Lake of Fire, Lethe, Phlegethon, The Pit, the Realm of Pluto, Styx, Tartarus, etc.

HELL

The wicked shall be turned into Hell, and all the nations that forget God.—*Psalms* XI:17.

....the fire is not quenched.—*Mark* IX:44.

The fire of Gehenna is sixty times as hot as the fire of this earth.—*The Talmud* (*Berachoth*).

Those who believe not shall have the garments of fire fitted unto them; boiling water shall be poured on their heads; their bowels shall be dissolved thereby, and also their skins; and they shall be beaten with maces of iron. —*The Koran* XXII.

Lasciate ogni speranza voi ch'entrate. [Abandon hope all ye who enter here.] —Dante, *Inferno* III.

Hell is a city much like London.—Percy Bysshe Shelley, *Peter Bell the Third* III.

If there is no Hell, a good many preachers are obtaining money under false pretenses.—"Billy" Sunday (1863–1936).

THE ORIGIN OF DEMONOLOGY

In *Parsifal*, Wolfram von Eschenbach (c. 1170–c. 1220) wrote:
> It is not in the land of Persia, but in a city called Persida, that magic was first conceived. Klingsor traveled to that place and from there he brought back the art of magically effecting whatever he wished.

Klingsor had a chip on his shoulder because he was "smooth between the legs": He had been caught in bed with the queen by the king himself and made into a eunuch.
> After the shameful thing done to his body he never again bore goodwill toward anyone, man or woman, and when he can rob

them of any joy, especially if they are honored and respected, it does his heart good.

This places the emphasis on the envy and malice that lie behind magical dealing with infernal powers, the weak becoming potent by sacrificing themselves to the devils and demons in exchange for the bitter fruit of revenge. That magicians are always cheated is clear. Chaucer refers to "Sathan, that ever us waiteth to bigile," to trick in a bargain.

NEMO REPENTE FUIT TURPISSIMUS

The shrewd satirist Juvenal (c. 55–c. 130) remarked that no one becomes depraved instantly. Bit by bit we get into the clutches of evil, once we get on the slippery slope. As Vergil (70–19 B.C.) put it, *facilis descensus Averni*, it is easy to go down into Hell.

DUAL DUTY FOR THE DEVIL

From St. Augustine's *The City of God* XV:427:
The Devil often transforms himself into an angel to tempt men, some for other instruction and some for their ruin.

DUAL DISGUISES OF THE DEVIL

From Martin Luther's *Table Talk* (1569), DCXVIII:
The Devil has two types of shapes or forms in which he disguises himself: either he appears in the shape of a serpent to frighten and to kill, or else in the form of a silly sheep to lie and to deceive. These are his two court colors.

PICTURING THE DEVIL AND HIS DEMONS

Christian art adapted the basilisk, bat, bird of prey, bull, centaur, dog, dragon, goat, lion, satyr, serpent, skeleton, and other guises to represent rampant evil. Evil creatures are often shown as hairy, scaly, pig-nosed, bat-winged, fanged and with talons, horned and with cloven hoofs, green and yellow like a frog or reptile, or blue. The Devil tends to remain anthropomorphic if grotesque. Minor demons can get more fantastic still. *El sueño de la razón produce monstros.* "The sleep of reason brings forth monsters."

THE DEVIL IN FOLK ART

Bayon, R. et al. *Revue des traditions populaires* 4 (1889), 5(1890), 6(1891), 9(1894).

Campany, R. "Demons, Gods, and Pilgrims...," *Chinese Literature* 7:1–2(1985), 95–115.

Cocchiara, G. *Il Diavolo nella tradizione populare italiana* (1945).

Grillot de Givry, Émile Angelo. *Picture Museum of Sorcery, Magic, and Alchemy* [trans. J. C. Locke, reprint 1963).

Reisner, Erwin, *Die Dämon und sein Bild* (1955).

Turnel, J. *Histoire du diable* (1931).

Villeneuve, R. *Le Diable dans l'art* (1957).

16.

١٦ـ قَالَ فَبِمَآ أَغْوَيْتَنِى لَأَقْعُدَنَّ لَهُمْ صِرَاطَكَ الْمُسْتَقِيمَ ٥

17.

١٧ـ ثُمَّ لَأَتِيَنَّهُم مِّنْ بَيْنِ أَيْدِيهِمْ وَ مِنْ خَلْفِهِمْ وَعَنْ أَيْمَانِهِمْ وَعَن شَمَآئِلِهِمْ وَلَا تَجِدُ أَكْثَرَهُمْ شَكِرِينَ ٥

18.

١٨ـ قَالَ اخْرُجْ مِنْهَا مَذْءُومًا مَّدْحُورًا لَّمَن تَبِعَكَ مِنْهُمْ لَأَمْلَأَنَّ جَهَنَّمَ مِنكُمْ أَجْمَعِينَ ٥

From the Koran VII:16-18. 16: He [Satan] said: "Because Thou hast thrown me off the correct path, behold I shall lie in wait for them [human beings] on the straight path." 17: "Then I shall attack them from before and behind and from their right and their left. Nor will You find in most of them any gratitude [to You]." 18: He [God] said: "Get out of here disgraced and expelled. If any of them follow thee, I shall fill Hell with all of you."

THE APPEARANCE OF THE DEVIL

Harpax, a demon disguised as a secretary, tells Theophilus in the first scene of the third act of Thomas Massinger's play *The Virgin Martyr* (1622) that The Devil has been lied about:

He's no such horrid creature, cloven-footed,

Black, saucer-ey'd, his nostrils breathing fire,

As these lying Christians make him.

Reginald Scot was one of the earliest writers to make fun of the horrible tales told of The Devil's appearance. In his *Discoverie of Witchcraft* he wrote:

In our childhood, our mother's maids have so terrified us with an ugly devil, having horns on his head, fire in his mouth, and a tail in his breech, eyes like a basin, fangs like a dog, claws like a bear, a skin like a Nig[g]er, and a voyce roaring like a lyon, whereby we are startled and afraid when we hear one cry Bough [boo].

DEVILS AND DEMONS IN VISUAL ART

There are many illustrations of demons, such as the Buddhist ones, which we cannot reproduce here because we are limited to black and white, and that does not render them well. Devils and demons are a major theme of oriental and a great deal of other visual art. See the works of Blake, Doré, Ensor, Fuseli, Goya et al. See relevant art books, the *Encyclopedia of World Art*, and such volumes as:

Castelli, Enrico, *Il Demoniaco nell'arte* (1952).
Cavendish, Richard. *Visions of Heaven and Hell* (1977).
Charcot, J. R. & Paul Richer. *Les Demoniaques dans l'art* (1887).
Grabar, A. *Christian Iconography* (1980).
Grillot de Givry, Émile Angelo. *A Pictorial Anthology of Witchcraft, Magic, and Alchemy* (University Books Library of the Mystic Arts, n.d.).
Lehner, Ernst and Johanna Lehner. *Picture Book of Devils, Demons and Witchcraft* (1972).
Waldo-Schwartz, Paul. *Art and the Occult* (1975).

THE DEVIL IN DISGUISE

When The Devil and his cohorts appeared among humankind, it was said, they most often wore disguises. In the iconography of the Middle Ages and on the stage of the Renaissance, for instance, devils appeared with horns, hooves, and a tail (sometimes with a sort of arrowhead on the end), suggesting that they were being confused with pagan deities such as Pan, with his goat hooves, or satyrs, half man and half beast. In Christopher Marlowe's great tragedy *Dr. Faustus*, Mephistophelis, "servant to Great Lucifer," first appears in horrible, hairy, animal guise and is told by anti-Catholic Marlowe (if not by Catholic theology professor Johann Faust) to assume a more apt disguise, such as that of a Catholic monk or friar. Lucifer is often shown in medieval art as a human form to which are added the wings of a bat. As an archangel originally, he ought to be extremely handsome but, as Oscar Wilde's Dorian Gray found out, evil can ruin one's appearance.

The devils and demons are shown most often as imps, grinning ferociously as they go about their nefarious business, horrible as the gargoyles (left over from earlier religions) that still lurk on the outside (for the most part) of Christian churches. Familiar spirits, devils in disguise, are most often thought of as taking animal shape. The Blessed Albertus Magnus was widely believed to be a magician and the large black dog that accompanied him wherever he went was popularly believed to be a devil in his service. There was a belief that though The Devil could create animals he could never do anything perfectly, so one looked for a deformed animal, a cat without a tail, a dog with some defect, even for a deformed person. Any of them might be devils in disguise.

At the Sabbat the demon Leonard appeared as a large black goat with three horns instead of two. The Devil himself at a Sabbat was supposed to appear in the same shape. Human beings who took his place at these rites sometimes dressed as a black goat. Most often they wore some sort of disguise and may often have made the ignorant peasants believe they were The Devil in person. The Devil was said to appear to poor people in the guise of a large black man who offered them promises of wealth. Various witches testified under oath that they had seen The Devil in various animal guises: bull, calf, cat, dog, foal, donkey, wolf, goat, etc. Some said he appeared as a handsome youth to seduce them. His phallus, however, was always ice cold, even painfully barbed.

From the goat disguise (tying The Devil in with lustful personages of the older mythology) came the conviction that The Devil had cloven hooves. The Basque for Sabbat was *Akhelarre* (Goat Pasture). Goya depicts The Devil (or Leonard? or a human in disguise?) as a huge goat at the Sabbat. In the eighteenth century some participants at the Sabbat came in goat masks and cloaks. The usefulness of attending proscribed rites with face concealed is obvious. Even in some few covens, small (thirteen) and regular groups of participants, members use first or even fake names only and keep their identities secret from all but the leader.

Father Martin Antoine del Rio, S. J., who wrote an encyclopedia of magic (1599), reports with confidence that:

The Sabbat is presided over by a demon, the Lord of the Sabbat, who appears in some monstrous form, most often as a goat or some hound of hell, seated upon a high throne. The witches who resort to the Sabbat approach the throne with their backs turned [all ceremonies involving The Devil are the reverse of common practice] and worship him...as a sign of their homage they kiss his rear end.

This last detail, the *osculum infame*, I suppose to be generated by the Jewish horror of homosexuality and the reputation of the Knights Templar as following this practice of the worship of Baphomet. After the submission came the wild dancing and an orgy, the music giving way to confused noise. Supposed experts from Salamanca report that food at these parties occasionally consisted of pies made of dead babies. In both Britain and Boston witches testified that a parody of Holy Communion took place at the Sabbat. What the Sabbat seems to have lacked most notably is the panoply of

Sex with The Devil, from Ulrich Molitor's *De Lamiis et phitonicis muleribus*.

the Mass, with its incense and holy water and vestments and transubstantiation so that the faithful can literally eat their god. Also, the god of the witches appears in person on occasion at the Sabbat while the bread and wine, though believed devoutly to be the body and blood of Christ, does not constitute the presence of Christ in exactly the same sort of way.

TWO AND THREES

Anything that is triple recalls of The Trinity. That's why you have bad luck if you walk under a ladder. The ground, the wall, the ladder—three. You are breaking through a trinity. A blessing is often given with three fingers up, like the salute of the Boy Scouts. A gesture to counter the evil eye, a piece of coral for the same purpose, requires two fingers, two points, because two reminds of the dichotomy God and The Adversary. Anything two-pointed is of The Adversary. Anything three-pointed is of God.

Of course in the "everything backwards" world of Satanism, a three-pointed host is used (instead of the regular round one)—but it is black, not white. Alternatively, a stolen, consecrated host can be used in a Black Mass—but it is broken into two, not three. In numerology, 2 is the number of The Devil, 3 of God, 3x3 or 9 especially powerful, 2x3 bad and 666 worst of all, which I explain elsewhere.

CHARLES LAMB ON THE DEVIL

In *Witches and Other Night-Fears* (1823), Charles Lamb wrote:
That the prince of the powers of darkness, passing by the flower and pomp of the earth, should lay preposterius siege to the weak fantasy of indigent eld—has neither likelihood nor unlikelihood *a priori* to us, who have no measure to guess at his policy or standard to estimate what rate those anile souls may fetch in the devil's market.

SATAN

The Devil can apparently assume any shape, though I repeat some say he can get nothing perfect. He is not only depicted as having cloven hooves and a tail and horns, though this is usual. He is sometimes represented by Cabalists as an angel with wings cut (his fallen state), with a star on his forehead (former star of the morning), bearing a torch (destruction by fire, or "bearer of light," Lucifer), and with the moon (changeableness) at his feet.

While the archangel Gabriel is symbolized by a five-pointed star (the six-pointed one is the seal of King Solomon or "the star of David"), The Devil's pentagram or five-pointed star is upside down, the two points sticking up like horns.

THE TRAGEDY OF THE DEVIL

Writing about the nature of tragedy in *The Forms of Drama* (1972), Robert W. Corrigan remarks that "the great tragedies of history...celebrate the fact that, while a man may learn to have to face and accept the reality of necessity, he also has an overpowering need to give a meaning to his fate."

The concepts of God and The Devil give substance to the inescapable awareness that there are positive and negative forces, good and evil, in our universe, indeed that the existence of one presupposes the existence of the other. The possibility of relying on God (Who presides over all) to protect us against The Devil gives us the comfortable assurance of an eventually happy outcome no matter how tragic our sufferings and death may be. To some, however, there is an appeal in the idea of being contrarian, of taking the side of The Devil, even if in the long run (they must suspect) that it has to be the losing side. Heretical as it may be in the Christian way of looking at the great questions of life and death and the meaning of the whole human experience, it is difficult not to see the world as a battleground of good and evil. And it is easy for many people to believe that, with the free choice that God has given us, we can choose evil and join The Adversary even as did some of the angels, sharing Satan's pride, though they must have known they would be cast out for their disloyalty to God.

Why any being would risk punishment in this way is puzzling, but to answer the question is simple if you can answer these other questions: Why do bad things happen to good people (tragedy)? Why is there sin? Are error and evil not necessary in the overall scheme of things?

BELIEF IN THE DEVIL AND HELL

Whether there is a personality called The Devil is a matter of debate today. Indeed, whether there is a God with a long white beard and a nasty temper, as in the Old Testament, or a nicer one, as in the New Testament, is debated. The Devil may be (say some) merely a convenient personification of a principle of evil (just as God may be just The Force, not a person). Most people seem to believe that malicious Evil and its negativity and also The Force and its creativity and love are active.

As for hell, David Margolick is quoted in *Harper's* Index as reporting that Americans who worry about money and health insurance outnumber those who worry about hell—five to one.

Oddly, many more Americans believe in The Devil than believe in hell, which raises the question (seldom addressed) as to where The Devil is a resident. Perhaps, as Walt Kelly's Pogo used to say, "We have met the enemy and he is us." The bull *Humani generis* of Pius XII, however, requires all Roman Catholics to regard The Devil as a person. And all demons are *real*—and after you!

TAKING OVER THE TEMPLES

Saint Bede (too often given the lower title of The Venerable) in his *Ecclesiastical History* quotes the letter that Gregory the Great wrote to the Abbot Mellitus, whom he was sending to help Saint Augustine convert the English. The wise pope advised that the "idol temples of that race" be converted to Christian shrines and, "because they are in the habit of slaughtering much cattle in sacrifices to devils," new ceremonies be given by the new magical agency to converts from the old one.

Do not let them sacrifice animals to the devil, but let them slaughter animals for their own food to the praise of God....It is doubtless impossible to cut out everything at once from their stubborn minds....

Keith Thomas in *Religion and the Decline of Magic* writes of "the notorious readiness of the early Christian leaders to assimilate elements of the old paganism into their own religious practice, rather than pose too direct a conflict of loyalties in the minds of the new converts." Thus did Christianity accommodate in the shift from paganism, and thus (when Christianity failed to take hold or otherwise was found wanting by some) witchcraft was facilitated in its growth as a heresy or (one might say) a religion to challenge Roman Catholicism.

There are many examples from the early days of Christianity of the new religion tearing down the pagan temples to get rid of the gods, turned demons, or building on the site to replace the old religion. One example will suffice, that of Saint Babylas, bishop of Antioch, who suffered in the persecution by Decius (250 A.D.). Gallus built a church in honor of Saint Babylas on the site of a famous temple to Apollo and at once the demons were banished, the oracle silent. Julian the Apostate tried to contact the oracle that used to be there. He was unsuccessful. In time the bones of Saint Babylas were transferred (it was claimed) to Cremona. There is no record of the Greek oracle reviving.

THE DEVIL OF A LOVER

Will Durant in *The Age of Faith* (Part IV of his wonderful introduction to history, *The Story of Civilization*):

> To common medieval imagination, and to such men as Gregory the Great, the Devil was no figure of speech but a life and blood reality, prowling about everywhere, suggesting temptations and creating all kinds of evil; he could usually be sent packing by a dash of holy water or other sign of the cross, but he left an awful odor of burning sulphur behind him. He was a great admirer of women, used their smiles and charms as bait to lure his victims, and occasionally won their favors—if the ladies themselves might be believed. So a woman of Toulouse admitted that she had frequently slept with Satan, and had, at the age of fifty-three, given birth, through his services, to a monster with a wolf's head and a serpent's tail. The Devil had an immense cohort of assistant demons....The monk Richalm described them as "filling the whole world; the whole air is but a thick mass of devils, always and everywhere in wait for us....It is marvelous that any one of us should be alive; were it not for God's grace, no one of us could escape."

See R. E. L. Masters' *Eros and Evil* (1962) and Roland Villeneuve's *Le Diable* (1963).

THE DEVIL IN THE CINEMA

Inevitably so dramatic a character as The Devil has often appeared onstage and, because of the tricks that photography can play, perhaps even more effectively on the silver screen. *Faust* in one version or another has attracted the talents of Emil Jennings, Andreas Tauber, Richard Burton, and perhaps a dozen other more or less leading actors. Variations on the theme have also been tried: Adolphe Menjou as a suave devil in *The Sorrows of Satan* (1927), Walter Huston as Mr. Scratch in *All That Money Can Buy* (based on Stephen Vincent Benét's story, 1941), Alan Mowbray in *The Devil with Hitler* (1942), Ray Milland as Nick Beal in *Alias Nick Beal* (1949), Stanley Holloway in *Meet Mr. Lucifer* (1953), Ray Walston as Mr. Applegate in *Damn*

Yankees (1958), Vittorio Gassman in *The Devil in Love* (1967), and on and on. Also, devil-worship was the theme (Leslie Halliwell's *Filmgoer's Companion* tells us) not only of *Rosemary's Baby* (1968) but also of *The Black Cat* (1934), *The Seventh Victim* (1943), *Night of the Demon* and *Back from the Dead* (both 1957), *The Witches* and *Eye of the Devil* (both 1966), etc. There are comic witches and warlocks in *I Married a Witch* and *Bell, Book and Candle* and *Bedknobs and Broomsticks* and serious ones in *Day of Wrath*, *The Witches of Salem*, *The Illustrated Man*, *The Brotherhood of Satan*, and many more films. Will Hammer's films liked to deal with devils, vampires, and the like.

Opinions will differ. Some may prefer Dreyer's somber medieval witch hunt in *Day of Wrath* or a semi-documentary by Benjamin Christensen or a pastiche narrated by William Burroughs or....Here are my candidates for the two most interesting films about witchcraft, one truly religious and one wild as only Ken Russell (whose very actors complained to their union about alleged obscenities on the set) could be wild. I'll let two professional film critics describe them for you.

Harry Alan Potamkin on Carl Dreyer's *The Passion of Jeanne d'Arc* (1929):

> This profound and truly passionate motion picture concerns itself with the last day of Jeanne, the day of excruciating torment....The torment of the young peasant girl...convinced in her childishness and mysticism of her divine mission, becomes the emotional experience of the spectator. Her fears, persistent under the insistent examination, become heavy with the burden of the torment, become luminous with the momentary glamor and memory stirred by the queries. The heavy tear imparts to the spectator the sense of the days and months of anguish the girl has endured in her steadfastness to her inspiration. The luminous tear elucidates the girl's origins, her free fields, her home, and the momentum of the inspiration that has urged her into this betrayal. The tears of Falconneti, the portrayer of Jeanne, are not the tears of a Clara Bow, insipid, irritating, fraudulent. Her eyes enamored of God borrow no stage-pantomime, but with the grained skin and parched lips, the clipped hair, and chained walk, reveal the entire enterprise of God within the girl's body. Falconneti faithfully submits to the intensity of the unit, enters into it, and expresses it while she expresses Jeanne. She is the conception. She is the film.

Pauline Kael on *The Devils* (1971):

> The critics were turned off by the madness of *The Devils;* the audiences were turned on by it. They wanted the benefits of the sex-

ual pathology of religious hysteria: bloody tortures, burning flesh, nuns violated on altars, lewd nuns stripping and orgying, and so on.

It is from the cinema and television that most Americans today get their thoughts and thrills of The Devil. It is from such stimuli as those that people get their fear of Satan—or their urges toward Satanism.

SATANISM ON THE TUBE

So alert to Satanism in the modern world is the television audience in both Britain and America that they had no problem accepting the premises of Daniel Boyle's two-part Inspector Morse *Mystery* program called "The Day of the Devil." In it, John Peter Barrie, a sadistic serial murderer and Satanist, escapes from life imprisonment, where he was "writing a book, a black bible," confronts the witch hunter Canon Humphrey Appleton, and commits other crimes. The audience is expected not to share Inspector Morse's belief that all the rigamarole about Satanists, Lammas (a day in August when The Devil is traditionally worshiped), the demon Astaroth, etc., is inappropriate nonsense as we are about to begin "the third millennium." The canon mildly remarks that Satanists not only exist but think of themselves as more realistic, more honest, than convinced Christians.

WARDING OFF DEVILS AND DEMONS

Tradition says that various colors and sounds and smells can ward off demons. Thus the Mediterranean peoples paint a certain blue around doors and windows to keep out vampires and wear blue beads to defend against the evil eye, and so on. Various ritual magic ceremonies and supernatural powers have their appropriate colors and must be used just as vestments of various colors are used at Masses commemorating martyrs (red), the dead (black, more recently violet or even white), expressing hope (green), and so on.

The ringing of bells is supposed to repel devils and demons, and we ring church bells, hand bells at the consecration of the Mass, etc. The garments of the High Priest of the Jews used to be decorated with tinkling bells to drive away evil spirits. (The most distinctive feature of his dress was probably the jeweled breastplate—behind it were secreted devices for fortune-telling.) Small bells are used this way in other cultures to this day. A hand bell is used in the exorcism of "bell, book, and candle" and in various other magical operations. Music repels evil by its order and harmony.

Evil creatures smell bad and incense drives them off, but "hellish" odors such as sulphur, brimstone, and tar attract them. Incense also represents purification and prayer rising to God (if sweet smelling) or The Devil (if repulsive). A new abode should be fumigated by burning camphor and myrtle and aloes or nutmeg. Camphor is of the Moon, myrtle of Venus, aloes of the Sun, nutmeg of Jupiter, and the house itself of Virgo, but the magical rite to protect it should be that of Saturn (in case that is any help to you). It is also said that angels were originally created out of fire, that *jinn* and spirits called up in necromancy and spiritualism's séances are assisted to become visible by the production of smoke, and that incense can be hallucinogenic (burning datura and henbane and other such drugs greatly assist people to "see things"). Most of all, perhaps, color and sound and incense create the atmosphere in which visualization, the key to magic, is best supported.

NEEDED TO CALL UP THE DEVIL

Eliphas Lévi has stringent rules about conditions for calling up devils and demons. You must have:
1. Invincible obstinacy.
2. Hardened conscience without fear or remorse.
3. Hatred or ignorance of all goodness.
4. Complete trust in The Devil.
5. The Devil as your god.

If you meet those conditions, I think, in a phrase from Stephen Sondheim's song *Call in the Clowns*, "Don't bother, they're here."

STORIES OF THE DEVIL

To any reasonable person, it is perfectly clear that much is said about the Devil that is the pure invention of persons who know they must be lying, that they could never really know what they pretend to be certain truth. To reasonable persons, also, it is pretty clear that much is said about The Devil that is more or less obviously nothing but illusion, that some people are insane, deluded, wholly untrustworthy, when it comes to this topic.

History has lied, religion has lied, saints and sinners have lied, and the truth is much obscured. Nonetheless, behind it all any honest person will have to admit that she or he senses that there is indeed something factual, palpable, undeniable, about evil, if not the personification of evil, that there is something we might call The Devil if not actually someone we might call The Devil.

In Charles Maturin's *Melmoth*, a shipwreck brings to The Wanderer the Spanish character called Moncada. He utters at one point a sentence that rings frighteningly true in connection with the tales (however unfounded or exaggerated) that we hear told about the Devil. The sentence is this: "There is no more horrible state of mind than that in which we are forced by conviction to listen on, wishing every word to be false, and knowing every word to be true."

You may doubt the tale of the archangel thrown out of Heaven for his overweening pride. You may reject the idea of the Adversary who rules in Hell, the argument that "misery loves company" and that the demons seek the souls of men. You may think it absolutely silly that some people think (or ever thought) that The Devil has horns and a tail. But down deep you know, you feel, that there is an evil force constantly at work in the world, and that there is, there must be, some kind of intelligence behind that evil force.

That is The Devil—or whatever else you want to call him, or her, or it.

The demon Baphomet in a drawing signed by Eliphas Lévi.

2

A Host of Demons

About the middle of the fifteenth century, Alphonsus de Spina published at Strasbourg his *Fortalicium Fidei* (Fortress of the Faith), defending Christian principles against Jews, infidels, and devils. He himself was a *converso*, a Jew who became first a humble Franciscan and later a professor at the University of Salamanca and a bishop. He was father confessor to John of Castille and was very well connected. He was considered to be a sane and sensible authority on matters theological.

De Spina calculated the number of devils in the high millions. However, things are getting better for the beleaguered innocents. Because we can reproduce and devils cannot, the population of the world today (in billions) outnumbers the devils (in millions), though there were fewer humans than devils in his day, De Spina calculated. In line with various Doctors of the Church, De Spina saw the world as threatened by hordes of fallen angels and other dangers.

DEMON MASKS

Superstition offers a plausible explanation for the inexplicable. If you know nothing of germs, you may ascribe disease to demons. If you believe that demons cause specific diseases, then using the masks portraying those demons may cure the diseases. So Chinese children are made to wear measles masks, and both Chinese and Burmese children sometimes are given cholera masks to wear. Similarly, a masked dancer could summon the *kachinas* (spirits) of the Pueblo Indians, protect the Iroquois from the *Gahado-goka gogosa* demons, drive off a demon of disease among the Singhalese, bring the powers of the invisible world to African tribes, etc. Masks portraying the gods and goddesses may bring those powers down to earth. Masks portraying dead ancestors will placate them and cause them not to plague the living. Horrible false faces can frighten away demons just as they frighten the enemy in war. Portrait masks placed on the corpses of the dead can assist the soul to recognize its body when it wishes to return to it. The skull could be made into a mask of power. Maskers pretending to be the dead returning to visit the living can exact tribute from them. This is done in Africa both as a joke and seriously and, of course, in America we have the "trick or treat" masked characters of Halloween. Finally, wearing a mask assists the magician in giving up his own personality to be taken over by some devil, demon, or good spirit.

BABYLONIAN DEMONS

Nina, the Babylonian serpent goddess, was combined with features of the dragon Tiamat, and what was to become the "Old Serpent" of *Revelations*, the embodiment of all evil, was born. See L. W. King's *Babylonian Magic* and R. C. Thompson's *Devils and Evil Spirits of Babylonia*.

THE DEMONS OF XENOCRATES

This Greek philosopher of the fourth century before Christ was a pupil of Plato. His works exist in only a few fragments but they are enough to show his thoughts on demonology, especially his interest in the continual opposition of good and evil and his division of the universe into gods (Titanic and Olympian), men, and demons. He said that these demons were propitiated by what most people thought of as religion, like philosophy created to relieve our anxieties and quell our fears. He set the stage for Christianity to look upon pagan deities as devils and demons.

In addition, the ancient world had Pluto and other powers of the underworld, Serapis, various versions of Venus and Mars, Proserpina, Priapus, and other gods of the Egyptians (such as Isis and Osiris), the Greeks, the Romans, and more. Of ancient deities my personal favorite happens to be Mithras. Mithras appears as a lion killing bulls, as a handsome youth in a Phrygian cap, etc., and his religion (which appealed to Roman soldiers, who took it to Britain and elsewhere) looks something like early Christianity, which followed it. Any of these pagan gods could be resented—King David said all the pagan gods were demons!—and could be condemned by those who wanted worship to be given only to their own deity or deities. "Cast aside foreign gods," Jacob commanded his household, who gave up their idols (and their gold earrings), which Jacob buried under a tree. Nonetheless *Judges* X says Israel "did evil in the sight of the Lord" by honoring a series of idols of their neighbors. *Exodus* XXXII:4 says the Levites went on a rampage and killed 3,000 of their fellow Jews in one day because they worshiped the Golden Calf. This was apparently in the service of their God and violence approved by Him.

The Jewish God said right up front that He wanted no "other gods before Me." Or "Us," to be more exact, because at the beginning of the Bible He is *Elohim*, which is a Hebrew plural. He seems to have been very touchy about rivals, which is why the archangel who led a rebellion was quickly dispatched to Hell. There he, too, put on great pomp: "High on a throne of royal state exalted Satan sat," says Milton, who as Latin secretary to Oliver Cromwell, The Lord Protector of The Commonwealth, did not think much of regal panoply.

For the Jews to overturn the glittering throne of a rival idol is understandable. But to declare that the gods of others are devils and demons was a bit much.

DEMONS IN THE JEWISH SCRIPTURES

In all of the Mishnah the only reference to *mazzikim* (harmful spirits) is one that says they were created on the eve of the Sabbath of creation. Both Rabbi Hillel and his pupil Rabbi Johanan ben Zakkai were said to understand the speech of *shedim* (devils).

There are two principal Talmuds: that of Jerusalem and that of Babylonia. The Jerusalem Talmud adds to *mazzikim* and *shedim* the word *ruhot*, also signifying "demons." The Babylonia Talmud has more demonology (according to the *Jewish Encyclopedia*): "The Babylonia Jews lived in a world which was filled with demons and spirits, malevolent and sometimes benevolent, who inhabited the air, trees, water, the roofs of houses, and privies." These creatures outnumbered human beings and had specific goals and times of greatest activity. Reciting Psalm 91 kept them at bay. The encyclopedia warns of drinking water from pools on Wednesday and the eve of the Sabbath, from drink left under the bed, from cups in pairs, etc., and Solomon is said to have forced demons to bring him water from

India to grow exotic plants which otherwise would not have grown in Israel. "The talmudic commentators and codifiers accepted the belief in demons; Maimonides alone opposed it," the encyclopedia states. The cabalists codified more and added Arabic, Christian (especially Slav), and other demonologies.

WHERE THE DEVILS AND DEMONS CAME FROM AND WHAT TO DO ABOUT THEM

It's difficult to say where gods came from (but not impossible), while the origins of devils and demons is simple. The Judeo-Christian tradition gets our devils and demons from the Jews (who regarded the deities of all other peoples as evil), and the Christians modified the Jewish beliefs somewhat and added their own remakes of the figures of pagan mythology. Once these were all in place, rituals conducted according to certain agreed-upon rules could generate more devils and demons or put into action already extant entities. Everywhere was rich in devils and demons, hard at work. So magicians got to work, too.

If you are not Jewish and you are not Christian, and you aren't a follower of Islam (which undertakes to update and improve those older religions), you probably don't worry about all the infernal enemies that bedevil followers of those religions. You may even embrace the beliefs of some magicians (and some other religions), which include defining evil as not merely prevalent but necessary and to be incorporated into one's thinking, accepted as a balance of the world.

Julio Caro Baroja in *The World of the Witches* traces occult performers back to the matriarchal societies of worshipers of the moon, the Goddess, Diana, fertility, etc. Margaret Murray in *The God of the Witches* posits a horned divinity, god of hunting and other male pursuits, driven underground by Christianity. Female or male to begin with, magic is likely to be, I think, an

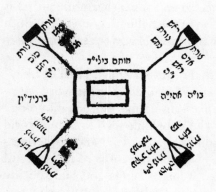

Sigil of the demon Bilad from *Sefer Berit Menuhah* by the cabalist Abraham ben Isaac ha-Sefardi Berdichev, 1807. *JNUL*, Jerusalem.

expectable if uncomfortable by-product of religious irrationality and mysticism. Rudolph Steiner, in *In Bluebeard's Castle*, asserts that magic is the product of decaying religion. This, I believe, is on the right track: Magic comes from religion as it moves through superstition toward myth. Magic represents the stage at which people rise up (Jules Michelet's theory) to oppose the oppression of religion and determine to take matters into their own hands. It may be helped along by ego trips, drug trips, or other factors, but it always seeks practical solutions, however radical or ridiculous, to real problems. Magic wants something and, to get it, it is willing to risk challenging and is excited about challenging moribund tradition and entrenched powers that be.

Someone once criticized Protestantism by saying that "every butcher boy can be his own pope." A magician can become his own god. "A sound magician is a mighty god," gloats Dr. Faustus. "Curse God, and die," wails Job. "Fight God and win," replies the magician. He has to fight The Devil and his dominions as well. The very world *religion* is about community; it speaks to what ties people together, connects them. Magic (as you see in English *The Great Work*, German *Zauber*, etc.) addresses itself to breaking away by taking individual action. Religion takes faith. Magic takes courage. Magic gets into action.

CLEMENTINE HOMILIES

Early in the history of the Christian faith, perhaps as early as the second century, perhaps as late as the fourth, a theory was put forth that Tertullian and Athenagoras and other authorities accepted, though Saint John Chrysostom seems to have been on the right track to reject it. The theory appears in what have been called *Clementine Homilies*; it concerns the origin of the pagan gods, good and bad. It is therefore related to Christian demonology, for the pagan gods were often said to have become the devils and demons of the Christian world. (For early Christian demonology, start with E. H. Zaug's *Genetic Study of Spirit Phenomena in The New Testament*, 1917.) Over the centuries the numbers and powers of devils and demons increased rapidly in Christian thought. Duns Scotus suggests that even The Devil, originally created good (because the Creator is good), could do good things as well as evil deeds, if he wished, and that the pagan gods had the same powers. In the Renaissance, renewed interest in pagan gods and also turmoil in Reformation and Counter-Reformation debates focused more attention on the pagan gods and their relationship to the spiritual world of the Christians, who not only built their churches on the sites of pagan temples but in many cases took on some of the pagan ideas, putting halos on a statue to Venus and Cupid to make it into the Blessed Virgin and the Infant Christ and otherwise altering pagan holidays (such as Saturnalia to Christmas) and pagan religious beliefs for Christian uses.

Reading *Genesis* and the story of the Flood, the Clementine commentaries made new use of the old. They suggest that although the Flood destroyed the offspring of lustful angels and human women, the souls of these semi-supernatural creatures were not destroyed. The idea that demons could mate with humans and produce offspring continued for a long time in Christian thought. It may still be inconveniently inescapable within the structure of the dogma, but over the centuries the conviction that fallen angels bred with humans has given way to the argument that demons, called *incubi* and *succubi*, were sterile and that semi-supernatural creatures were not possible. Still, the faithful were ready to accuse Martin Luther, after he started to give the Roman Catholic Church such trouble, of being the outcome of a demon-human copulation. This was not metaphorical. Those who hated Luther and his Reformation were not saying that his ideas came from The Devil and were mixed with good Christian ideas. They were saying he was part demon and part human.

To put it briefly, the early products of demon-human intercourse became the gods of the Greeks and other peoples. That was the argument. Far more people believed that than ever subscribed to the allegation that Luther was semi-supernatural. This theory of angel-human was supported by the misconception in the *Book of Enoch* of details of *Genesis* and strengthened by the fact that the *Book of Enoch* on supernatural creatures is noted in the New Testament literature of *Corinthians* and *Jude*.

In the Jewish tradition of *kosher*, of course, a mixture of half supernatural and half human is unacceptable. In my view, that is why the Jews rejected the divinity of Christ, quite apart from His unsatisfactory performance as a political leader. A prophet or messiah in the Jewish view must be from God but not God Himself in human form. The *Clementine Homilies* are also in direct opposition to the Christian view that the mixture of the human and the divine consists solely of the immortal soul resident in a temporary human body, and that Jesus Christ, the Son of God born of woman, was the only true combination of the divine Word and humanity: "and the Word was made flesh, and dwelt among us," later to go to heaven to rule. Roman Catholic dogma is forever to say that angels and demons on the one hand and human beings on the other are different species. An angel or a demon may take human form, we are told. A human cannot ever become an angel, or a fallen angel. Humans can become saints and join the angels in heaven; they can be damned and join the devils in hell. But they cannot become angels or devils.

The miscegenated children of fallen angels and mankind were said to have died in the Flood, going then to rule as gods and goddesses of pagan times. This is as heretical in traditional Christianity as the doctrine of Origin (the final redemption of the fallen angels and their being restored to heaven). The official view of the Roman Catholic church is that the fallen angels will never be forgiven or return to heaven, as was made clear by the Fourth Lateran Council's profession (1215). Devils are devils, angels are angels, and humans can be guided by one or the other but will always be human souls.

DEMONS BORN OF WOMAN

The Book of Jubilees extends habitual. Hebraic misogyny when it says that a race of demons that survived the Flood here mated with human women. The medieval encyclopedist Rabanus Maurus (Raban the Moor) thinks this likely. With the frailness of femininity and the shrewdness of demons, women didn't stand a chance. By the Middle Ages the term *demon* meant not just any spirit but an evil spirit, and what was more evil to a Christian, especially a celibate cleric (who could read and write and whose views were therefore recorded and preserved), than the sins of the flesh?

Valerie I. J. Flint in The Rise of Magic in Early Medieval Europe writes that the enormous variety of religious cults which had survived into this [Roman] empire—Zoroastrian, Neoplatonic, Jewish, Gnostic, Christian—had one strong link between them... demons as spirits of evil. Demons, whether they lived in the upper or the lower air, in the known world, in people, or in hell, were held to be real and powerful agents of human misfortune, and the possessors of supernatural powers. They flew or floated about, awaiting their many opportunities. There were armies of them. They caused plagues and famines, tempests, stormy seas, sicknesses, and deaths. The apocryphal Book of Enoch and the Pseudo-Clementine Hommilies (believed, of course, to be by the real Clement, Saint Peter's successor) were largely responsible for the spread of a story about demons that gained especially wide credence...and extension of the account of the illicit intercourse between lustful fallen angels and the daughters of men. The daughters bore giants, whose souls, surviving the flood, became demons, eternally tormented and tormenting.

How to cope? Two ways. Be sanctified and safe or be bold and manipulate the demons by magic, using them rather than letting them use you. Demons, the writer says in another place, "remain a necessary part of the cosmos as long as irrational and forbidden magical divinations, marvels, and cures are sought after and are thought surely to work."

JEWISH WOMEN DEMONS

Alexander, Tamar. "The Woman Demon in Jewish Customs and Folktales," *Jewish Folklore and Ethnology Review* 12:1-2 (1990), 21.
————"Theme and Genre: Relationships between Man and She-Demon in Jewish Literature," *Jewish Folklore and Ethnology Review* 14:1-2 (1992), 56-61.
————"LeSh'elet Halztuv HaJaneri Shel Sipurney Shedim," *Dappim-LeMehkar-BeSifrut* 8 (1992), 203-219.

THE WORST NIGHTS FOR DEMONS
ACCORDING TO THE TALMUD

Pesachim: "Never go out alone on Wednesday or Saturday nights, for demons are abroad then, and eighteen legions of them, commanded by Agrath the daughter of Machlath, seek whom they may devour."

TACITUS ON THE JEWS

"A people given to superstition and opposed to religion." *Annals* V (c. 110 A.D.) Any worse than any other people?

FOREVER DAMNED

Satan was, of course, cast from the presence of God forever immediately upon his rebellion, but it was not until 553 A.D. that the Roman Catholic Church decided that demons were forever condemned to hell with him, never able to repent, never to be forgiven. Actually, the Greek for "demon" is the same as that for "spirit," so all spirits of any kind were meant, though this was not made clear until the fourteenth century.

Tertullian, a Doctor of the Church, did not doubt that "certain spirits do exist" and that "the magi also agree with the existence of angels and demons." Soon scholastics were arguing whether angels or demons could breed with themselves or with humans, whether they had physical existence at all (the famous question of how many could dance on the head of a pin), whether they could or should be contacted if that is possible, and so on. But no one was allowed to doubt that demons are forever damned and, because misery hates to be lonely, actively seeking to bring humans to eternal damnation.

THE RANKS OF HELL

Just as archangels and angels, Dominions, Principalities, and Powers are in heaven, so it is said demons and devils are in a hierarchy of hell, Princes, Ministers, Ambassadors, Justices, The House of Princes, and the Trivial Spirits. Alphonsus de Spina (that convert who brought into Christianity a lot of Jewish lore) says there are ten orders of demons. Some other authorities say there are nine orders of devils, some six, some four. This was an idea that was especially appealing to the hierarchical mind-set of the Middle Ages. At the top is God's Adversary himself, Satan. At various times he is confused with Lucifer, The Angel of Light, The Prince of Darkness, The Dark Angel, and others but it is Satan we usually mean when we speak of The Devil. All the others are demons, not devils, though our language tends to regard devils and demons as synonymous. Here are the principal personages in the infernal kingdom. I'll give them in alphabetical order because there is some disagreement about their exact placement. What is more interesting than that, however, is how it is imagined that the kingdom of hell mirrors other kingdoms. It is also interesting how and why students of demonology hit upon the very specific numbers of infernal legions commanded by this or that power. *Mark* V:7 says Christ was attacked by a legion of demons in the form of pigs. They were drowned.

But to our hierarchy: Here, collected from a number of sources, is probably the most complete—I do not claim "the most accurate"—list to be found anywhere:

ABADDON. King of the Demons. Better known by his Greek name, *Apollyon*.

ABIGOR. A horseman with a lance and scepter, commanding sixty legions of devils.

ADRAMELECH. Chancellor of Hell and President of The High Council of Devils.

AGUARES. Grand Duke of Eastern Hell, commanding thirty legions of devils.

ALOCER. Grand Duke of Hell, commanding thirty-six legions of devils.

AMDUSCIAS. Grand Duke of Hell, commanding twenty-nine legions, popular with black magicians.

ANDRAS. Marquis of Hell, commanding thirty legions of devils.

ASMODEUS. Head of the Casinos of Hell, banished to the desert by Raphael.

ASTAROTH. Grand Duke of Western Hell, Lord Treasurer of Hell.

ASTARTE. One of a number of heathen gods and goddesses sometimes consigned to Hell.

AYM. Grand Duke of Hell, commanding twenty-six legions of demons. Also *Haborym*.

AYPEROS. Prince of Hell, commanding thirty-six legions of devils.

AZAZEL. Standard Bearer of the armies of Hell. Also *Satanael*.

BAAL. Commanding General of the Infernal Armies.

BAALBERITH. Chief Secretary and Archivist of Hell, a second-order demon. Also *Berith*.

BALAN. Prince of Hell.

BEARDED DEMON, THE. His name cannot be given lest people deal with him in search of the Philosopher's Stone (as King Solomon and Paracelsus are said to have done).

BEELZEBUB. Prince of Demons, Lord of the Flies, second only to Satan.
BELIAL. Prince of Trickery, Demon of Sodomy, sometimes called The Antichrist. It is likely he is also the one called *Zephar* by the German demonologist Weir.

BELPHEGOR. Demon of Ingenious Discoveries and Wealth.

BUER. Second-order demon but commanding fifty legions of devils.

CAYM. Grand President of Hell.

CHARON. Boatman of Hell who ferries souls across the Styx or Archeron.

CHAX. Grand Duke of Hell. Also *Scox*.

CRESIL. Demon of impurity and slovenliness (according to Sebastien Michaelis, 1613).

DAGON. Baker of Hell, member of the House of Princes.

EURYNOMUS. Prince of Hell who feeds on corpses.

FURFUR. Count of Hell, commanding twenty-six legions of demons.

GERYON. Giant centaur who (Dante said) guards Hell. Others say the guardian is a dragon.

HECATE. Queen of the witches.

JEZEBETH. Demon of Falsehoods.

KASDEYA. According to *The Book of Enoch* (LXIX:12) "the Fifth Satan."

KOBAL. Entertainment Director of Hell, patron of comedians.

LEONARD. Inspector-General of Black Magic and Sorcery, The Great Negro of the witches' sabbats as a giant black goat. In Germany, *Urian*.

LEVIATHAN. Grand Admiral of Hell; androgynous, he is said to have seduced both Adam and Eve.

LILITH. Princess of Hell, first wife of Adam.

MALPHAS. Grand President of Hell, commanding forty legions of devils. Same as *Caym*?

MAMMON. A word misunderstood was personified as the Demon of Avarice.

MASTEMA. Leader of the offspring of fallen angels by human beings.

MELCHOM. Treasurer of the House of Princes of Hell.

MEPHISTOPHELES. In some versions, servant of Lucifer; in others, The Devil himself.

MERIHIM. Prince of Pestilence.

MOLOCH. Another demon inherited from Jewish belief.

MULLIN. Servant of the House of Princes, lieutenant to Leonard.

MURMUR. Count of Hell, Demon of Music.

NABURUS. Marquis of Hell, connected with Cerberus.

NERGAL. Chief of Secret Police of Hell, a second-order demon, married to Allotu.

NYBRAS. Grand Publicist of the Pleasures of Hell, an inferior demon.

NYSROGH. Chief of the House of Princes of Hell, a second-order demon.

ORIAS. Marquis of Hell, Demon of Diabolic Astrologers and Diviners.

ORTHON. A minor demon familiar to the Comte de Corasse and the Comte de Foix. Another personal demon known by name is *Sybacco*, rather unreliably said to have attended Adriano Lemmi, connected with the alleged Satanic-Masonic cult of Palladinism in nineteenth-century Italy (see Domenico Marggiotta's *Le Palladinisme*, 1895), and then there are all sorts of demons (usually with French names) that possessed French nuns, etc.

PAYMON. Master of Ceremonies of Hell.

PHILOTANUS. Demon assisting Belial in furthering pederasty and sodomy.

PROSERPINE. In some accounts, Princess of Hell.

PYRO. Prince of Falsehood.

RAUM. Count of Hell, commanding thirty legions of demons.

RIMMON. Ambassador from Hell to (Czarist) Russia, Chief Physician of Hell. Also *Damas*.

RONWE. Minor demon commanding nineteen legions of devils.

SAMAEL. Angel of Death, Prince of the Air, perhaps the one who tempted Eve.

SEMIAZAS. Chief of the Fallen Angels.

SHABRIRI. Demon who struck people blind. The Jews also had goat demons *Schirim, Seirim*), demon monsters (*Behemoth, Leviathan*), and *Lilim, Nazzikim, Ruchoth*, and many more.

SONNEILLON. Demon of Hate (Michaelis).

SUCCORBENOTH. Chief Eunuch of the House of Princes, Demon of Gates and Jealousy.

THAMUZ. Ambassador of Hell, Creator of The Holy Inquisition, Inventor of Artillery.

UKOBACH. Stationary Engineer of Hell, Inventor of Fireworks, maybe Cooking Out.

UPHIR. Head of the HMO of Hell, Demon physician and apothecary.

VALAFAR. Grand Duke of Hell "in charge," say Tondriau and Villeneuve (1972), "of good relations among brigands."

VERDELET. Master of Ceremonies of the House of Princes of Hell.

VERIN. Demon of Impatience.

VETIS. A devil who specializes in tempting and corrupting the holy.

XAPHAN. Stokes the furnaces of Hell, a second-order demon.

ZAEBOS. One of many animal-human combinations in Hebrew imitation of the Sumerians. This one is part crocodile, part human.

ZAGAM. Demon of Deceit and Counterfeiting. He can do Christ's first miracle, changing water into wine.

I omit in the list above the information allegedly revealed by Baalberith to Soeur Madeleine de Demandoix in the early seventeenth century. She had pretty familiar names in her first hierarchy but her second (*Carreau, Carnivean, Oeillet, Rosier, Verrier*) and their hierarchy (*Belial, Olivier, Juvart*) look incredibly French.

My list is long enough, though if Weir (who wrote in the sixteenth century) is to be believed, Hell as 66 princes, each commanding 6,666 legions, each legion comprising 6,666 devils. That would amount to about half the world's population in his time. This looks suspiciously like a riff on the number of the Beast of The Apocalypse, 666, which some cabalists say is 600 (false religion), 60 (greed), and 6 (this world).

It might be added that some devils or demons refuse to give their names even when summoned by magical means because in their names is power. On the other hand, having a name always makes communications of any sort easier.

DEVILISH TIMETABLE

Now that you know names and addresses, you might be interested in the best times to contact these infernal beings. Demonologists, ever willing to provide detailed information (of questionable accuracy), have published the following calendar. Here are the months in which these individuals are most busily going about their evil work:

JANUARY: Belial
FEBRUARY: Leviathan
MARCH: Satan

APRIL: Astarte
MAY: Lucifer
JUNE: Baalberith
JULY: Beelzebub
AUGUST: Astaroth
SEPTEMBER: Thamuz
OCTOBER: Baal
NOVEMBER: Hecate
DECEMBER: Moloch

Persons claiming personal knowledge assure me that Astaroth is the most easily reached and Hecate, Leviathan, and Moloch may not be taking calls at all, or these may not be the right names for infernal creatures. I should not advise you to try to get in touch with any of these. It is (a) too dangerous or (b) too ridiculous. Maybe both.

NIGHT STALKERS

Helped by religions that worshiped the sun as the source of good, the concept that evil walks by night has been firmly established. Everyone who has seen a vampire film knows about it. Here are some devils and demons of the night, the forces of darkness, from cultures around the world. I omit gods and goddesses that are in whole or in part good even though they rule the darkness. The Chinese god *Hsuan T'ien Shang Ti* actually exorcises demons. The Hawaiian *Kane-i-ka-wai-ola* waters plants and makes the earth fruitful.

APEP(I). Serpent-crocodile monster in opposition to Ra, the sun god, in Egyptian religion.

APOPHIS. Serpent demon similar to *Apep*, also representing the battle between day (good) and night (evil).

CHERNOBOG (The Black God). Evil, misfortune, death and night to the Baltic and Slavic peoples.

ELATHAN. Celtic god of darkness, one of the evil Formors.

EREBUS. Son of Chaos, guardian of the darknesses surrounding Tartarus (hell) in Greek mythology.

GRAND BOIS (Big Woods). Haitian master of the forests of the night.

HATU-ATU-TOPUN. Dangerous goddess at twilight and dawn in Polynesia.

HETU-AHIN. Same as or similar to Hatu-atu-topun.

LUCIFER,
Empereur.

BELZÉBUT,
Prince.

ASTAROT,
Grand-duc.

LUCIFUGÉ,
prem. Ministr.

SATANACHIA,
grand général.

AGALIAREPT.,
aussi général.

FLEURETY,
lieutenantgén.

SARGATANAS,
brigadier.

NEBIROS,
mar. de camp.

Hellish elite, *Le Dragon rouge* (1822).

IKWAOKINYAPIPPILELE. Causes headaches and other ills, say the Cunas of Panama.

ITZCOLIUHQUI. Aztec god that brought earthquakes, cold, destruction.

KARAU. Guards animals but also brings death to the world, say the Yupas of Panama.

LILITU. An ancient demon; she is mentioned elsewhere in connection with *Lilith*.

MANUVAL. Evil spirit of the night in New Guinea.

ME(T)ZLI. Aztec goddess of the night had an evil side.

MUSH. Iranian demon of eclipses and darkness.

NYX. Daughter of Chaos, sister and wife of *Erebus*.

OROAN. Demon of eclipses in Guyana.

PITKIS. Terrifying god of night of The Baltic.

PO-TANGOTANGO. Personified "gloomy night" of the Maori.

SAKARABRU. Demon of darkness who judges and can be nasty, West Africa.

SET. Egyptian god of the night, storms, evil, and more.

TCALYEL. Female controlling the night when "there is more of whatever is bad," say the Navajo of Arizona.

TEZCATLIPOCA. Aztec great god of "Smoking Mirrors." Has numerous oppositions in him but is bad in his Black manifestation as when the god of sorcerers, etc.

TLACATECOLOTOTL (Rational Owl). Toltec (Mexico) god of evil and night.

TROIAN. Night demon (with waxen wings) in the Baltic and Russia.

YAOTL (Enemy). An aspect of *Tezcatlipoca*.

YALOCAN TUMULU. Darkness and mischief, say some inhabitants of Surinam.

THE HINDU DEMONS

The Hindu demons are perhaps the most awesome of all and must be driven off by dancers wearing the most horrifying masks. The serpent Vritra is the enemy of the gods, Yama is the king of death (with his two dogs dragging off dying humanity), and Ravana is the Demon King served by terrifying *rakshasas*. The god of wealth, Kubera, is attended by demons both male (*yakshas*) and female (*yakshinis*).

In Hindu belief, an *asura* ("breath," or even "not god") is a divinity. In the oldest part of the *Rig*-Veda the word is tantamount to "Supreme Deity," just as Ahura is the god of the Zoroastrians. Later *asura* came to mean not divinity but demon and the Brahmanas speak of contests between the wicked *asuras* and the good gods.

Azuras came, it is said, from the breath of Pajapati (or from his belly when he became pregnant), who was the origin of "gods, men, fathers, Gandharvas, and Apsarases" from water; the bad creatures may be from drops of water spilled. Likewise we may more or less accidentally have got the Rakshasas and Pisachas. Manu, father of men, says the *asuras* derive from "Prajapati's groin." Vishnu Purana says they came from the groin of Brahma. The origins of these evil creatures is, as you see, debated.

In any case, *asuras* now is a term that covers "the enemies of the gods, including Daityas and Danavas and other descendants of Kasyapa, not including the Rakhasas descended from Pulastya." (That from John Dowson's *Classical Dictionary of Hindu Mythology and Religion*).

Let us start with Kasyapa. He was a Vedic sage who did much creation, both of hymns and creatures. Grandson of Brahma, father of Vishnu, grandfather of Manu, the progenitor of all mankind. That's Kasyapa. By Diti, Kasyapa gave birth to the Daityas, unpleasant demons who were *kratudwishas* (spoilers of sacrifices); they had to be defeated by the good gods. These Daityas are hardly distinguishable from other creatures fathered by Kasyapa, called Danavas, also demons. Then there are Darbas (Tearers), destructive demons.

And Rakshasas (Guardians), descended from either the sage Pulastya or (in another story) from the foot of Brahma. These Rakshasas are goblins and ghouls. They can be titans or smaller but they all haunt cemeteries, disturb sacrifices, animate corpses, devour people, harass the devout, and spread disease and disorder. Some scholars have suggested that they represent the barbarian peoples whom the Aryans first encountered, then defeated.

The Hindus have many devils and demons and, as with the Judeo-Christian tradition, there are questions about their origins but a common explanation is that they were first good and later bad (like the fallen angels).

HAITI

Haiti is famous for voodoo, and the supernatural enters every aspect of life, even politics. In addition to *Baron Saturday*, we could mention such dreaded personages as *Maître Carrefour* and the demons *Congo Zandor, Lima, Lingelson* (to whom sacrifices are made), *Olisha* (a pernicious goddess with a complete line in poisons and sorcery, much consulted by evil magicians), and such figures as *Grand Bois* of the forest and night and *Guéde Zarignis*. Haitian practice mixes up African and Christian and devil-worshiping elements into a heady brew of its own. Devils and demons and African deities and Christian saints are all consulted through magical means.

MAYAN EVIL SPIRITS

Mexico has evil spirits of the Aztecs, Toltecs, Zapotecs, and more. The Maya list includes such frightening characters as *Ah Uok Puc, Chac, Ekahau, Hapikern, Kisin, Paqok,* and *Xiba,* to name but a few. *Mam* presides over the five sort of leftover and definitely unlucky days at the end of each Mayan year. With their immense interest in measuring time, the Maya developed a wonderful calendar (associated with various spirits, some evil) and an elaborate astronomy and astrology (with some planets being tied to evil personalities).

DEVIL WORSHIPERS OF BRAZIL

Lebara is an evil god worshiped by the Yoruban cult of Maranhao, Brazil.

EVIL SPIRITS FOSTERING SODOMY

These crop up everywhere and include *Baphomet, Chin, Cavil, Chou Wang, Philotanus,* and *Maran.* Worshipers of evil gods have often been accused of sodomy. Demonizing again!

SOME UNUSUAL DEMONS

It is a subjective call but I think the following are unusually colorful even in the incredible world of devils and demons.

INMAI (say the Chin people of Burma) lives in the post at the front of the house and can cause you to be injured with thorns.

JILAIYA (say the Charmar of India) flies as a bird of night and sucks the blood out of people whose names it has heard.

KOK-LIR (say some Dyaks of Borneo) preys on men only.

MARA (a Buddhist demon) constantly strives to "damn the human soul".

MOKO-NUI and MOKO-TITI are evil lizard demons of the Maori.

SATAN exists under names as different as *Satanael, Kahu, Nitne Kamui*, etc.

DEMONS AND THE WEATHER

Mark Twain observed that everybody talks about the weather but "nobody ever does anything about it." Demons do. Chinese dragons create water-spouts and storms. Witches can call up storms, as we see in *Macbeth*. In Japan, *oni* demons live in the center of tempests. In Akkadian and Egyptian and later mythologies there are demons who create floods—and droughts. Nature spirits in all mythologies can cause bad weather and some specialize in storms at sea or hail.

Demons are given the task of explaining the mysterious and often baleful forces of nature to the unlettered primitive.

ANIMAL FORMS

Demons are theoretically able to assume any shape, but in Africa they often are said to take the shape of crocodiles or leopards or other fierce creatures. Some popular witches' familiars are the forms of cat and dog, hare and pig, birds (especially black ones such as the raven), etc. Demons also inhabit the forms of bull and ox, lion and wolf, bats and other nocturnal creatures, and so on. Borrowing from the satyrs of classical times, perhaps, the more recent mythology related the goat to The Devil and in that form he was supposed to preside at the *Sabbat*. Unpleasant habits of one animal or another would suggest to the superstitious the possibility of that form for a devil in disguise. Of course such creatures as the Tasmanian Devil are not thought to be supernatural, just nasty.

A Babylonian demon of fatal disease, from a wall in Nineveh.

Evil has also been associated with mythological creatures (often half human and half animal, or composed of parts and therefore qualities of several animals). The dragon (or fiery and flying snakes, as in Russian demonology) appears as the embodiment of evil in many cultures and is The Devil himself in the combat with Saint George or the Archangel Michael, perhaps in *Revelation*, where a red dragon is mentioned. Black for evil and red for fire are the basic colors of The Devil and these colors in animal forms suggest evil creatures.

An old superstition says that The Evil One can create nothing perfect, as I have said before, so a devil or demon in animal form may lack a tail or have some other defect. An old woman with a one-eyed black cat was once upon a time easily suspected of being a witch.

THE TOP TEN

We like things in tens because we have ten fingers to count them on. That, in my view, is why there are Ten Commandments, not nine or eleven. Another view is enshrined in the old joke that has God offering Moses "some commandments." Moses asks how much they cost. God says they are free, Moses says, "I'll take ten."

Alphonsus de Spina (1467) who keeps turning up here because his work was so influential, grouped devils and demons in ten classes, with a little overlapping, it is true, but he reached the preferred number. Here is his list, from 10 to 1 in the recently popular TV fashion:

10. Those who persuaded old women to attend the Sabbat.
9. Those who assailed saints.
8. Those in disguise.
7. Those produced by sex with humans.
6. Nightmares.
5. Familiar spirits.
4. Armies.
3. *Incubi* and *succubi*.
2. *Poltergeisten*.
1. Fates.

There is a lot wrong with this list, not least the inclusion of No. 7 when De Spina was at pains elsewhere to deny that demons could breed with humans. He considered that gross superstition.

DEVILS AND DEMONS AS TOURIST ATTRACTIONS

It is odd that reports of appearances by devils and demons have not been publicized as tourist attractions the way, for instance, weeping statues of the Blessed Virgin have been. In 1995 a plaster statue of the Madonna in Cittavecchia (Italy) was reported to have wept blood. The bishop, Giralomo Grillo, was annoyed that communist city officials downplayed the story (as similar officials did in 1967 the Madonna of Czestochowa in Poland) and more annoyed when the blood was officially tested and proved to be male. Within weeks the Church had a dozen more weeping statues of the Virgin to investigate around Italy.

NINE KINDS OF DEVILS AND DEMONS

Anyone familiar with the mind-set reflected in the medieval encyclopedias such as those by Raban the Moor or Isidore, Bishop of Seville, will immediately recognize that nine (three times three) is a powerful number. Just as there are nine choirs of angels, and evil angels attending on us are countered by good and guardian angels, to match the good angels in heaven, there are nine kinds of devils and demons.

1. *False gods* such as Beelzebub.
2. *Lying spirits* such a Pytho.
3. *Iniquitous spirits* such as Belial.
4. *Vengeful spirits* such as Asmodeus.
5. *Deluding spirits* such as Balban.
6. *Creators of tempests*, "the powers of the air".
7. *Furies*, "powers of evil, discord, war, and devastation."
8. *Accusers* such as Christ cast out.
9. *Tempters* such as Mammon.

There does seem to be some fuzzy categorization here, but it was important to someone to get that number nine. Some evil spirits are said to haunt dismal places, some harry but do not greatly injure mankind, some attack physically and some assail spiritually. Some spirits have no corporeality; some have entered the living or the dead and work within their bodies. All evil spirits have one thing in common: They work for The Enemy of Mankind.

MAD AS HELL

Demons come from a broken home and a place of din and discomfort. They are, as Lactantius says (*Divinae institutiones*, quoted in *Ritual Magic* by

"David Conway"), "defiled and abandoned" and they "roam across the face of the earth seeking comfort in their perdition by destroying men. Thus they fell everything with their tricks and stratagems, their deceits and wiles." They are pure malice, like the witch who was caught in London in the eighteenth century, clearly under their baleful influence, slipping poison into the stew pot at a soup kitchen to murder the hungry poor.

I DREAM OF GENII

To have dreams of devils and demons, put laurel leaves under your pillow. Rub your eyelids with the blood of bats. (Be careful. Bats are often rabid.) Omit your nightly prayers, which call for guarding the sleeping one:

> Now I lay me down to sleep.
> I pray The Lord my soul to keep.
> If I should die before I wake,
> I pray The Lord my soul to take.

THE EVIL WATCHERS

The Book of Jubilees says that God created Watchers and some of these He sent to earth to watch and instruct the children of men. The ones who stayed in heaven still live in the fifth heaven (where Satan once lived) but the ones who came to earth were corrupted by mankind, bred with mankind, and were consigned to perdition. They are now in hell (or, some say, the third heaven). Here are some of the Watchers (and what they taught mankind):

AMAROS (resolving enchantments).
ARAKIEL (signs of the earth).
AZAZEL (war equipment, cosmetics, ornaments).
BARAQUEL (astrology).
KOKABEL (the constellations).
PENEMUE (writing, "bitter and sweet, and the secrets of wisdom" to children).
SARIEL (the course of the moon).
SEMJAZA (enchantments, root-cuttings, etc.).
SHAMSHIEL (signs of the sun).

SEPHIROTH

From the left side of God came unholy creatures (and from the right, their opposites). According to A. E. Waite in *The Holy Kabbalah*, here are the bad (and the good) guys:

THAUMIEL (Kether).
CHAIGIDIEL (Chochma).
SATHARIEL (Binah).
GAMCHICOTH (Chesed).
GOLAB (Geburah).
TOGARINI (Tiphereth).
HARAB SERAP (Netzach).
SAMMAEL (Hod).
GAMALIEL (Jesod).
LILITH (Malkuth).

Sammael is Satan. Gamaliel was the middle name of President Warren G. Harding.

THE FALLEN ANGELS

The Dictionary of Angels creates an amazing list of the angels that fell—it took nine days—from heaven, a third of the heavenly hosts (says *Revelation*). De Spina is elsewhere quoted as numbering the fallen angels at 133,306,668, a figure so precise that one hardly knows what to say. *The Book of Enoch* says there were 200 but lists far fewer. The dictionary lists just over 100 names culled from I *Enoch*, the Apocrypha, the Cabala, goetic, rabbinic, patristic, and other writings. Here they are as they appear in the appendix there:

1. Abbadona (once of the order of *seraphim*).
2. Adramelec.
3. Agares (Agreas).
4. Amezyarak (Amiziras; also alternate for Semyaza).
5. Amy (once partly of the order of powers and partly of the order of angels).
6. Anmael (identified with Semyaza).
7. Arakiel (Araqiel).
8. Araziel.
9. Ariel (once of the order of virtues).
10. Arioc(h).
11. Armaros (Abaros, Armers, Pharmaros).
12. Armen.
13 Artaqifa (Arakiba).
14. Asbeel.
15. Asmoday.

16. Asmodeus (Sammael) (once of the order of *seraphim*).
17. Astaroth (once of the order of *seraphim* and of thrones).
18. Astoreth (Astarte).
19. Atarculph.
20. Auza (Oza).
21. Azaradel.
22. Azazel (once of the order of *cherubim*).
23. Azza.
24. Azzael (Asael).
25. Balam (once of the order of dominations).
26. Baraqel (Barakel, Baraqijal).
27. Barbatos (once of the order of virtues).
28. Barbiel (once of the order of virtues).
29. Batarjal.
30. Beelzebub (once of the order of *cherubim*).
31. Beliar (Belial) (once partly of the order of virtues and partly of the order of angels).
32. Busasejal.
33. Byleth (Beleth) (once of the order of powers).
34. Balberith (once of the order of *cherubim*).
35. Caim (Caym) (once of the order of angels).
36. Carnivean (once of the order of powers).
37. Carreau (once of the order of powers).
38. Dagon.
39. Danjal.
40. Ezekeel (Ezequeel).
41. Flauros (Hauras).
42. Gaap (once of the order of potentates).
43. Gadreel.
44. Gressil (once of the order of thrones).
45. Hakael.
46. Hananel (Ananel).
47. Harut (Persian).
48. Iblis (Eblis, Haris) (Mohammedan Satan).
49. Ielahiah (once of the order of virtues).
50. Iuvart (once of the order of angels).
51. Jeqon.
52. Jetrel.
53. Kasdeja.
54. Kawkabel (Kokabel).

55. Lau(v)iah (once partly of the order of thrones and partly of the order of *cherubim*).
56. Leviathan (once of the order of *seraphim*).
57. Lucifer (often, but erroneously, identified as Satan).
58. Mammon.
59. Marchosias (once of the order of dominations).
60. Marut (Persian).
61. Mephistopheles.
62. Meresin.
63. Moloc(h).
64. Mulciber.
65. Murmur (once partly of the order of thrones and partly of the order of angels).
66. Nelchael (once of the order of thrones).
67. Nilaihah (once of the order of dominations).
68. Oeillet (once of the order of dominations).
69. Olivier (once of the order of archangels).
70. Ouzza (Usiel).
71. Paimon (Paymon) (once of the order of dominations).
72. Penemue.
73. Procell (once of the order of powers).
74. Pursan (Curson) (once of the order of virtues).
75. Raum (Raym) (once of the order of thrones).
76. Rimmon.
77. Rosier (once of the order of dominations).
78. Rumael (Ramiel or Remiel).
79. Sammael (Satan, Asmodeus).
80. Samsaweel.
81. Saraknyal.
82. Sariel.
83. Satan.
84. Sealiah (once of the order of virtues).
85. Semyaza (Shemhazai, Azaziel) (once of the order of *seraphim*).
86. Senciner (once partly of the order of virtues and partly of the order of powers).
87. Shamshiel.
88. Simapesiel.
89. Sonneillon (once of the order of thrones).
90. Tabaet.
91. Thammuz.

92. Tumael.
93. Turael.
94. Turel.
95. Urakabarameel.
96. Usiel (Uzziel) (once of the order of virtues)..
97. Verrier (once of the order of principalities).
98. Verrine (once of the order of thrones).
99. Vual (Vvall) (once of the order of powers).
100. Yomyael.
101. Zavebe.
    also
102. Belphegor (Baal-Peor) (once of the order of principalities)
103. Forcas (Foras).

MORE ABOUT SOME OF SATAN'S
COMPANIONS IN DAMNATION

Johannes Weyer's *De Praestigiis daemonum* learnedly cites the names demons bore as recorded by the first-century historian Diodorus Siculus, the second-century philosopher Apuleius, and the third-century fathers of the church Origen and Tertullian. Weyer states that "the special aims and interests of the demons are generally revealed by the explanation of those names." Much more important is this: The Jews made the gods of their enemies into the devils and demons of their own religion. They even made place-names (*Astaroth*) and qualities (*Remmon*) into personages. They likewise abhorred the practices of their enemies in worshiping the Golden Calf and the seven golden idols (The Nymphs of the Amorites, of which the historian Philo tells us, and who had "names of women who were the wives of seven sinful men who consecrated them as deities after The Deluge. The men were Chanaan, Phut, Selath, Nembroth, Abiron, Elat, and Defuat.") Moreover, they objected to the worship of the Queen of Heaven and more. King Solomon himself worshiped Astarte and Astaroth (whom he later banished) and the Jews were led astray into the worship of the Golden Calf at one point.

Here are some of Weyer's (or Weir's) explanations and his interesting comments on the origins of these infernal powers in the order in which Weyer takes them up:

BEL ("old," "nothing," "confused") "was considered a god of the Babylonians."

BEELZEBUB (in II *Kings*, *Matthew*, and *Luke*) was "the foul idol of the Acharonites," Beelzebub "lord of the fly," "who spreads his net for all and catches at least the fly, that is, the weak individual."

BAAL ("dominating or subjecting," "possessing"), "an idol which proceeded from the Siddonians to the Jews, a divinity of Samaria and the Moabites."

BELPHEGOR ("the lord who gapes, who exposes, who is naked"), "a god of the Moabites."

ADRAMELECH ("robe of the king") "was an idol of Sepharvaim...a city of the Assyrians."

ANAMELECH ("affliction or response of the king"), "a god of the Sepharvaim."

BENOTH. "Succot Benoth, 'the tents or tabernacles of the daughters,' was a divinity of the Babylonians."

NERGAL ("the one who explores," "lantern of the tomb") "was an idol of the people of Cutha, who came from Persia and Media."

ASIMA ("offense against the law") "was an idol of the men of Emath."

NEBAS ("the one who relates a vision") "was a god of the Hevites."

TARTAC ("the enchained") "was a divinity of the Hevites."

NISROC ("alluring temptation") "was an idol adored by Sennacherib, king of the Assyrians."

CHAMOS ("stroking, flattering," "withdrawing or taking away") "was a god of the Moabites and the Ammonites."

MELCHOM ("their king," "their Counselor") "was an idol which the sons of Ammon worshiped."

DAGON ("their gain," "their sorrow," "their fish") "was an idol of the Philistines."

ASTARTE ("sheepfold," "flock, herd"), "name of a goddess of the Siddonians."

ASTAROTH ("flocks, wealth," "the one making an exploration," "the worm or moth eating at the law") "a god of the Philistines, according to Josephus."

BAALBERITY ("lord of the covenant").

REMPHA "in the Bible" [the Egyptian name for the planet Saturn].

REMMON "(loftiness")."

ADONIS (Hebrew *Thamuz*, "the one consumed," "a burning"), "a god of the Syrians."

THE MANY FACES OF LILITH

Lilith was a demon, the wife of Adam before Eve came along. Elijah, says Jewish lore, met Lilith and forced her to reveal the various disguises she used when she worked evil on mankind. Here are the names of Lilith, in alphabetical order, that he elicited:

ABEKO	IZORPO	PARTASAH
ABITO	KALI	PATROTA
AMIZO	KEA	PODO
BATNA	KOKOS	SATRINA
EILO	LILITH	TALTO
ITA	ODAM	

I suspect that these odd names are not purely arbitrary,—that some pattern or message is contained in them, but I cannot find it. Can you?

Then J. E. Hanauer in *Folk-Lore of the Holy Land* gives these names of Lilith:

ABRO	'ILS	PETROTA
AMIZ	KALEE`	PODS
AMIZU	KAKASH	RAPHI
AVITU	KEMA	SATRINA(H)
BITUAH	LILITH	THILTHOH
'IK	PARTASHA	

There is some overlap (counting variant spellings also) but there is no explanation of the difference between this list and the former. In addition, a *Dictionary of Angels* adds "from sundry sources" these names:

ABYZU	GALLU	LAMASSU
AILO	GELOU	ZARIEL
ALU	GILOU	ZEPHONITH
ARDAD LILI		

Even allowing for spelling variations (transliteration from Hebrew is as chancy as from Arabic, which Sir Richard Burton suggested was an art rather than a science), there are new names here, too.

THE SEVEN ARCHANGELS OF THE YEZIDIS

It is famous that these alleged devil worshipers of Kurdistan regard God ("Sole Almighty Creator of Heaven") as passive and believe the world to be ruled actively by seven archangels. If you consider that devil worship, then these are seven major devils:

SHAMS-EL-DIN (Sun of the Faith)
FAKR-EL-EIN (Poor Person of the Faith)
NASR-EL-DIN (Help of the Faith)
SIJ-EL-DIN (Mercy of the Faith)
SHEIKH ISM (Power of Mercy)
SHEIKH BAKRA (Power of Mercy)
KADIR RAHMAN (Power of Mercy)

Cornelius Agrippa lists seven angelic rulers (over 196 provinces of heaven) as *Araton, Bethor, Hagith, Och, Ophiel, Phaleg,* and *Phul.* These are different officials. *The Testament of Solomon* (a fake) lists the seven rulers of the divisions of hell as fallen archangels named *Kushiel* (Rigid One of God), *Lahatiel* (Flaming One of God), *Shoftiel* (Judge of God), *Makatiel* (Plague of God), *Puriel* (Fire of God), and *Rogziel* (Wrath of God) plus one other apparently added solely to make the magical number of seven. Elsewhere the archangels of punishment are called *Kezef* (wrath and destruction), *Af* (anger and death of mortals), *Hemah* (death of domestic animals), *Mashhit* (death of children), and *Meshabber* (death of animals), only five.

The main object of worship of devil worshipers everywhere, not only in Kurdistan, is Satan (also called *Samael,* Poison Angel, a name the rabbis use for the angel of death, the angel God sent to call Moses when his years were up, the guardian angel (says *Yalkut* I:110 in the Talmud) that God provided for Esau, maybe (if the *Zohar* is correct) the angel with whom Jacob wrestled. He occurs also in Jewish writings as *Salmael.*

In *The Sayings of Rabbi Eleazar* the angel Samael is the serpent who tempted Eve and by her was the father of Cain. (Satan is also supposed to have a son named Salpsan, according to the apocryphal *Gospel of Bartholomew.*) In A. E. Waite's *The Holy Kabbalah* the angel Samael is the "fifth of the archangels of the world of Briah," which another authority equates with "the sefira Geburah." Cornelius Agrippa calls Samael another appearance of the Greek god of destruction Typhon, and, to cut to the chase, Samael is Satan and Satan is The Adversary and that is the archangel who defied God, preferred ruling in hell to serving in heaven, and was cast into everlasting perdition with all his angelic followers. In II *Enoch* he is

Prince of Demons, an evil magician. In Jewish legend he rules the Seventh Heaven (others say the Fifth Heaven) and with two million angels is one of the seven rulers of the world. In Christian theology he rules hell. To the Yedizis he rules the earth.

DEVILS AND DEMONS ARE "PERSONAL BEINGS"

We Protestants may choose sometimes to look upon the sacrifice of the Mass as merely commemorative of the Last Supper. Roman Catholics must believe it is magic. We Protestants, and some others, may choose to some extent to consider the discussion of devils and demons to be a convenient way of expressing a recognition of forces of evil and chaos in the universe. But Roman Catholics must believe that devils and demons have personal existence, just like you and me. Pius XII's bull *Humani generis* made is clear that Roman Catholics have no freedom to think of devils and demons as merely symbolic. They are as real as you and I and have very nasty personalities and are incorrigible. Also, *they are after you!* I reiterate this.

LIBER PERDITIONIS

This was a medieval Book of Damnation which listed all the damned spirits, a sort of Who's Who of demons.

AZRAEL

In Muslim belief, Azrael (Whom God Helps) is the angel of death. He writes your name in his book when you are born and erases it when you die. *Encyclopedia of Religion and Ethics* (IV:617) credits Azrael with "70,000 feet and 4,000 wings, while his body is provided with as many eyes and tongues as there are men in the world." And women and children, too, one assumes.

In Jewish tradition Azrael is the embodiment of evil but, as the angel of death, does God's work. He is not to be confused with Azriel (also known by the name Mahniel) of the *Zohar*, one of the chief angels of destruction. In the East, however, amulets with the name of Azriel on them are used to ward off destruction. Nor is Azreal to be confused with Azazael, one of the *makkim* or destructive forces. This evil angel taught human beings how to bring the sun and the moon closer to the earth so that they could worship those planets better. It is said the ancient Jews sacrificed goats to him. The *Midrash Petirat Mosheh* seems to advise staying as far as possible away from Azazael. But, because we all must die, we cannot avoid Azrael.

Devils with fire and brimstone torture the lustful in hell. *Le grant kalendrier et compost des Bergiers* (1496).

BELIAL

Belial's name is also rendered as Beliel and Beliar. He seems to be a god of some enemies of the Jews who was made into a demon in Jewish estimation and appears to be confused with the chief of the fallen angels, that is Satan. Saint Paul appears to equate Belial with Satan when he asks, "What concord hath Christ with Belial?" (II *Corinthians* VI:15). Belial is not to be confused with another fallen angel called Bileth, Beleth, Byleth, etc., whose sigil A. E. Waite offers in *The Book of Black Magic and Pacts* and who is evil, or Beliael, who is a good angel. Another good angel is Bedaliel; he is a good angel invoked to exorcise bad angels like Belial.

BEELZEBUB

Still another fallen angel who is confusing. He is Beelzebub, a god of the Philistines who in the Jewish thinking becomes the chief of the nine hierarchies of devils and demons in Hell. To three of the evangelists (Matthew, Mark, Luke) Beelzebub is the chief of the demons and *Matthew* XII:24 calls him the "prince of the devils," but Beelzebub is not the Prince of Darkness, not Satan himself.

In the *Gospel of Nicodemus* there is a story about the Harrowing of Hell in which Christ, during his three-day stay in the underworld, makes a deal with Beelzebub and allows him to be chief of the demons, despite the objection of Satan, because Beelzebub agrees to permit Christ to take Adam and others who went to Hell before the birth of Christ with Him out of Hell to dwell henceforth in Heaven.

To complicate matters, Dante's *Inferno* equates Beelzebub with Satan himself.

But this is enough to show, with a few angels and devils, how the names are confusing. Who made up these names is not known, but some of them have been much mangled since then.

Ochosias, King of Israel, according to *Kings* II, perished because he sent agents to consult Beelzebub.

EFFECTS OF DEMONIC POSSESSION

No, your head doesn't spin around like that of the little girl in *The Exorcist*, but you do vomit up foul matter and foul words, have incredible strength, speak strange languages and in the voices of demons, have ringing in the ears, palms reversed, and—many demonologists have sworn they have witnessed this—spit up needles.

AMULETS AGAINST DEMONS

Sapphires are good, but you can also wear coral, preferably with two branches. Medals of saints are dangerous. A demon might heat one instantly to red hot and burn you badly. Garlic is powerful, but you need the *flowers*, and angelica works as well and smells better. The phallus-shaped ornament (sometimes with wings, in imitation of one found in the ruins of Pompeii, I believe) is called the *satyrica signa* (satyr sign) and, though sometimes regarded by Italian-Americans especially as a protection of virility, actually is basically a protection against the evil eye. Greeks wear blue beads with spots like eyes on them, blue being used throughout the Mediterranean to ward off vampires. (That's the meaning of the blue trim windows and doors of their white houses that I mentioned earlier.)

An eye set in a ring also wards off demons. Medieval people recommended the (left) eye of a weasel.

Various formulas can be written on paper or parchment and carried on the person. The Muslims call these *fatihat*. They also use The Hand of Fatima, inscribed with magical writing. Many Jews no longer nail up a *mezzuzah* by their door. Now that Saint Christopher has been dropped from the list of saints of the Roman Catholic Church because they belatedly discovered that he never existed, a Saint Christopher medal or figurine in your car may not work. In vampire movies, you may have noticed, even the Crucifix doesn't work reliably any more against the demonic undead.

Confronting an evil force with a scapular, a blessed medal, a crucifix, holy water, and so on worked only so long as both the defender and the aggressor had faith in the power of such things. It is your faith that protects you, not the symbol itself. Vampires do not seem to be as religious as they once were, and of course when, as someone did in a funny vampire film, you hold up the Christian cross against a Jewish vampire, you may get the Yiddish for "This will not help!"

Fetish has taken on new meaning now; it seldom is used to mean an amulet any more. *Charm* originally meant a kind of prayer or spell. A real charm requires some writing to be used on or in the amulet. One of the most unusual charms must be the kid-skin belt on which in the first century A.D. Saint Martha (one of the patron saints of Provence) wrote the 31st Psalm as a protection. She used it, in an emergency, to strangle a *tarasque*, a monster that was ravaging the villages along the Rhône.

If it contains bits of bone, or graveyard dirt, or hair, or such, even if there is some scrap of writing, it is more likely to be a *gris-gris*, like a fetish, a small and portable protector derived from the guardian idol of the tribe.

These are still worn in Louisiana and are sold to tourists. I would suggest that you adopt the rule applicable to gumbo (which is the basic word for "mixture"): Don't bother with it unless you trust the maker and can recognize what's in it.

AHRIMAN

The Zoroastrians saw the world as the battleground between the forces of light and the forces of darkness, a dualism that influenced a number of other religions, and the god of darkness they called Ahriman. With him we associated our Satan. There is at least one functioning New York coven, as I write, dedicated to the worship of Ahriman as a Satanist figure rather than as a Persian god.

SETH

The Egyptian lord of the underworld we tend to associate with our Satan. In the sixties and seventies, Seth study was popular among hippies but they could hardly be described as Satanists. So little is known by the average person about Seth that his name can be given to children (and has been) without arousing the opposition that would greet *Lucifer, Satan*, or even *Adolf*.

MEPHISTOPHILIS

Christopher Marlowe's tragic Dr. Faustus exclaims in one of those "mighty lines":

Had I as many souls as there be stars
I'd give them all for Mephistophilis!

I do not include Mephistophilis (whose name may be Greek "destroyer-liar") among the Top Devils elsewhere because Mephistophilis is more a literary figure than a personage in ritual magic. He seems to have been invented by the Byzantine scholar Michael Constantine Psellus. By the time the Abbot of Tritheim got to him, Mephistophilis is confidently described as "a mysterious kind of demon, dark through and through, malicious, restless, stormy"—much, indeed, like all other demons. Soon Mephistophilis was assigned to the planet Jupiter to tie him to astrology and his name began to crop up in magical formulae and rituals. Marlowe's tragedy (posthumously printed 1604), written considerably earlier) and Goethe's *Faust* (the first part of which was published 1808, the whole finished only a short time before his death in 1832) are the chief places to consider Mephistophilis (Goethe spells his name Mephistopheles), not a book on devils and devils *per se*. There are also the musical *Mephisto Walts*, the modern German film *Mephisto*, and other references to this melancholy, sly demon.

PREVENTIVE MEDICINE

Wearing a topaz or jasper will help you to preserve continence, the medieval experts said, just as holding one kind of gemstone or another in the hand during sex prevents pregnancy. Try agate. Most of all, engraved gems with certain designs on them were confidently believed to ward off the demons responsible for disease. Albertus Magnus (1193–1280), perhaps the greatest scientist of his time—if that was not Roger Bacon (c. 1214–1292), who like Albertus was widely believed to be a black magician—had a full belief in the magic power of various gems.

SUPERSTITIONS CONNECTED TO DEMONOLOGY

I have written a whole book, *The Complete Book of Superstition, Prophecy and Luck* about such things as superstitions, but here I may mention a few common beliefs that are connected with long-forgotten beliefs in black magic: It is unlucky to have a black cat cross your path; hold your breath while driving by a cemetery; at the end of the rainbow is a pot of gold.

DEMONS USED TO BE GOOD

Not only were demons once good angels in the Judeo-Christian way of thinking, they also were good in the days of the Greeks. Socrates had a personal demon. In Greek myth, demons were beneficent spirits, angels, and inspirations. Hesiod in his *Works and Days* speaks of these good demons, comparable to what we used to mean by "genius."

"EVIL CANNOT BE AS EVIL AS IT WILLS TO BE"

According to Max Picard:
   If evil did not make its dwelling in man, it would be much more
   evil than it is. Evil cannot be as evil as it wills to be because it is
   tied to man. Because it is in man, a watch is kept on evil. In man,
   the image of God, evil is constricted; it is there under custody as

in a prison. The destructive power of evil would be unlimited if it were on the earth alone, unsheltered by God's image. The earth is saved from destruction because, in God's image, a watch is kept upon evil.

FLYING

The wings of angels, good and bad, must be purely imaginary, symbolic of their speed, that's all. Crawford H. Greenewalt, an expert on hummingbirds, calculated that if angels had wings and were built like humans in other ways, an angel weighing about 154 pounds would have wings 4 feet long. However, he could not fly, because human pectoral muscles would provide only about a third of the power needed to flap the wings.

If you see an apparition that has wings but otherwise looks human, it is not an angel or a devil but something your imagination has made out of a false tradition.

NOTHING TO SNEEZE AT

Roman Catholics are specifically instructed by an old papal admonition to refrain from trying to foretell the future by counting sneezes. The rest of us go on saying "God bless you" and "*Gesundheit*" when people sneeze without ever thinking how this relates to demons. The old superstition said that, when you sneeze, your soul flies out of the body. To protect you from having it seized by a passing demon, we wish you well until it can get back where it belongs.

MONSTERS

The Bible regards some monsters (such as Leviathan) as demons, but not all monsters are devils or demons. For a survey of the whole field, see Daniel Cohen's alarming *Encyclopedia of Monsters* (1987) and similar works.

Francis Barrett and others have undertaken to draw the portraits of devils and demons, most of whom look monstrous. Behind it all, I suppose, is the age-old assumption that an ugly exterior bespeaks an ugly interior, but the Puritans (who were so wrong about so many things) were probably correct in assuming that beauty ought to put us more on our guard. In any case, Shakespeare, as in so many other instances, sums it up authoritatively: "There is no art to catch the mind's construction in the face." As the arch-deceiver, Satan ought to be expected to have appearance belie reality.

Remembering that, like so many other aspects of demonology, assertions are made by people who offer no evidence whatever to back up their extraordinary opinions, we can list some of the physical descriptions of famous devils and demons. As in the case of pagan idols (some of which we turned into demons), odd attributes and equipment may be intended not as reporting but as merely representative of powers ascribed. Recall that Janus (after whom we named what is now the first month of the year) was supposed to have two faces; actually, he was supposed to look both forward and back. Horus had the head of a bird. The Holy Spirit (a.k.a. The Holy Ghost) is depicted as a bird. Abraxas, a god of the Gnostics, from whom the famous magical *abracadabra* comes, had the head of a rooster. Andras has the head of an owl.

You will note that monstrous combinations abound in ancient mythology. Like The Sphinx and the griffin, the centaur and such, devils and demons are often combinations of human and animal or two or more animals. Animal-bird combinations or animal-snake combinations are common. The results are monstrous. In a related vein, children born grotesquely deformed were said to be of The Devil, and some unfortunate women were put to death for bearing these children.

Not all devils and demons look unattractive. For example, Abigor among the males and Astarte among the females are said to be overwhelmingly attractive and, when Beelzebub and Belphegor and such

Behemoth, from William Blake's *The Book of Job.*

take on female form for their nefarious purposes, they are gorgeous. Astaroth has a good physique but looks a trifle unwell, pale. Some demons are especially well endowed for sexual tempting, the males with extraordinary phalluses and the females (such who tempted Saint Anthony and other sex-starved hermits in the desert) with huge breasts and even scented thighs.

Attributing manifold powers to supernatural beings creates some monstrous representations, as with the multi-limbed creatures of Indian religions or the three faces or three heads of certain Christian devils and demons. Baal is said to have three heads, for example: that of a cat (like certain Egyptian and other deities), that of a king (wearing a crown to indicate power), and that of a toad (a creature much connected with witchcraft and spells). You'll see his picture at the end of this chapter.

For the first thousand years of what the Jews persist in calling not *Anno Domini* but the *Common Era*, Satan himself was depicted as handsome and sporting a false exterior of beauty and holiness. But in the later Middle Ages and in the Renaissance, Satan was described as hideous. He appeared in various forms to Martin Luther, mostly animal. Once Luther threw an inkwell at him, and you can see the mark on the wall to this day. Recall that the Roman Catholics said Satan was the father of Martin Luther and looked just like him.

GARGOYLES AND OTHER DEVILS IN CHURCH

These represent devils and demons as monsters. They are usually on the outside of churches and are frequently used for rain spouts. The demon most frequently seen inside churches is probably the dragon that Saint George is depicted as killing, representing evil and heresy, just as Saint Michael the Archangel is shown defeating The Devil.

An old prayer said after Mass invoked Saint Michael and underlined the dangers of evil in the world:

Saint Michael the Archangel, defend us in the battle, be our safeguard against the wickedness and snares of The Devil, whom God rebuke, and do thou, O prince of the heavenly host, cast back into Hell Satan and all the other wicked spirits who roam through the world seeking the ruin of souls.

SPIRIT RAPPERS

These are not like the *Poltergeists*, who throw things around and make a terrible racket, but a kind of British fairy who, in the mines, leads miners by their tapping to rich veins. There are bad spirits underground as well, especially (say Paracelsus and others) in German mines. The mineral cobalt is named for them.

GETTING BAALBERITH ON YOUR SIDE

To get the demon Baalberith (about whom demonologists disagree , ranking him anywhere between lord and librarian) on your side for twenty years, all you have to do is take a black chicken to a crossroads at night and sacrifice it. As you cut its throat, say: "Berith, do my work for twenty years." Then bury the chicken so deep that it will not be dug up by animals or otherwise disturbed. If you can manage to chuck it into a pothole that soon will be repaired by your local authorities, you are especially lucky.

In fact, you'll be lucky to get any pothole repaired.

DEMONS IN RINGS AND BOTTLES

In 1523, Don Alfonso Manriquez, Grand Inquisitor, gave orders to arrest "any person [who] made or caused to be made mirrors, rings, phials of glass or other vessels therein to contain some spirit who should reply to his inquiries and aid his projects." It looks as if Christians in formerly Muslim Spain were picking up the idea of an imp in a bottle, the *djin* (as we sometimes spell it) who is "the slave of the lamp," and a lot more hocus-pocus from the fairy tales of *The Arabian Nights* and "Alladin's Wonderful Lamp." There's an interesting short story you should seek out; it's called "The Bottle Imp."

A DICTIONARY OF DEVILS AND DEMONS

Julien Tondriau (author of *Occultism*) and Roland Villeneuve produced a work with the above title which, because of its French origins, naturally stresses the French aspects of the topic. It is chock full of items of French demonology and Satanism you will not find even in larger compendia than their little paperback.

Among French personalities in this subject they note Eliphas Lévi (1810–1875, the ritual magician who claimed not to have dabbled in practice); a number of possessed nuns (remembered in such works as *Soeur Jeanne des Anges* 1886, *Proces Verbal...a Louvier* 1883, *Histoire admirable... possession...d'une penitent* (1613); authors of works on the Sabbat and evil spells such as Pierre Lancret (1553–1631), who crushed the Basque witches with fierce efficiency); the Comte de St.-Pol (who "committed numerous crimes and was afterwards changed into a werewolf"; Jacques Roulet, who while a were-wolf killed a boy and was condemned to death but had his sentence reduced to two years in jail; two men who were burned at the stake in Dôle for being "bankers of the Devil"; judges determined to root out witchcraft (Jean Bodin 1529–1596); Paul Grillandus, with an important tract on heresy and witch-craft of 1536; Le Sieur Bouvet, with an influential book of 1659; and Bishop François Sadoval, who pardoned a witch who gave him proof of her pow-ers by flying on a broomstick for him; not to mention the judge who con-demned Pierre Gandillon to be burned alive because he changed himself into a hare; the man who claimed he was sent to "exorcise the Roman Church" (Jean-Antoine Boullan); men and women put to death for witchcraft (Angela de Labarthe may have been the first French witch burned alive, 1274, and the last French execution for witchcraft was in 1856); the Château of St.-Croix of which The Devil himself took title, and evil French cemeteries, mountains, etc.; and many obscure and of course famous Frenchmen such as the infamous Gilles de Rais (the Marshal of France who raped and killed many small boys for The Devil), Robert *Le Diable* of Normandy (whose bas-tard son became William the Conqueror), Charles IX (who, dying, had a teraphim made out of a beheaded young Jew in the hope of foretelling his future), Jacques de Molay (Master of The Knights Templar), Father Urbain Grandier (of the Witches of Loudon fame), and on and on.

There are *grimoires* mentioned (such as *Le Petit Albert*) and a host of other French words less familiar than *grimoire* concerned with the subject unknown to most French speakers today, such as *breiche, burbot, corrigans, coulombe, drac, embarrer, gaffe* (not in the sense of error), *gerulf,* and so on down the alphabet to *vaudoiserie.* We learn that the French for *poltergeist* is *rabbat.* We learn that the seventh son of a seventh son (sometimes the ninth son) is supposed to have magical powers; in the United States we used to call him *Doctor* and in France they gave him the name *Marcou.*

They also note the works on the diabolic published in the nineteenth century by Charcot and his pupils, including *Le Sabbat des Sorciéres* by Bourneville and Teinturier 1882, Collin de Plancy's popular *Dictionnaire infernal* (half a dozen editions from 1818 to 1863), up to more modern works such as Robert Amadou's exposé of *Les Grands Mediums.* One misses such big names in the field as Gillot de Givry, Jules Michelet, Leloyer's *Histoire des Spectres,* Tranquille's *Relation de Loudon,* Salverte's *Sciences occultes,* but no small book can encompass a topic which has fascinated writers for so many centuries.

Every country, every language, has its own major and minor figures, its own stories, its own vocabulary. For France, Michelet's *Satanism and*

Witchcraft: A Study in Medieval Superstition (available in English) is a good place to start. *A Dictionary of Devils and Demons* is a useful handbook.

THERE ARE NO DEMONS

From Eliphas Lévi's *Transcendental Magic: Its Doctrine and Ritual* (trans. A. E. Waite, reprint 1968):

> Man is himself the creator of his heaven and hell, and there are no demons except our own follies. Minds chastised by truth are corrected by that chastisement, and dream no more of disturbing the world.

This is to suggest that, like the Tibetans, we must learn to create *tulpas* (demons) with our imaginations and determination, evoke them fearlessly, and banish them utterly, freeing ourselves thereby from their real power to harm us. All their terrible power lies in superstition and credulity; it lies in our false belief that they have an objective existence about which we can do nothing. With the control of the self, one controls the universe: "I myself am Heaven and Hell." Give no control to the demons you create and defend yourself against the demons that spring from the evil minds of others.

APOLLO AS A DEMON

The *Leggenda aurea* of Jacopo de Voragine tells us that when Saint Benedict took over the temple of Apollo and made it into an oratory to Saint John, the god was so angry he turned himself into a black demon with flaming eyes and tormented Saint Benedict.

GHÂYA OR *PICATRIX*

Composed in Arabic and known as the *Ghâya*, an important manual of magic was translated into Spanish at the court of Alfonso X, and under the title *Picatrix* was widely circulated in Latin in the Middle Ages. (The Warburg Institute published a translation in 1927.) It gives prayers and rituals by which the magician can get the stars to help him and provides *sigila* or pictures of the astral powers. Engraved on previous stones, these figures could work astrological magic. In a time when Cecco d'Ascoli died at the stake for calculating the date of birth of Christ, it is amazing that astrology and the calling upon pagan astral powers were allowed. Leo X founded a chair of astrology in the Sapienza University and there were

other such professorships at The Sorbonne and in several Italian univer-
sities. Everyone, from the popes who used horoscopes to plan their coro-
nations and consistories, down to the most ignorant peasant, believed in
astrology more or less and in the devils, demons, gods and goddesses of
antique legend associated with the stars and planets.

SMOKING THEM OUT

Quite apart from the hallucinations attributable to the burning of psychotropic substances at magical rites, smoke has other uses in demonology.

Perfumed smoke, incense, can attract and calm down devils and
demons. They especially like sandalwood and cinnamon and myrrh. Specific incenses are often noted in instructions for ritual magic along with
the suitable colors, metals, and so on.

Smoke at magical ceremonies may give spirits called to show themselves substance out of which to form apparitions. It may also cloak charlatanism, of course. You have heard the expression "smoke and mirrors."
I have seen combinations of smoke and gauze on strings produce marvelous
imitations of ectoplasm. In one séance that was as rowdy in its conclusion
as it was elaborate in its fakery, dry ice vapor filled the room and produced
not only beautiful effects of light from the single candle in a milk-glass
shade but a good cover for the medium, who left her chair to manipulate
her effects.

When she tried to get back to her seat, however, she found that I had
put out my hand, and, discovering she had left her place, I had moved to
occupy it. When the lights came up, I offered her the seat I had vacated.

Books on magic say a lot about driving away devils and demons with
smoke. The Bible recounts the advice of the archangel Raphael to Tobias
to burn the heart and liver of a fish to drive off the fearful demon Asmodeus,
who had killed off seven successive husbands of Sara. For most demons,
burning asafoetida will suffice to get rid of them. In the nineteenth and
early twentieth century, children in the United States often were made to
wear little bags of his unpleasant-smelling stuff around their necks. That
was supposed to ward off germs and was considered to be a magical protection. I suspect it worked principally by keeping at a distance people who
might be carrying germs.

KNOWLEDGE FROM DEVILS AND DEMONS

Having been around a very long time, devils and demons were supposed
to have great knowledge, the way gnomes and trolls had stored up great

wealth. Carmelite monks in Bologna in the fifteenth century taught that there was no sin at all in obtaining knowledge from infernal spirits. In 1474, Sixtus IV put them right and outlawed the practice. Ten years later, Innocent in *Summis desiderantes* completely forbade dealing with devils and demons but at the same time he stayed clear of making belief in the powers of witches and sorcerers a matter of faith and dogma.

EBLIS

Eblis (Despair) is the Persian Satan, the chief of the fallen angels. William Beckford in *Vathek* says Eblis was once the angel Azazael, whom St. Augustine and others say was condemned by God for refusing to worship God's new creation, Adam. God appointed three angels (Aebel, Anush, and Shettel) to look after Adam, according to *Yalkut Reubeni* and *The Book of Adam and Eve*, but some angels were not happy with God's new work. In Guinzberg's *The Legends of the Jews* I:63, the angel Azazel was supposed to have said to God: "Me Thou hast created of smokeless fire, and shall I reverence a creature made of dust?" For this disobedience God cast him from heaven.

MUSLIM DEMONOLOGY

The Muslims especially feature among spirits both good and bad the *jinn* (demons). If you look at the singular, *jini*, you are reminded of *genii* and maybe *I dream of Jeannie* on television. These demons famously were made of smoke, "the slaves of the lamp," and sometimes imprisoned in bottles, as you know from stories you must have read as a child. In Muslim theology they are thought to antedate Adam by 2000 years or more and were first like our angels. But Iblis and his five sons rebelled against God, were cast out of heaven, and became devils. In addition there are the *gul*, like our ghouls consuming the bodies of the dead; the *sealáh* inhabiting the forests; and the odd *skikk*, like half a human being, among others. There are said to be forty troops of assorted devils and demons, 600,000 in a troop. There is something of numerology in these numbers, but the main thing is that the Muslim world is full of invisible and often rapacious and dangerous creatures. It is a world of marvels, of magicians, a world where (as in the *Arabian Nights* tale of a man who is tricked into thinking his donkey has turned "back" into a human being) the supernatural is ever present and totally taken as fact.

DEMON GUARDIANS

Frightening, monstrous, often hybrid demons are represented in many cultures as guardians of the home (on metal plaques or carvings, in Bali), of the sacred shrines (giants outside Chinese Buddhist temples), on amulets, on the dragon prows of ships (copied from the East by the Vikings in the eighth century), on personal jewelry (many demoniacal attributes being derived from ancient gems and seals); architectural design (the Gothic style used grotesque gargoyles and other *droleries*), masks and vestments in painting (particularly scenes from the temptations of saints such as Saint Anthony), etc., though in some cultures picturing or even mentioning demons, it is feared, will draw them and bring disaster. One must guard against that, too.

PRACTICALITY

Natives of Madagascar, when it was objected that they offered more sacrifices to the evil gods than to the good gods, pointed out to anthropologists that it is from the evil gods that they have the most fear.

MALAY DEMONS

Malaysia has a host of demons. W. W. Skeat's *Malay Magic* mentions many of them. The worst is the *penanggalan* (an especially horrendous vampire). But the most peculiar may be the demon of a murdered person. If the blood of such a victim is placed in a bottle and prayed over, the ghost will not come back as a destructive demon. After a week the magician may hear a sound. Then he puts his finger into the bottle for the *polong* (demon) to suck. The *polong* looks like a tiny female figure and flies through the air accompanied by a *pelesit* (a tinier demon in grasshopper form).

SUPERVISION OF DEMONS

It is often jokingly said that "God is not dead. He is living in South America under an assumed name and doesn't want to get involved." The Kimbunda tribe of Africa have a belief rather like that. They say that Suku-Vacange, the creator, stands aloof from his creation and has handed over day-to-day operations to demons, many of them bad. From time to time the supreme deity hurls a thunderbolt or two to straighten out the worst ones.

DEVIL DANCES OF SRI LANKA

For centuries the country that used to be called Ceylon has exorcised demons and devils with dances that involve hideous masks and grotesque costumes (said to represent the demons' appearance), fire, prophetic utterances, interspersed little playlets, and characteristic music which a Westerner might find clangorous. These dances are not performed with the same highly controlled gestures as the Kandyan dances of Hindu inspiration, but they have a practical purpose and an enthusiasm which appeal to the folk. The dancers do not perform on stilts to achieve more impressive "supernatural" effects, as they do in China and Tibet, for example, but their demons and devils are energetic and, mostly due to the masks worn, scary.

THE INKWELL

Grimorium verum, a handbook for magic, says that in order to protect myself from devils and demons (and also to put power into my writing) I must have "engraved on my inkwell" these names:

YOD HE VAU HE (the famous Tetragrammaton or four letters from which our "Yahweh" or "Jehovah" comes).

METATRON (the name of the angel who guided the Israelites through The Wilderness).

YOD (the first consonant in the Hebrew from which we get "Yahweh," "I Am").

CADOS (this must be Hebrew "Kadosh," "The Holy One").

ELOYM (this must be "Elohim," a Hebrew plural meaning "Gods," a name of God).

SABAOTH (another substitute for the real name of God).

But I write on computer keyboards, so I have had to write the names on labels and stick them on, up near "Scroll Lock."

In case you are wondering how that angel's name crept in among substitutes for the name of God, "Metatron" adds up to 314 in gematria and so does "Shaddai," and "Shaddai" is another substitute for the name of God ("The Almighty"). OK?

A Talmudic scholar who is a friend of mine argues that the labels ought to go on the EPSON *printer*. I argue in return that "EPSON" does not add up to a propitious number. The keyboard seems best to me.

THE CHIEF CONTRIBUTION OF CHRISTIANITY

Colin Wilson in *The Occult* writes: "The belief in hordes of spirits and demons may be considered the chief contribution of Christianity to the study of magic."

EVIL GODS AND GODDESSES OF THE PHILIPPINES

I was astounded at the number of evil creatures Marjorie Leech found in the Philippines for her *Guide to the Gods*. Filipinos appear to have more trouble with the supernatural than with their ludicrous, internationally notorious politicians. If you think the Hos (of India) are plagued by evil spirits, look at these Filipino fiends (as if the flying monsters called *Taiyaban* were not enough):

AKOP, who preys on widows and widowers.

ANGUL, "who kills people with the helve of his ax."

ANLABBANG, an evil spirit who encourages quarrels.

APO, who "devours the kidneys of people who die of dysentery."

BULANGLANG, who has to be countered with "magical incantations."

BUMALIN, evil god of the underworld.

HUKLOBAN, a killer. She also destroys houses.

IBWA, who feeds on corpses.

INARXAY, who kills people at the harvest.

KADONGAYAN, who preys on the dead.

KAKAYAN, who teaches and tempts people to commit evil.

KIBAYEN, who appears at curing ceremonies to attempt to take the person's life.

MANGAMIAN, an evil spirit who attempts to kill.

MANKUKULAM, "an agent of Sitan who causes fire beneath the house."

MAXABLAY, who "comes after the harvest with intent to kill."

XA-MUL, "who swallows people alive without crushing them between his teeth."

Fortunately, some of these horrors can be pacified with betel nuts and fought with nets and other measures.

ORIENTAL DEVILS

All the religions of the world represent evil in some way, but the devils and demons of the religions of Asia are perhaps the most frightening in appearance. The Balinese hang grotesque devil masks on their sanctuaries. The Siamese have a huge statue of the guardian at the royal temple in Bangkok. Its hideous face, its winged ears, its huge sword, even its shoe tips belligerently upturned (a style that was briefly copied in the West centuries ago) are supposed to discourage demons from approaching this sacred place of pilgrimage. The Tibetan demons are said to be especially powerful and have to be counteracted by priests wearing skirts made of human bones and waving hundreds of strands of hair taken from corpses. Chinese demons often appear in the pictorial and dramatic art of that ancient culture.

Asian demons are supposed to be particularly adverse to noise. That explains the blaring trumpets of the Tibetan lamas, the firecrackers thrown at Chinese processions (out of which came our recipe for gunpowder), and the cacophony that so often accompanies religious rituals and funerals in the East. In World War II slang a number of British and American expressions linked the Chinese with noise, such as *Chinese attack* (loud attack), *Chinese national anthem* (loud explosion), *Chinese landing* (loud crash). The late slang-expert Stuart Berg Flexner once explained such terms as coming into use "perhaps because English-speaking servicemen found the Chinese language and ways of doing things very foreign and confusing."

In return the Chinese find Westerners strange. "Blue-eyed devils" is one of the common derogatory ways they refer to white people.

THE FOUR CORNERS OF THE EARTH

In Chinese cosmology, the heavens are round and the earth is square. At each corner of the Chinese earth stand guardians. At the north a "black warrior" or tortoise. At the south a red bird. At the east a white tiger. At the west a blue dragon. Both the colors and the creatures are symbolic.

In Christianity for a long time there was resistance to the idea (originally pre-Christian, and Greek) that the earth was a globe. *Revelation* speaks of presiding spirits at the four corners of the earth, so it had to be square, as well as having the sun move around it (because God is said in Scripture to have stopped the movement of the sun long enough for Joshua to fight the battle of Jericho and bring the walls tumbling down). The great beasts of *Revelation* are our Western version of the Eastern guardians of the "far corners" of the world.

THE CHINESE HELL AND ITS DEMONS

The Chinese hell (*Naraka* in Sanskrit) is the Chinese *Shi-tien Yen-wang* (Ten Palaces of Kings of Hell). It is not a place of permanent retribution, because compassionate Buddhas come to rescue sinners from torment there. The minimum stay, however, is 500 years. This Buddhist hell is 280,000 miles below the Great Seat at *Wu-chiao Shih* (Rock of Purification), which is Mount Meru (perhaps the Himalayas) and surrounding it are great mountains, a wide sea, and a ring of iron. This Hindu hell was inconvenient to China so it was moved, insofar at the Chinese are concerned. It was transferred by Taoists to the Chinese province of Szechuan and lies under a high mountain near the city of Fêng-tu Hsien. Hell has ten courts or palaces, from 5,000 to 8,000 feet on a side, and each is presided over by a demon with special functions:

1. Ch'in-kwang Wang.
2. Ch'u-chian Wang.
3. Sun-ti Wang.
4. Wu-kuan Wang.
5. Yen-lo Wang.
6. Pien-ch'êng Wang.
7. T'ai-shan Wang.
8. Tu-ti Wang.
9. P'ing-têng Wang.
10. Chuan-lun Wang.

The Chinese tell the tale of a governor of the province of Szechuan, one Kuo, in the reign of the Emperor Wan Li of the Ming dynasty (which began with a former Buddhist monk turned warrior in 1368 and lasted until 1644). Kuo actually ventured into the mountain and had himself lowered hundreds of feet to a verdant landscape underground where the gate of hell, a studded, strong gate of gron was shut on the first court of hell. Kuo knocked at the gate. It was opened to him by Kuan Yi, the Chinese god of war, who showed him the first court and then the second, third, and fourth. At the fifth court, Kuo was offered tea by its ruler, Yama, who explained that erring souls were collected at their deaths on earth and brought to him and his infernal companions for punishment. Kuo then had to return to the upper world and never did see the rest of the palaces and their governors. A monument with an inscription commemorating Kuo's spectacular visit was erected at the city of Ku'ei-chou Fu in the northern part of Szechuan.

Kuo did not get a really good tour of the hells, which were at first eight and then sixteen, the *Mahayana* (Northern) School adding the extras so that there were eight hot hells and eight cold hells. In another version of the story, there are eight large hells each with sixteen smaller divisions plus a hell for females (on the right of the ninth court) and a hell for suicides, making a total of 130 hells. Another version has 180 hells. The ten courts are from the Sung dynasty (which lasted from 960 until the conquest by the Mongol hordes in 1279) and the first and last of them are not places of torture but a sort of reception area (good people are checked in a great book and sent immediately to court ten) and a final processing area (where those who have expiated their sins are handled). Sinners if regenerate are rehabilitated and sent on to rebirth as a human being, an animal, a fish, a bird, or an insect. Those who are unregenerate undergo the ten departments another time. An entity can exist in one of six possible states: gods or *devas*, human beings, *asuras* or demons, animals, *prêtas* (of which there is more later), and those tormented in hell. All beings pass eventually to personal extinction in *Nirvana*, the bliss which everything seeks.

No one who survives the ten hells recalls any of the experiences of those hundreds of years because on passing out of the last hell they are taken to a Hall of Oblivion. There Mêng P'o makes them partake of a drink like the waters of Lethe: They forget everything.

The Chinese hell is really a correctional institution rather than a penitentiary and the demons are fierce but not malicious, more like mandarins with a dirty job to do who undertake to do it as efficiently as possible.

PRÊTAS

Much of the information about the Chinese hell comes from E. T .C. Werner's *Dictionary of Chinese Mythology*, and to him we can turn also for information on the peculiar Chinese institution of the *prêtas*, hungry ghosts something like our vampires. They haunt cemeteries. There is but one class—but it will do as a sample—of the half-dozen varieties of *Gati* demons. Werner says:

Thirty-six classes of demons with huge bellies, large mouths, and tiny throats, suffering inappeasable hunger and thirst, but unable to appease either on account of their contracted gullets, and living either in hell, in the service of Yama, or among men (but visible only at night). Avaricious persons are to be reborn as *prêtas*....The *prêtas* of Buddhist legend have mouths too small to eat with, and can only emit a thin whistling cry. This whistling sound is often associated with spirits.

It was the Hindus who first started to feed with sacrifices the unfortunate hungry ghosts of ancestors and strangers and when the custom reached China in the third century, with its ancient traditions of ancestor worship, it caught on quickly. After the arrival of Amogha (733) it became practically universal. Offerings called *tsu-ya* are made on the sixteenth day of the first month of the year and may be made on the second and sixth day of each month in the Chinese calendar. It was once believed that as prayers and offerings could get a Christian soul out of Purgatory so prayers and offerings to hungry ghosts could get them out of their unpleasant state of punishment in the Chinese hell. Today feeding these hungry ghosts, ancestors or not, is practiced (says Werner) "by all sects, Confucianists, Taoists, and Buddhists." Food and paper clothes (burned for the benefit of those who have been drowned) are offered with prayers and requiems otherwise foreign to ancient Buddhism.

Werner concludes:

In China *kuei*...demons, are the inhabitants of the *narakas* or subterranean and "other prisons" called *ti-yü*...hells. Many of them formerly belonged to the world of men. Some are condemned by Yama to certain prisons. Others haunt the graves where their former bodies are interred. The *prêtas* hunger for food, and hence the custom, so prevalent in China, of feeding the hungry ghosts both of relatives and others.

Only in our vampire and werewolf and a very few other ideas can human beings turn into devilish or demoniacal personages and go lusting after "food," usually blood. It is not our custom generally to feed the hungry ghosts, though the gifts to "trick or treat" costumed children at Halloween may recall the concept of keeping the ghosts fed, maintaining Grateful Dead in our world. In many ways we feed the memory of the dear departed or create endowments and find other ways by which we can be remembered after we die.

FAR-OUT AND FARAWAY

Elliott, A. J. A. *Chinese Spirit-Medium Cults in Singapore* (1955).
Oke, Isaiah and Joe Wright. *The True Story of Demon Worship and Ceremonial Murder* [in Nigeria] (1989).
Skeat, W. W. *Malay Magic* (1900).

AN INTERNATIONAL SELECTION OF DEVILS AND DEMONS

There are hundreds, perhaps thousands, of significant evil creatures in world religions and mythology. Here are fifty-two selected examples, two for each letter of the alphabet.

A, evil and with some control over other evil spirits among the Samoyeds of Siberia.

AZIDAHAKA, Iranian three-headed god of witchcraft and "horrible sins."

BATIN, one of the four chiefs of the world of demons of the Sakai of the Malay Peninsula.

BENG, as *oBeng* (The Devil) the Satan of the Romanian gypsies and the Kalderash gypsies.

CHEMOSIT, evil spirit "half man, half bird" of the Nandi of Kenya.

CHU KWAI SHEN CHUN, malevolent "creator of freaks" in Chinese belief.

DOGAI, frustrator of human enterprise, can be male or female, from Melanesia.

DURISSA, omnipresent creator of demonic possession among the Darassa of Ethiopia.

ELEL, chief of the evil spirits among the Puelche of Argentina.

ER MO, King of Demons in Szechuan, China.

FALEKAHO ATUA, evil god who kills at Makefu, Niue Island, Polynesia.

FREFTAR, deceiver who seduces mankind. Iran.

GAUNAB, supreme god of evil among what used to be called the Hottentots of South Africa.

GUARICANA, devil honored by flogging young men until the blood flows, among the Yurimagua of Brazil.

HERENSUGUE, serpent (sometimes with seven heads), an evil spirit in the Basque country of Spain and France.

HUECUVOE, chief evil spirit of the Auraucanians of Chile.

INGRATH BAT MAHALATH, early Hebrew goddess of evil.

IRVENE, demon in the form of a dog from Las Palmas, Canary Islands.

JAHI, female demon of debauchery in Persian tradition.

JURIPARI, evil spirit of the *pampas* near Buenos Aires, Argentina.

KAHU, the Satan of the Cunuana of Venezuela.

KERON-KENKEN, Patagonian evil spirit who eats newborn babies and drinks the tears of their mothers.

LHA-MO, evil (and only) goddess of the Dharmapalas of Tibet and Mongolia.

LOGON, evil god to whom the Dusans of Borneo make sacrifices to propitiate him.

MOKO-NUI, evil spirit of the Maoris.

MUTO, cruel and evil god of Japan.

NEFAS, nefarious evil god of the Romans.

NGYAN SPAR BA DUNG MGO GYU'I THOR TSHUGS CAN, Tibetan evil deity.

OLETHROS, Greek personification of destructive forces.

ORUSULA, evil spirit in the form of a giant pig whose "foam gives people a rash that kills them" in Costa Rica.

PAIRIMAITI (Crooked Mindedness), female demon who denies religion in Persia.

POMSA, with evil brother Apom lives in rubber trees and must be propitiated in time of sickness. India and Tibet.

QANEL, among the Chimalteco of Guatemala a deity of the seventeenth day of the calendar, which is good only for praying for sheep.

QUEJ, the strongest and most prominent of the Yearbearers of the Mayans; in his years expect "business losses and many illnesses."

RAGEORAPPER sets trees on fire and enforces *tabu* against those (for example) touching wood from a tree blasted by lightning or imperfectly burned funeral-pyre bones.

ROTA, the source of all evil in the lives of the Lapps.

SATANAEL, whom the Bogomils believed was God's first-born, elder brother of Jesus.

SUTEKH, god of evil identified with the Egyptian Set.

TA HSIEN FU SHEN and TA HSIEN FU JEN, male and female Great (Fox) Fairy evil spirits that must be propitiated. China.

TANDO, chief (evil) deity of the Ashanti, demanding human sacrifice, seven men and seven women at a time.

UDDAGUBBA, the messenger ("vengeance and destruction") of Enlil to the Sumerians.

ULI, Hawaiian goddess of sorcery and "praying to death" for evil purposes.

VATIPA, god of evil, immediate minister of the Great Spirit, worshiped by the Aricoris of Guyana.

VERENO, Zoroastrian demon of lust. Persia.

WATAMARAKA, goddess of evil and "mother of all demons." South Africa.

WELE GUMALI (The Black God), evil presence among some of the Bantu of Kenya.

XIC, a god of the underworld bringing sudden death to men, the Quiché of Guatemala.

XOTSADAM, female demon (formerly wife of the sky god) of the Yet of Siberia.

YETAITA, chief of the evil spirits of the Yaghan of Tierra del Fuego.

YUSH, the evil power defeated by any Kafir wearing the national weapon. Afghanistan and Kafiristan.

ZAM'BI-A-N'BI, the Satan of the good god Zambi among the Bafioti of Gabon.

ZLYDNI (Bad Luck), personification of ill fortune of the Doljas of Russia.

The three-headed demon Baal, as shown in Collin de Plancy's *Dictionnaire infernal*.

The Tragicall History
of the Life and Death
of Doctor FAVSTVS.

With new additions

Written by *Ch. Marlot*,

Printed at London for *Iohn Wright*, and are to be sold at his
shop without Newgate. 1628.

3

Dealing with the Devil

HOW WITCHES SOLD THEIR SOULS TO THE DEVIL

So long as witches stayed with spells and curses and did not turn to poisoning and blasting crops and cattle, people were pretty much content to let them be. After all, the love philters and the home-brew medicines and the herbal extracts were much appreciated. But when the witches undertook to sell their souls to The Devil, this was intolerable to both church authorities (who wanted to stamp out heresy) and secular authorities (to whom the church turned over heretics for punishment). William Perkins in *A Discourse of the Damned Art of Witchcraft* (1608) saw witches as a threat to all ecclesiastical and secular authority, writing that:

> though the witch were in many respects profitable, and did not hurt but procured much good, yet, because he hath renounced God his king and governor and hath bound himself by other laws to the service of the enemies of God and his church, death is his portion justly assigned to him by God: he may not live.

Now, the Bible really meant that a poisoner, a sorcerer who killed, should not be permitted to live, but with this objection to witchcraft the witch need not be accused of murder, just of serving another other than God. And rapidly proof of submission to that power in terms of legal contracts made with The Devil began to appear. These were taken as proof of heresy and high treason, both capital offenses, whereas offenses from blasphemy to practicing medicine without a license would deserve lesser punishments. Once witches were regarded as, in effect, citizens of another country, the kingdom of dark-ness, sworn in fealty to another prince, The Devil, they were political ene-mies, and all that was fair in war was fair in dealing with them.

By the time the faculty of The Sorbonne decided that witches entered into pacts with The Devil (1398), the stage was set for the punishment of *maleficia* as treason to God and country.

So witches were accused of denying the Christian faith, denying their Christian baptism (and sometimes being baptized by The Devil) and replac-ing their godparents with colleagues in witchcraft, surrendering a piece of clothing and blood (in signing an oath) to The Devil in token of submis-sion to him, accepting the mark of The Devil on their bodies and being recorded in his black book as his, promising to pay The Devil annual taxes and to sacrifice infants to him and to bring up their own children in his service, and in every way to work against Christianity and its adherents. He was their god and their king. Witches became a fifth column of evil within every kingdom—and they were persecuted just as Jews and others considered dangerously disloyal were persecuted.

Black, S. Jason and Christopher S. Hyatt. *Pacts with the Devil: A Chronicle of Sex, Blasphemy and Liberation* (1993).

Peters, Ted. *Sin: Radical Evil in Soul and Society* (1994).

Pulling, Pat and Kathy Cawthon. *The Devil's Web* (1989).

Victor, Jeffrey S. *Satanic Panic...* (1993).

MAKING THE PACT WITH THE DEVIL

It is alleged that you cannot call The Devil for this purpose but that, if you are in the way of being damned, he will send a messenger to arrange things.

The *Formicarius* (1435) gives the earliest if not the most complete description of what happens. Supplied with friends who have already for-sworn God, the applicant arrives at a church on a Sunday morning very early and renounces God and the One, Holy, and Apostolic Church. He pays homage to The Devil, drinks the blood of sacrificed children, and sub-scribes to the rules of the damned, which cover many things from diet to cursing and sacrificing. He expresses the desire to trade his soul for one or more favors from The Evil One, often wealth or power for a specified number of years.

The Devil (as it were) takes a reverse mortgage on the person's body. The person can continue to live in it and draw benefits, but when he dies The Devil takes possession of it.

The *professio* with terms proposed by The Devil must be signed in the person's blood, drawn from the left arm. If it will not flow easily—human nature resists such an act—it is warmed with fire (representing passion overcoming intellect) and the person is inscribed in the "red book" of death.

SIGNED IN BLOOD

In olden times in the West, people used to say, "I put my hand and seal" on a document when signing it. In the East, this was literal in some cases: The emperor of Japan in ancient days "signed" important documents by dipping his hand in blood (presumably someone else's) and putting a full bloody handprint on the page.

In the history of pacts with The Devil, people were supposed to sign their names in blood. I have seen a couple of alleged pacts of the sort from earlier centuries and neither, as far as I can tell, was signed in blood, though they do bear signatures of people.

Blood undoubtedly stressed the seriousness of the signing. You were giving away your soul. "The blood is the life," says the Bible. That's why vampires are after your blood: They want your soul. That's why we have kosher chickens for people who do not want to consume the soul of a fowl.

An aspect of Satanism seldom discussed is the connection between blood and soul and the consequent need for signing the pact with The

This must be one of the most obvious forgeries ever accepted into evidence in a court. It is a document presented in the trial of Father Urbain Grandier at Loudun in 1634 and it purports to record "the alliance" of the priest with signatories as follows: Satan, Beelzebub, Lucifer, Elimi, and Astaroth, with signature of the recorder, the demon Baalberith. It is written backward and often in abbreviated Latin, but it says Father Grandier "is on our side" and is guaranteed "the love of women, the flower of virgins, the chastity of nuns, worldly honors, pleasures, and riches" and that he will fornicate "every three days." He will get twenty years of this and "finally will come among us to curse God." This document states that Lucifer is The Devil and the others are princes of Hell.

Devil in blood and letting blood thereafter. While spittle is one bodily product used in magic (and in the miracles of Christ, as the New Testament reports) blood is the most important and powerful.

In America, the Creek, Cherokee, and some other nations refused to eat the blood (soul) of any animal, and everyone knows the Jewish prescription about *kosher* meat. In *Leviticus* and *Deuteronomy* the connection between blood and soul and the taboo of drinking blood (as in some Satanist ceremonies) are clear. In many societies (Islamic, African, Chinese, etc.) consuming blood is forbidden and that on which blood is spilled (even the ground) becomes imbued with the soul. This explains a number of gruesome Satanic ceremonies in which someone or something is claimed by bloodying it. There are aspects of real Satanism (of the kind practiced by Gilles de Rais and other monsters) that would horrify the pseudo-devil worshipers who like to shock by saying they belong to Satanic cults. Satanic cults are murderous, not play-acting. They spill blood, not crack open eggs like some more sensitive practitioners. No one involved in a Satanic cult would confess it to outsiders. As in many aspects of the occult, those who tell, don't know; those who know, don't tell.

SELLING YOUR SOUL TO THE DEVIL

First you need a piece of virgin parchment. That comes from the first calf a cow bears and is not, as many people think, simply a piece never written on before.

Write on it in your own blood: I promise GREAT DEMON to repay him in seven years for all he shall give me. In witness whereof, I sign my name.

Sign it in your own blood.

Then, within the magic circle (you'll need a book on ritual magic to construct that), holding the document in your hand, recite the invocation:

LUCIFER, Emperor, Master of All Rebellious Spirits, I beseech thee to be favorable to me in calling upon thy GREAT MINISTER which I make, desiring to make a pact with him.

BEELZEBUB, Prince, I pray thee also, to protect me in my undertaking.

ASTAROTH, Count, be propitious to me and cause that this night the GREAT DEMON appear to me in human form and without any evil smell, and that he grant me, by means of the pact which I shall deliver to him, all the treasures of which I have need.

GREAT DEMON, I beseech thee, leave thy dwelling, in whatever part of the world you may be, to come speak with me; if not, I shall thereto compel thee by the power of the mighty words of the Great Key of Solomon, whereof he made use to force the rebellious spirits to accept his pact.

Appear then instantly or I shall continually torment thee with the might words of the Key: *AGLON, TETRAGRAMMATON, VAYCHEON, STIMULAMATHON, EROHARES, RETRASAM-MATHON, CLYORAN, ICION, ESITION, EXISTIEN, ERYONA, ONERA, ERASYN, MOYN, MEFFIAS, SOTER, EMMANUEL, SABAOTH, ADONAI. I call you.* AMEN.

When the demon appears, throw him the pact. Do not step outside the circle on any account.

BREAKING WITH THE DEVIL

Saint Alphonso Maria de Ligouri (1696–1787), founder of the Redemptorists, says in *Moral Theology* III:28 that if one wishes to break a pact with The Devil one doesn't have to feel bound to keep one's word, even if signed in blood. Rather, one must:

1. Renounce and abjure any contract with The Evil One.
2. Destroy all charms, talismans, writings, etc., connected with the black art.
3. Burn the written contract if you have it or just declare you regret and reject it.
4. Make restitution for any harm done, insofar as is possible.

DEVILISH "COMPACTS WITH WICKED MEN"

Devils and demons are only a comparatively small part of the 1,100 pages of Ebenezer Sibly's compendious *New and Complete Illustration of the Occult Sciences* (1790). Dr. Sibly died in 1800 but by 1807 this big book was in its tenth edition. It is chiefly devoted to astrology "founded on Natural Philosophy, Scripture, Reason, and Mathematics," but it also delves into "The Black Art." Sibly discusses apparitions, charms, divinations, exorcisms, and how to "raise up spirits" with "various instances of their Compacts with wicked men." He distinguishes a number of types of spirits:

ASTRAL SPIRITS haunt abandoned places, especially sites of violence;

IGNEOUS SPIRITS are monsters of a "middle vegetative nature" and "very apt for conjuring" but extremely malicious and dangerous;

TERRENE SPIRITS haunt chasms, mines, caves, etc., and are hateful to mankind.

Spirits must be evoked, says Sibly, at the proper time, in the proper manner, in the proper place. He recommends the traditional lonely dungeon, cursed crossroad, deserted wasteland, "or amidst the ruins of ancient castles, abbeys, monasteries, etc., or amongst the cruel rocks on the seashore, or in some private and detached churchyard, some solemn melancholy place, between midnight and one o'clock, either when the moon shines very bright and full, or else in a storm of thunder, lightning and rain."

I am delighted at the penchant of devils and demons for the Gothic gloom and romantic scenery of the turn of the nineteenth century, but moderns have malls, though a Sibly magician would be perhaps out of place in such a setting in his gown of black bombazine, covered with an ephod of white linen, girt with a consecrated girdle, and topped with a high-crowned cap of sable silk. (Sibly neglects the wand, the sword, and other paraphernalia that also would cause comment.)

Completing the costume, Sibly goes wrong entirely on the shoes. The magician's shoes are (he says) supposed to be embroidered all over with the Tetragrammaton (*JHVH* or *YHVH*), but this would not work. The four letters suggesting the secret name of God are supposed to be *on the soles* of the shoes: Only by treading sacrilegiously on the name of God can the magician invoke evil spirits. Sibly gives useful information about how to incense the demons when they appear, how to command them, and how to get rid of them (very important) without mishap. I doubt, however, he really ever got the "experience" he claims to have had; he could never get any devils or demons or suicides or other gruesome creatures to come in the first place—not in the wrong shoes.

Just as well, because some of them require blood from ritual murder and all of them are devious and dangerous to deal with, dangerous to sanity if nothing else.

A medical doctor and fellow of a royal society ought to have paid attention to that little detail in risking his own mind trying out his instructions and the minds of those who might ape his efforts.

SELLING YOUR SHADOW TO THE DEVIL

Louis-Charles-Adelaide Chamisso de Boncourt (1781–1838) was a French nobleman who became famous as the Romantic German writer "Adalbert von Chamisso" principally for his story of *Peter Schlemihls wundersame Geschichte* (1814). The young man sells his shadow to The Devil. The climactic moment here is in the translation of Sir John Bowring (1874). This translation is very clumsy English but closely follows the German of a Frenchman not writing in his own language. Style is not Chamisso's strong point, but his plot has power.

What could I make of this singular proposal for disposing of my shadow? He is crazy! I thought; and yet with an altered tone, yet more forcible, as contrasted with the humility of his own, I replied, "How is this, good friend? Is not your own shadow enough for you? This seems to me to be a whimsical sort of bargain indeed."

He began again, "I have in my pocket many matters which might not be quite unacceptable to the gentleman; for this invaluable shadow I deem any price too little."

A chill came over me; I remembered what I had seen, and I knew not how to address him whom I had just ventured to call my good friend. I spoke again, and assumed an extraordinary courtesy to set matters in order.

"Pardon, sir, pardon your most humble servant, I do not quite understand your meaning; how can my shadow—" He interrupted me: "I only beg your permission to lift up your noble shadow, and put it in my pocket; how to do it is my own affair. As a proof of my gratitude to the gentleman, I leave him the choice of all the jewels which my pocket affords; the genuine divining rods, mandrake roots, change pennies, money extractors, the napkins of Rolando's Squire, and divers other miracle-workers—a choice assortment; but all this is not fit for you—better that you should have Fortunatus's wishing-cap, restored spic and span new; and also a fortune-bag which belonged to him."

"Fortunatus's fortune-bag!" I exclaimed; and, great as had been my terror, all my senses were now enraptured by the sound. I became dizzy—and nothing but double ducats seemed sparkling before my eyes.

"Condescend, sir, to inspect and make trial of this bag." He put his hand into his pocket, and drew from it a moderately sized, firmly stitched purse of thick cordovan, with two convenient leather cords hanging to it, which he presented to me. I instantly dipped into it, drew from it ten pieces of gold, and ten more, and ten more, and yet ten more; I stretched out my hand. "Done! the bargain is made; I give you my shadow for your purse." He grasped my hand, and knelt down behind me, and with wonderful dexterity I perceived him loosening my shadow from the ground from head to foot; he lifted it up; he rolled it together and folded it, and at last put it into his pocket. He then stood erect, bowed to me again, and returned back to the rose grove. I thought I heard him laughing softly to himself....

"WILL YOU SIGN THE PARCHMENT?"

In a climactic scene from *The Monk*, the classic Gothic thriller, The Devil gets Ambrosio to sign away his soul—and then betrays him. More of the author, "Monk" Lewis, later, but here see what excitement he, at age nineteen, could put into a long novel he dashed off in ten days, a novel which forever gave him his nickname and his fame.

At first the monk rejoiced at having resisted the seducer's arts, and obtained a triumph over mankind's enemy; but as the hour of punishment drew near, his former terrors revived in his heart; their momentary repose seemed to have given them fresh vigour; the nearer that the time approached, the more did he dread appearing before the throne of God: he shuddered to think how soon he must be plunged into eternity—how soon meet the eyes of his Creator, whom he had so grievously offended. The bell announced midnight: it was the signal for being led to the stake. As he listened to the first stroke, the blood ceased to circulate in the abbot's veins; he heard death and torture murmured in each succeeding sound: he expected to see the archers entering his prison: and as the bell forbore to toll, he seized the magic volume in a fit of despair. He opened it, turned hastily to the seventh page, and as if fearing to allow himself a moment's thought, ran over the fatal lines with rapidity.

Accompanied by his former terrors, Lucifer again stood before the trembler.

"You have summoned me," said the fiend. "Are you determined to be wise? Will you accept my conditions? You know them already. Renounce your claim to salvation, make over to me your soul, and I bear you from this dungeon instantly. Yet is it time. Resolve, or it will be too late. Will you sign the parchment?

"I must—Fate urges me—I accept your conditions."

"Sign the parchment," replied the demon, in an exulting tone.

The contract and the bloody pen still lay upon the table. Ambrosio drew near it. He prepared to sign his name. A moment's reflection made him hesitate.

"Hark!" cried the tempter; "they come—be quick. Sign the parchment, and I bear you from hence this moment."

In effect, the archers were heard approaching, appointed to lead Ambrosio to the stake. The sound encouraged the monk in his resolution. "What is the import of this writing?" said he.

"It makes your soul over to me for ever, and without reserve."

"What am I to receive in exchange?"

"My protection, and release from this dungeon. Sign it, and this instant I bear you away."

Ambrosio took up the pen. He set it to the parchment. Again his courage failed him; he felt a pang of terror at his heart, and once more threw the pen upon the table.

"Weak and puerile!" cried the exasperated fiend. "Away with this folly! Sign the writing this instant, or I sacrifice you to my rage."

At this moment the bolt of the outward door was drawn back. The prisoner heard the rattling of chains; the heavy bar fell; the archers were on the point of entering. Worked up to frenzy by the urgent danger, shrinking from the approach of death, terrified by the demon's threats, and seeing no other means to escape destruction, the wretched monk complied. He signed the fatal contract, and gave it hastily into the evil spirit's hands, whose eyes, as he received the gift, glared with malicious rapture.

"Take it!" said the God-abandoned man. "Now then, save me! snatch me from hence!"

"Hold! Do you freely and absolutely renounce your Creator and His Son?"

"I do! I do!"

"Do you make over your soul to me for ever?"

"For ever!"

"Without reserve or subterfuge? without future appeal to the Divine Mercy?"

The last chain fell from the door of the prison. The key was heard turning in the lock. Already the iron door grated heavily upon its rusty hinges.

"I am yours for ever, and irrevocably!" cried the monk, wild with terror; "I abandon all claim to salvation. I own no power but yours. Hark! hark! they come! Oh, save me! bear me away!"

"I have triumphed! You are mine past reprieve, and I fulfil my promise."

While he spoke, the door unclosed. Instantly the demon grasped one of Ambrosio's arms, spread his broad pinions, and sprang with him into the air. The roof opened as they soared upwards, and closed again when they had quitted the dungeon.

In the meanwhile, the gaoler was thrown into the utmost surprise by the disappearance of his prisoner. Though neither he nor the archers were in time to witness the monk's escape, a sulphurous smell prevailing through the prison sufficiently informed them by whose aid he had been liberated. They hastened to make their report to the grand inquisitor. The story, how a sorcerer had been carried away by the Devil, was soon noised about Madrid; and for some days the whole city was employed in discussing the subject. Gradually it ceased to be the topic of conversation. Other adventures arose, whose novelty engaged universal attention, and Ambrosio was soon forgotten as totally as if he never had existed. While this was passing, the monk, supported by his infernal guide, traversed the air with the rapidity of an arrow, and a few moments placed him upon a precipice's brink, the steepest in Sierra Morena.

Though rescued from the Inquisition, Ambrosio as yet was insensible of the blessings of liberty. The damning contract weighed heavy upon his mind; and the scenes in which he had been a principal actor had left behind them such impressions as rendered his heart the seat of anarchy and confusion. The objects now before his eyes, and which the full moon sailing through clouds permitted him to examine, were ill calculated to inspire that calm of which he stood so much in need. The disorder of his imagination was increased by the wildness of the surrounding scenery—by the gloomy caverns and steep rocks, rising above each other, and dividing the passing clouds; solitary clusters of trees, scattered here and there, among whose thick-twined branches the wind of night signed hoarsely and mournfully; the shrill cry of mountain eagles, who had built their nests among these lonely deserts; the stunning roar of torrents, as swelled by late rains they rushed violently down tremendous precipices, and the dark waters of a silent sluggish stream, which faintly reflected the moonbeams, and bathed the rock's base on which Ambrosio stood. The abbot cast round him a look of terror. His infernal conductor was still by his side, and eyed him with a look of mingled malice, exultation, and contempt.

"Whither have you brought me?" said the monk at length, in a hollow, trembling voice. "Why am I placed in this melancholy scene? Bear me from it quickly! Carry me to Matilda!"

The fiend replied not, but continued to gaze upon him in silence. Ambrosio could not sustain his glance; he turned away his eyes, while thus spoke the demon:

"I have him then in my power! This model of piety! this being without reproach! this mortal who placed his puny virtues on a level with those of angels! He is mine—irrevocably, eternally mine! Companions of my sufferings! denizens of hell! how grateful will be my present!"

He paused—then addressed himself to the monk: "Carry you to Matilda!" he continued, repeating Ambrosio's words: "Wretch! you shall soon be with her! You will deserve a place near her, for hell boasts no miscreant more guilty than yourself. Hark, Ambrosio! while I unveil your crimes! You have shed the blood of two innocents; Antonia and Elvira perished by your hand. That Antonia whom you violated was your sister! that Elvira whom you murdered gave you birth! Tremble, abandoned hypocrite, inhuman parricide, incestuous ravisher! Tremble at the extent of your offences! And you it was who thought yourself proof against temptation, absolved from human frailties, and free from error and vice! Is pride, then, a virtue? Is inhumanity no fault? Know, vain man! that I long have marked you for my prey: I watched the movements of your heart; I saw that you were virtuous from vanity, not principle; and I seized the fit moment of seduction. I observed your blind idolatry of the Madonna's picture. I bade a subordinate but crafty spirit assume a similar form, and you eagerly yielded to the blandishments of Matilda. Your pride was gratified by her flattery; your lust only needed an opportunity to break forth; you ran into the snare blindly, and scrupled not to commit a crime which you blamed in another with unfeeling severity. It was I who threw Matilda in your way; it was I who gave you entrance to Antonia's chamber; it was I who caused the dagger to be given you which pierced your sister's bosom, and it was I who warned Elvira in dreams of your designs upon her daughter, and thus, by preventing your profiting by her sleep, compelled you to add rape as well as incest to the catalogue of your crimes. Hear, hear, Ambrosio! Had you resisted me one minute longer, you had saved your body and soul. The guards whom you heard at your prison-door came to signify your pardon. But I had already triumphed: my plots had already succeeded. Scarcely could I propose crimes so quick as you performed them. You are mine, and Heaven itself cannot rescue you from my power. Hope not that your penitence will make void our contract. Here is your bond signed with your blood; you have given up your claim to mercy, and nothing can restore to you the rights which you have foolishly resigned. Believe you that your secret thoughts escaped me? No, no—I read them all! You trusted that you should still have time for repentance. I saw your artifice, knew its falsity, and rejoiced in deceiving the deceiver! You are mine beyond reprieve: I burn to possess my right, and alive you quit not these mountains."

During the demon's speech, Ambrosio had been stupefied by terror and surprise. This last declaration roused him.

"Not quit these mountains alive!" he exclaimed. "Perfidious! what mean you? Have you forgotten our contract?"

The fiend answered by a malicious laugh.

JULES-AMEDÉE BARBEY D'AUREVILLY

This writer (1808–1889) is a good example of the connection between ultra-montane Catholicism, dandyism, and dabbling in the occult that produced a whole school of French fiction in the nineteenth century. Of interest here are such works as his short story *Les Diaboliques* (1874). He influenced Léo-Marie Bloy, Georges Bernanos, Petrus Borel d'Hauterive, and many others. All these writers were fascinated with the diabolical, with possession and the like.

DIABOLICAL OBSESSION AND DIABOLICAL POSSESSION

It was believed by the Jews that Sarah was attacked by the demon Asmodeus, who killed seven of her husbands in a row. Asmodeus had to be trounced by an angel and consigned to a remote desert. Saint Paul claimed to be picked on by The Devil himself "lest the greatness of the revelations should puff me up" (II *Corinthians* XII: 7-8), though keeping Paul from becoming too proud seems like a service to God and all of us that Satan is performing, not a depredation on the saint. Paul had to request repeatedly that "the thorn in the flesh" be taken away, three times before God reacted. (God was also slow to relieve Job when he was sorely tried.) Moderns who claim that they are being assailed by supernatural forces generally ascribe them to rival magicians, not to The Devil in person.

Diabolical possession sees the human being as taken over by, rather than attacked from outside by, devils or demons. Unless "the evil spirit that troubled" King Saul can be regarded as diabolical possession (which I doubt), there is not much about possession in the Old Testament. But Christianity's advent saw more and more of it until the individual exorcisms performed by Jesus look minor when compared to the need for dealing with, say, a whole convent of possessed nuns. As science progressed, fewer and fewer sexual extravaganzas, diseases of body and mind (boils, blindness, epilepsy, melancholy, various manias, everything from depression to darkest despair, suicidal and homicidal drives, and more) were attributed to possession by evil. At first the church was glad to be of service. It saw putting down The Devil as strengthening faith. However, it may be true to say that in time the church, embarrassed perhaps by the excesses of the superstitious past, went almost to the other extreme, trying every explanation besides The Devil to account for extraordinary phenomena. The church closely questioned every alleged case of possession. It drastically cut down on exorcism. It produced apologists such as Herbert Thurston, SJ (author of *Ghosts and Poltergeists*), explainers-away rather than explainers. It was embarrassed by the credulity of some of its own ministers. It placed an emphasis on finding non-devilish explanations of speaking in tongues, incredible physical strength, and other signs of diabolical possession that, in earlier times, would have marked the speaker as a heretic and blasphemer, for in earlier times it was almost as bad to doubt that one could be possessed of devils and demons as it was to welcome The Devil. Both actions were absolute heresy.

Today the Roman Catholic Church particularly is as pained to hear that another person has complained of being possessed as it is to hear that some lower-class people in New Jersey have been vouchsafed a personal visit in their backyard by the Blessed Virgin Mary.

A FRENCH CLERIC'S EXPERIENCE
WITH DEMONIC POSSESSION

J. H. Crehan in an encyclopedia article on signs of possession notes that Father J. de Tonquedec, "a modern exorcist...who acted for the archdiocese of Paris from 1919 to 1939," found that 90 percent of supposed cases of possession were not real. That leaves 10 percent he could not doubt.

PHYSICAL SIGNS OF DEMONIC POSSESSION

From Francesco Maria Guazzo's compilation of hundreds of works on witchcraft and demonology, *Compendium maleficarum* (1605), the physical signs of possession:

The following is the customary practice to determine whether a sick man is possessed by a demon. Secretly apply to the sick man a writing with the sacred words of God, or relics of the saints, or a blessed waxen Agnus Dei, or some other holy thing. A priest places his hand and his stole upon the possessed and pronounces sacred words. Thereupon the sick man begins to shake and shudder with fright, and on account of his pain makes many confused movements, and says and does many strange things. If the demon lodges in his head, he feels the most piercing pains in his head, or else his head and his face are suffused with a red hot flush like fire. If the demon is in his eyes, he makes them roll wildly. If in the back, he brings on convulsions in his limbs, in front and behind, and sometimes makes the whole body so rigid and inflexible that no amount of force can bend it.

Sometimes the [possessed persons] fall down as if dead, as if they were suffering from tertiary epilepsy and a vapor rushing into their head; but at the priest's command they arise, and the vapor goes back where it came from. If the demon is in their throats, they are so constricted that they appear to be strangled. If the devil is in the nobler parts of the body, as about the heart or lungs, he causes panting, palpitations and syncope. If he tends more to the stomach, he provokes hiccoughs and vomiting, so that sometimes they cannot take food, or else cannot retain it. And he causes them to pass something like a little ball by the anus, with roarings and other discordant cries; and afflicts them with wind and gripings in the abdomen. They [demons] are also sometimes known by fumes of sulphur or some other strong-smelling stuff.

You must also be on the lookout for any disease difficult to pin down or that is intermittent or grows worse with treatment, or that the patient cannot explain or despairs of, or keeps patients from taking medicine or nourishment, or gives them a pain like "being torn in two," or produces a visible pulse in their necks, or produces hot flashes and "an ice-cold wind," or creates impotence, or brings up a light sweat, or twists the patient in knots, or causes them to waste away, or turns them yellow (or ashen), or gums up their eyelids, or makes them afraid of the nearness of priests or witches, or ....Well, lots of things. And if the priest applies some holy ointments and the patient reacts with heat, rash, etc., then you know he or she is bewitched, possessed, and needs exorcism.

SEIZURES

The term reminds us that a theory of demons seizing or possessing the person was once used to explain attacks of epilepsy.

EXORCISM

For driving out devils, as with other magic, one needs a master word, powerful and precise. In the New Testament we are told that the name of Jesus drove out devils but that the Pharisees, priests of the Jews, accused Christ of driving out devils by the name Beelzebub, "the Lord of the Flies."

The official exorcism rite of the Roman Catholic Church is in the *Rituale Romanum* prepared at the beginning of the seventeenth century for Paul V. After being informed by a spokesman for the archdiocese of New York that there was no such formula available, I found one in a copy of the *Rituale Romanum* that bore the *imprimatur* of Francis, Cardinal Spellman of New York. The *Rituale* stresses that the exorcist resist being too easily convinced of demonic possession but that, having reached the conclusion that a person is possessed, the exorcist must proceed with care and courage. The exorcist should look for a possessed person having diabolical strength, speaking in unknown languages, and knowing things that the person could not legitimately know. The exorcist must be wary, for devils and demons are subtle and horribly dangerous.

The big book on the subject is the *Thesaurus Exorcismorum* by Maximillian von Eynatten. It goes well over 1,000 pages and covers all conceivable problems.

Exorcism has been noted in numerous medical books as effective in convincing disturbed patients to give up delusions and psychotic behaviors. In law, testimony given by demons is traditionally inadmissible. As The Sorbonne decided (1620), demons lie! Other high points in the history of exorcism in France are the mass exorcisms of Laôn (1569) and the famous matter of the devils of Loudon (1634), the subject of a sensational film by Ken Russell more or less based on Aldous Huxley's novel.

EXORCISMS IN SCANDINAVIA

Scandinavians thought of storms as Odin and his Wild Hunt rushing across the sky with noise and lights and clouds. On occasion, a storm left a hound dog whining on your hearth. You couldn't order it out. You had to feed and tend it until and unless you exorcised it. To do that you had to brew beer in eggshells. Then the magical cur would run off.

Beer brewed in eggshells was also sovereign in getting rid of *maras* (nightmares) who might appear, or dwarfs who might come and change your beautiful baby for an ugly, deformed one of their own. To correct that problem you simply held the changeling's feet to the fire or, more dramatically, threatened to put it into the oven. The dwarf mother would come to rescue her child and you would get your own child back.

VICTIMS OF DEMONIC POSSESSION

The official view of the Roman Catholic Church—one of the few churches that has an official view on the subject—is that The Devil cannot possess a person unless, like a vampire, he is invited in. So, in the current culture of victimization, note that if you are possessed it is your own fault; you are not a victim but vicious. The exorcist should get you to confess your sins and explain why you got yourself into such a bad situation. The Devil's power does not extend over the righteous. You have nothing to fear if you resist temptation.

TAKING THE LAW INTO ONE'S OWN HANDS

At Sologne in France in 1885, a daughter and her husband burned her mother; they said she was a witch. The number of persons murdered by those who think they are doing us all a favor by ridding the world of a witch will, of course, never be known, but people even today take the law into their own hands—against the law.

EXORCISING HOBGOBLINS

These minor annoyances can be easily banished. Just throw flaxseed on the floor.

SAY "UNCLE"

One of the simplest exorcisms will rid you of the Indian demon which eats people both alive and dead. It is a *rakshasa* (destroyer) and, to get rid of it, you just say "Uncle."

BEANS

The Roman festival of Lemuria used beans to propitiate and exorcise the spirits of the dead, and at the *calends* of the next month (June) offered beans as food for the dead. In American folklore, if you want to deal with The Devil for the information, you can take a handful of beans and a shovel to the cemetery at midnight. Place the shovel on the ground round side down and throw the beans up in the air. Then carefully pick up the shovel and carry it out of the cemetery without dropping any beans that landed in it. Once outside the cemetery, not before, you can count the beans in the shovel. That will be the number of locals who will die during the coming year. It is unclear whether by limiting the number of beans thrown in the air you can affect the number of possible deaths.

"A LITTLE BOOK IN WHICH EXORCISMS ARE WRITTEN"

The earliest mention of exorcism in the Christian church is from The Council of Carthage (A.D. 256). It says that when exorcists were ordained (on the way to the priesthood) they were given "a little book in which exorcisms were written" by the bishop, who also by the laying on of hands confirmed in them the power to drive out demons with the words provided. No one, as far as I can tell, now knows what was in the "little book."

FAITH HEALERS

If we are not very brief here, we are likely to tread on many toes, for faith healing is a large part of a number of American religions. To the extent that it is believed to be the driving out of demons of disease, it is witchcraft of the old "leech-craft" type, exorcism. Or it might be auto-suggestion.

BANISHING MONSTERS

Folklore provides with a couplet a simple solution to problems of monsters. Say:

Criss-cross, double cross!
Tell the monster to get lost.

A FORMULA FOR EXORCISM

Jeffrey Burton Russell (whose trilogy anatomizing the subtle changes over time in the nature of the concept of The Devil constitutes essential reading) translates a Galician manuscript of the eighth century which offers a formula for exorcism (different from the much longer one in the *Rituale Romanum*, which would be used by the Roman Catholic Church today). I omit some text, especially a long boast of successes of the Jews over the enemy (who was, it seems to me, not always The Devil or inspired by him).

> I accost you, damned and most impure spirit, cause of malice, essence of crimes, origin of sins, you who revel in deceit, sacrilege, adultery, and murder! I adjure you in Christ's name that, in whatsover part of the body you are hiding you declare yourself, that you flee the body which you are occupying and from which we drive you with spiritual whips and invisible torments. I demand that you leave this body which has been cleansed by the Lord. Let it be enough for you that in earlier ages you dominated almost the entire world through your action on the hearts of human beings. Now day by day your kingdom is being destroyed, your arms weakening. Your punishment has been prefigured as of old....Through the power of all the saints you are tormented, crushed, and sent down to eternal flames....Depart, depart, wheresoever you lurk, and nevermore seek out bodies dedicated to God; let them be forbidden to you forever, in the name of the Father, the Son, and the Holy Spirit.

WIDE SELECTION AVAILABLE

Tantric Buddhism has spells available for the control of more than 60,000 different kinds of devils and demons.

EXORCISING DEVILS AND DEMONS

Driving out devils and demons was performed in Old Testament times: Josephus says that King Solomon's "forms of exorcism" were used in such a situation by one Eleazar performing before the Emperor Vespasian. In the New Testament, Christ exorcised devils and demons and gave His apostles and disciples the power to do so. Saint Paul in *Acts of the Apostles* is reported to have driven the evil spirit out of a girl who was being used to prophesy. The early fathers of the church (Tertullian, Origen, and others) and the great Saint Thomas Aquinas, of the *Summa theologica*, and medieval popes all speak of and defend the rite of exorcism. The Roman Catholic Church has been using exorcism ever since it cleansed in this way the catechumens who wished to become full members. The sacrament of baptism is a rite of exorcism. So is the blessing of the water used in baptism, sanctifying of churches and holy water and holy oil and altars and holy vessels, and so on. This reminds us that devils and demons have long been thought to reside in objects as well as in persons, somewhat the way gods lived in trees or stones of old or trolls in mountains.

The Roman Catholic Church undertakes to exorcise even noncommunicants and excommunicants. In an emergency, any Catholic can perform an exorcism, though increasingly the church has restricted exorcism and calls upon ordinaries (superiors) to select only careful and well-adjusted priests for the rite. All priests are exorcists. Exorcist is the third of the four minor orders leading up to Holy Orders, the ordination of a priest.

Exorcism is simply a prayer to God to banish the creatures He permits to torment mankind. He may delay or refuse or quickly grant the boon. Devils and demons do not go quietly and the rite is dangerous.

Exorcism is performed with breathing on a person (the breath traditionally carrying the soul, and suggesting creation), the laying on of hands (a traditional method of conveying power or blessing), the sign of the cross, the Holy Name, the cursing of The Devil (with demands to unclean spirits to depart), and the reading of Holy Writ. There used to be a *Book of Exorcisms*. Now the formula for exorcism is in the *Rituale Romanum* approved by seventeenth-century authorities and reprinted often, though not usually consulted by the laity. It is "the book" used in exorcism by "bell, book, and candle."

THE ROMAN CATHOLIC EXORCISM
TRANSLATED FROM THE *RITUALE ROMANUM*
FIRST PUBLISHED IN THE REIGN OF PAUL V

The priest, robed in surplice and violet stole, one end of which is placed round the neck of the possessed person, bound if he is violent, sprinkles those present with holy water. Then the service begins.

1. *The Litany.*
2. *Psalm 54* ("Save me, O God, by Thy name").
3. *Adjuration* imploring God's grace for the proposed exorcism against the "wicked dragon" and a caution to the possessing spirit to "tell me thy name, the day, and the hour of thy going out, by some sign."

4. *The Gospel* (John I; and/or Mark XVI; Luke X; Luke XI).

5. *Preparatory Prayer.*

Then the priest, protecting himself and the possessed by the sign of the cross, placing part of his stole round the neck and placing his right hand on the head of the possessed, resolutely and with great faith shall say what follows.

6. *First Exorcism:*

"I exorcize thee, most vile spirit, the very embodiment of our enemy, the entire specter, the whole legion, in the name of Jesus Christ, to ✠ get out and flee from this creature of God ✠ ✠.

"He himself commands thee, who has ordered those cast down from the heights of heaven to the depths of the earth. He commands thee, he who commanded the sea, the winds, and the tempests.

"Hear therefore and fear, O Satan, enemy of the faith, foe to the human race, producer of death, thief of life, destroyer of justice, root of evils, kindler of vices, seducer of men, betrayer of nations, inciter of envy, origin of avarice, cause of discord, procurer of sorrows. Why dost thou stand and resist, when thou knowest that Christ the Lord will destroy thy strength? Fear him who was immolated in Isaac, sold in Joseph, slain in the lamb, crucified in man, and then was triumphant over hell.

(*The signs of the cross* ✠ *should be made on the forehead of the possessed.*) "Depart therefore in the name of the ✠ Father, and of the ✠ Son, and of the Holy ✠ Ghost; give place to the Holy Ghost, by the sign of the ✠ Cross of Jesus Christ our Lord, who with the Father and the same Holy Ghost liveth and reigneth one God, for ever and ever, world without end."

7. *Prayer for Success*, and making the signs of the cross over the demoniac.

8. *Second Exorcism:*

"I adjure thee, thou old serpent, by the judge of the quick and the dead, by thy maker and the maker of the world, by him who has power to send thee to hell, that thou depart quickly from this servant of God, N., who returns to the bosom of the Church, with fear and the affliction of thy terror. I adjure thee again (✠ on his forehead), not in my infirmity, but by the virtue of the Holy Ghost, that thou depart from this servant of God, N., whom Almighty God hath made in his own image.

"Yield therefore; yield not to me, but to the minister of Christ. For his power urges thee, who subjugated thee to his cross. Tremble at his arm, who led the souls to light after the lamentations of hell had been subdued. May the body of man be a terror to thee (✠ on his chest), let the image of God be terrible to thee (✠ on his forehead). Resist not, neither delay to flee from this man, since it has pleased Christ to dwell in this body. And, although thou knowest me to be none the less a sinner, do not think me contemptible.

"For it is God who commands thee ✠.

"The majesty of Christ commands thee ✠.

"God the Father commands thee ✠.

"God the Son commands thee ✠.

"God the Holy Ghost commands thee ✠ .

"The sacred cross commands thee ✠.

"The faith of the holy apostles Peter and Paul and of all other saints commands thee ✠.

"The blood of the martyrs commands thee ✠.

"The constancy of the confessors commands thee ✠.

"The devout intercession of all saints commands thee ✠.

"The virtue of the mysteries of the Christian faith commands thee ✠.

"Go out, therefore, thou transgressor. Go out, thou seducer, full of all deceit and guile, enemy of virtue, persecutor of innocence. O most dire one, give place; give place, thou most impious; give place to Christ, in whom thou hast found nothing of thy works, who hath despoiled thee, who hath destroyed thy kingdom, who hath led thee captive and hath plundered thy goods, who hath cast thee into outer darkness, where for thee and they ministers is prepared annihilation.

"But why, truculent one, dost thou withstand? Why, rash creature, dost thou refuse?

"Thou art accused by Almighty God, whose statutes thou hast transgressed.

"Thou art accused by his Son, Jesus Christ, our Lord, whom thou didst dare to tempt and presume to crucify.

"Thou art accused by the human race, to whom by the persuasion thou hast given to drink the poison of death.

"Therefore I adjure thee, most wicked dragon in the name of the ✠ immaculate lamb, who trod upon the asp and basilisk, who trampled the lion and dragon, to depart from this man (✠ let the sign be made on his forehead), to depart from the Church of God (✠ let the sign be made on those standing by). Tremble and flee at the invocation of the name of that Lord at whom hell trembles, to whom the virtues of heaven, the powers and dominions are subject, whom cherubim and seraphim with unwearied voices praise, saying, Holy, holy, holy, Lord God of Sabbath.

"The word made flesh ✠ commands thee.

"He who was born of the Virgin ✠ commands thee.

"Jesus of Nazareth commands thee, who, although thou didst despise his disciples, bade thee go, crushed and prostrate, out of the man, and in his presence, when he had separated thee from the man, thou didst not presume to go into a herd of swine.

"Therefore, adjured now in his ✠ name, depart from this man, whom he has created. It is hard for thee to wish to resist. It is hard for thee to kick against the pricks ✠. Because the more slowly thou go out, the more the punishment against thee increases, since thou despisest not men but him who is Lord of the quick and dead, who shall come to judge the quick and the dead and the world by fire."

9. *Prayer for Success.*

10. *Third and Final Exorcism:*

"Therefore, I adjure thee, most vile spirit, the entire specter, the very embodiment of Satan, in the name of Jesus Christ ✠ of Nazareth, who, after his baptism in Jordan, was led into the wilderness and overcame thee in thine own habitations, that thou stop assaulting him whom he hath formed from the dust of the earth to the honor of his glory, and that thou tremble not at the human weakness in miserable man but at the image of Almighty God.

"Therefore, yield to God, who by his servant Moses drowned thee and thy malice in Pharoah and in his army in the abyss.

"Yield to God, who made thee flee when expelled from King Saul with spiritual songs through his most faithful servant, David.

"Yield to God ✠ who condemned thee in Judas Iscariot the traitor. For he beats thee with divine ✠ scourges, in whose sight, trembling and crying out with thy legions, thou hast said: What are thou to us, O Jesus, Son of the most high God? Art thou come hither to torture us before our time? He presses on thee with perpetual flames, who shall say at the end of time to the wicked: Depart from me, ye cursed, into everlasting fire, which is prepared for the devil and his angels.

"For thee, impious one, and for thy angels are prepared worms which never die.

"For thee and thy angels is prepared the unquenchable fire; because thou art the chief of accursed murder, thou art the author of incest, the head of sacrilege, the master of the worst actions, the teacher of heretics, the inventor of all obscenities. Therefore, O impious one, go out. Go out, thou scoundrel, go out with all thy deceits, because God has willed that man be his temple.

"But why dost thou delay longer here?

"Give honor to God, the Father Almighty, to whom every knee is bent.

"Give place to the Lord Jesus Christ ✠ who shed for man his most precious blood.

"Give place to the Holy Ghost, who through his blessed apostle Peter manifestly struck thee in Simon Magus, who condemned thy deceit in Ananias and Sapphira, who smote thee in Herod the King because he did not give God honor, who through his apostle Paul destroyed thee in the magician Elymas by the mist of blindness, and through the same apostle by his word of command bade thee come out of the pythoness.

"Now therefore depart. ✠ Depart, thou seducer. Thy abode is the wilderness, thy habitation is the serpent. Be humbled and prostrate. Now there is no time to delay. For behold the Lord God approaches quickly, and his fire will glow before him and precede him and burn up his enemies on every side. For if thou hast deceived man, thou canst not mock God.

"He expels thee, from whose eye nothing is secret.

"He expels thee, to whose power all things are subject.

"He excludes thee, who has prepared for thee and thy angels everlasting hell; out of whose mouth the sharp sword will go, he who shall come to judge the quick and the dead and the world by fire."

11. *Final Prayers*, including canticles, creed, and various psalms.

Evil spirits plague a seventeenth-century house at Tedworth because the owner took the drum away from a demobilized drummer of the Civil War. The drummer set devils and poltergeists on him. He was "condemned to transportation."

PART OF THE FORMULA FOR EXORCISING A HOUSE, TRANSLATED FROM THE SEVENTEENTH-CENTURY *RITUALE ROMANUM*

I adjure thee, O serpent of old, by the Judge of the living and the dead; by the Creator of the world, who hath power to cast into Hell, that thou depart forthwith from this house. He that commands thee, accursed demon, is He that commanded the winds, and the sea, and the storm. He that commands thee is He who ordered thee to be hurled down from the height of heaven into the lower parts of the earth. He that commands thee is He who bade thee to depart from Him. Harken, then, Satan, and fear. Get thee gone, vanquished and cowed, when thou art bidden in the name of Our Lord Jesus Christ, who will come to judge the living and the dead and all the world by fire. Amen.

Christ casts out an evil spirit from a man into swine. Illuminated Gospels of Czar Ivan Alexander, Bulgaria, fourteenth century, now in the British Museum.

BOOKS ON EXORCISM FROM 1618 TO 1974

"Brognolus, Candidus." *Alexicacon* (1668).
Ebon, Martin. *The Devil's Bride, Exorcism Past and Present* (1974).
Eynatten, Maximillian van. *Thesdaurus exorcismorum* (1626).
Nauman, St. Elmo. *Exorcism through the Ages* (1974).
Osterreich, T. K. *Possession and Exorcism* (reprint 1974).
Sargant, William. *The Mind Possessed* (1974).
Wolley, Reginald Maxwell. *Exorcism and the Healing of the Sick* (1932).
Zacharias, Father. *Compendium artis exorcisticæ* (1618).

EXORCISM

This must be one of the most underreported activities in United States's publications. They seem to notice exorcisms only when something goes disastrously wrong, such as when the *Houston Post* reported (3 September 1993) the death of the Harris County (Texas) person who died in a botched attempt. The person being exorcised (Servando C. Rodriguez) and the ill-instructed woman performing the ceremony (in which she set fire to him and herself with a bottle of alcohol that tipped over) were badly burned. He died.

Generally the press is content to ignore the exorcisms conducted by priests of both traditional and alternate religions and to get by with DIY advice around Halloween, as when a Denver witch (30 October 1993) told in "Spirits Be Gone" in the *Denver Post* how you could exorcise your house. The evangelicals are strongly at the task. In the United States in 1984 alone, for example, were published M. I. Brubeck's *Overcoming the Adversary*, M. Harper's *Spiritual Warfare*, and J. L. Murphy's *Darkness and Devils*.

DEMON MASKS OF EXORCISTS

The Encyclopedia of World Art has a series of excellent articles by various hands on the iconography of demons, and typical is Frederick W. Funke's article on the Asiatic East. It follows the basic research of Paul Wirz's

Exorzismus und Heilkunde auf Ceylon (1941). Funke discusses how the Sing-halese (like the Balinese) believe the world is a constant battleground of good and evil spirits where animism, Buddhism, Hinduism, folk medicine and native superstitions have merged to create a colorful demonology that involves spiritual and physical health and disease demons. (Compare the Jewish view that illness is from God, *Amos* III:6.) The disease demons are descended from ancient evil deities (just as the Canaanite god Resheph becomes a Jewish demon) and seem to be outside the control of the good deities (unlike Dever, "Pestilence," which goes with God into battle but which God controls absolutely). The dancing in spectacular masks attracts and disarms disease demons.

Exorcist healers try to free anyone who is possessed by a demon of disease by means of an ecstatic dance in which they wear the mask of the appropriate demon. With this dance they seek to coax him from the sick man's body. These masks are generally more than life size and are carved from soft wood. Hideously protruding eyes are believed to strengthen the magical potency, and painting in bright, variegated colors lends further efficacy to the masks. The *raksasa* masks of Ceylon are characteristically adorned with many bodies and heads of serpents. On their heads are placed high crowns made of wreathed cobras, while from their nostrils, from the corners of their mouths, and from between their teeth protrude the repulsive heads of other cobras. The demon Mahasanny, as the supreme head of the spirits of disease, bears on both his cheeks, like ornamental plaques, representations of the sixteen most dangerous diseases to which man is subject, among which are leprosy and syphilis.

HOW THE EVIL SPIRIT DEPARTS

Various cultures provide various ways for the spirit conjured out—which is what *exorcism* means—to travel away, either on the back of a scapegoat or up in the smoke of incense or (my favorite) in a little boat, which is the center of exorcism ceremony as performed in certain parts of the East Indies. The boat receives the evil spirit and then is set adrift.

Three witches convicted of attempting to kill the family of the Earl of Rutland. They are shown with their familiars: an owl, a white dog, a mouse, and a black cat called Pusse.

4

In the Service of Satan

WHY WITCHES AND WITCHCRAFT?

I have taken up this subject before, as the title of *The Complete Book of Magic and Witchcraft* shows, and I shall take it up again from still another perspective when I follow this book you hold in your hand with a companion volume, as I said in the preface to the present work. There I shall survey the practice of witchcraft, religions such as spiritualism and voodoo, magical rites such as necromancy, etc. Here I offer a chapter on the servants of Satan in witchcraft (and some of the persecutions they have suffered) and at the end of this present book we shall return to those who in the modern world are, or want to be, Satanists.

It is worth noting that traditionally those accused of witchcraft (as opposed to many modern Satanists) were "midnight hags," hideous old crones, helpless and perhaps even senile old women. In sexist societies one would have expected witches to make personal beauty a part of the deal with The Devil. In fact, beauty might well have aided them in doing evil work. However, just as those who claim to be experts in astrology and numerology seem not to be doing extraordinarily well in winning the lottery or playing the stock market (or at any other sort of betting), so witches seem to have benefited little from dealing with evil forces and selling their immortal souls. True, they got invited (they say) to parties with other harridans and old wizards, and a male master who might have been "horny" but whose semen was reported to be ice cold and his sexual technique painful. Satan was nobody's idea of Mr. Right, no woman's dream.

Even Dr. Faustus, pulling in a great deal of cash in his medical practice (unlike psychics, who you would think could get so wealthy they would not have to charge fees for their services!), obtained very little from his diabolical bargain and wasted the magical powers he was given. The Devil neither answered his spiritual questions nor truly improved his physical life. Dr. Faustus might well have asked still another question: Why were his two magician friends, who urged him to conjure and risk his soul, themselves neither powerful nor rich? They appear to be too timorous to take the chance they urge him to take. Perhaps they have not tried the conjurations themselves, out of fear. Or perhaps they have and, as Mephistophilis frankly tells Faustus, "misery loves company."

Witches, joining the company of the damned, got precious little for doing the work of The Devil. But that should surprise no one. "The workman is worthy of his hire," and other sound business practices, are of God, not of The Devil. Crime may pay. The Devil never pays. Those who want to serve him want to do *maleficia*, malice, evil for evil's sake. And to do that they subject themselves to dealing with horrific demons.

Do they turn to demons out of some kind of internalized hatred projected on them by others?

"THOU SHALT NOT SUFFER A WITCH TO LIVE"

If this is indeed translated correctly from the inerrant Word of God— "witch" and not "poisoner"—then witches have much to fear from fundamentalist Christians. In fact, those Christians have been woefully lax, because witchcraft ceased to be a hanging offense in Britain in 1736, and in the United States today you are more likely to be prosecuted (if at all in connection with witchcraft) for *not* delivering the goods, for consumer fraud, and certainly never threatened with the death penalty.

QUESTIONABLE PRACTICES

Many will question if service to The Devil is in fact possible at all, and others will say that there are questionable and even evil practices that cannot by any stretch of the imagination be called true witchcraft. Is the use of amulets and talismans dealing with The Devil? Are blessed medals and phylacteries and the Hand of Fatima, superstitious nonsense, diabolical crime? What about mesmerism and trance states and clairvoyance and automatic writing and psychic practices generally—telepathy, second sight, astral pro-jection? Are these witchcraft? Surely not. Nobody—well, it is always dangerous to say "nobody," but practically nobody, then—gets involved in blibliomancy today (fortune-telling by picking a word at random out of a book, such as the Bible), but I do know children whose parents, following religions strange to us, named them that way. I suppose there's a great decline lately in *sortes Virgilianæ* (picking words at random out of the works of Vergil), but I know many who use the *I Ching* and more who read tea leaves or playing cards and especially The Tarot. I read The Tarot myself (to get in touch with my unconscious, not infernal powers) but I do not read palms or bumps on the head (phrenology was very popular in the nineteenth century in America, but now we argue about intelligence in terms of the bell curve, the IQ tests, etc.). I know someone who will read for you the moles on your body. I know people who are not witches at all but use herbs or even crystals and aromas and read the signs of nature or the signs in the heavens. Have you seen your horoscope today? I predict that if someone offered you your horoscope you would say (a) you don't believe in such stuff and (b) you'd like to see it for a moment or two.

For more on the fascinating history of witches and witchcraft, read the companion volumes to this book, the previously published *The Complete Book of Magic and Witchcraft* and the forthcoming *The Complete Book of The Devil's Disciples*.

Here, let us conclude with a chapter that proves that superstition is far from dead in the world of modems and malls as the twentieth century gives way to the twenty-first. (If it does—re-reading this to proofread it on St., Valentine's day in 1996—I recall that this morning in the grocery I saw the headline in *The Sun* that proclaims the end of the earth in the year 2000. Rogue star or something. Don't worry. My crystal ball says "Not!")

WARNING

I am well aware that many of the readers attracted to this present book will be even more superstitious than the general run of mankind and that a considerable number of them, judging by the readership of *The Complete Book of Magic and Witchcraft*, will be approving of or even consider themselves adepts in witchcraft.

I can only say that, as for the legal aspect, I hope that they do not transgress laws reasonably constituted to protect individuals and society as a whole. As for the psychological element, in my way of thinking witchcraft is dangerous, and clearly it has attracted in the past many highly disturbed people. On the other hand, some great minds have grappled with it and the problems it raises, the questions it poses.

As for religion, every person must act according to the prescriptions of whatever religion she or he adheres to—or none, if that is the choice. For Jews, the concept of sin (if etymology can guide us to the origin of the concept in Hebrew thought), is missing the mark. For Jews, God has dictated the mark. Any serious Jew knows the Law, what is required and what is forbidden.

In Christian thought, there are proscriptions but motive is paramount. What you intend to do as a sin is a sin. What you do not think of as a sin is not a sin, for you. Conscience guides, and some people are invincibly ignorant or have what are called hardened consciences. They may commit what other people call sins or crimes; but if they do what they think to be right that is all God requires of them. On the other hand, there are sins of omission (not doing something you know to be right) as well as sins of commission (doing things you know to be wrong). Also, you must not invite or entertain temptations or put yourself into what are called occasions of sin.

Whether this means you cannot deal in witchcraft, white or black or a mixture of the two, is, as you see, not so simple to determine. It is, however, everyone's duty to examine motives and question both desire and actions.

Most of the witches I have encountered say they are trying to do good. Very few describe themselves as antisocial. In fact, many are drawn into witchcraft because it offers a kind of sisterhood or brotherhood.

In the early days, shamans served their societies, and women wise in herbs and other medicines distributed folk remedies (especially for female complaints, in which male doctors were insufficiently interested) and were regarded as useful members of the community—at least until envy or some other vice entered the picture. When the witches were poisoners, they were dealt with like other murderers.

Many religions assert (or recognize) the existence of devils and demons. Some religions forbid any willful contact with them. In British thought, for instance, from Henry Holland's *A Treatise against Witchcraft* (1590, England) and James VI's *Dæmonologie* (1597, Scotland), at least until the latter part of the last century, all dealings with devils and demons were anathema. But even Aleister Crowley, "The Beast," claimed he was only working white magic, doing good.

Clergymen looked at the religious aspects, lawyers and judges at the legal aspects, in books such as these:

George Giffard. *Dialogue concerning Witches* (1593).
William Perkins. *Damned Art of Witchcraft* (1608).
J. Mason, *Anatomie of Sorcery* (1612).
Alexander Roberts. *Treatise of Witchcraft* (1616).
John Cotta. *Trial of Witchcraft* (1616).
Thomas Cooper, *Mystery of Witchcraft* (1617).
Matthew Hopkins. *Discovery of Witches* (1647).
N. Hornes. *Dæmonologie and Theologie* (1650).
Henry More. *Antidote against Atheism* (1655).
Joseph Glanvill. *Sadducismus triumphatus* (1681).
Anthony Horneck. *Appendix to...Sadducismus triumphatus* (1681).

Wayne Schumaker has published eight important Renaissance treatises of various degrees of obscurity in *Renaissance Curiosa* (1982) and *Natural Magic and Modern Science* (1989). Students of the occult will be especially concerned with Dr. Dee's *Conversation with Angels*, Cardano's *Horoscope of Christ*, and the ones on the relationship of magic to science by Giordano Bruno, Tommasso Campanella, Martin Del Rio, and Gaspar Schott. This last is the least familiar. He wrote *Magia universalis*.

Publications continued in the eighteenth and nineteenth centuries, defending the theories of devils and demons and attacking those who consulted evil forces. Interesting books include Edward Fairfax's *Demonologia* (edited 1882) and the anonymous *Witchcraft Detected* (1826). Uncommon views are exposed in Reginald Scot's *Discoverie of Witchcraft* (1584), John Wagstaffe's *Displaying of Supposed Witchcraft* (1671), Margaret Murray's *The Witch Cult in Western Europe* (1921). In the twentieth century some English witches (of both sexes) have come forward to defend themselves, but the public generally thinks of them as kooks at best and dangerous at worst.

SOLOMON'S RING AND KEY

King Solomon was supposed to have worn a ring which gave him power over devils and demons, but it was buried with him. His magical secrets, though, are supposedly published in a *Key* in two parts. It tells you how to cast spells and to call up The Devil. It must be copied by hand, not printed, underlining the fact that a sorcerer must be closely associated with the text. One must fast for quite a long time before even opening the book and then summon up the courage to follow its instructions implicitly.

AMULETS

There is a country-western ditty that goes:

I don't care if it rains or freezes, 'long as I got my plastic Jesus
Sittin' on the dashboard of my car....

But get rid of your Saint Christopher. He is no longer a saint, poor fellow.

The Jews read the *Book of Raziel*, one of the seven great books of the secret lore, to get instructions for preparing amulets. King Solomon had some allegedly powerful ones, ones that magicians in the Middle Ages and Renaissance claimed to have rediscovered.

Bol'shaia Sovetskaia Entsiklopedia (Great Soviet Encyclopedia) takes a crack at those who do not agree that religion is superstition when it states:

Even the Christian Church, while condemning superstition, continues to use amulets in the form of crosses and medallions worn
on the body supposedly to protect believers from "dark powers."

In fact, followers of Islam wear the Hand of Fatima, Christians wear crosses and blessed medals and scapulars, and many other religions permit or encourage the use of amulets to protect against devils and demons. Jews with their phylacteries and *mezzuzahs* and Buddhists with their prayer wheels incorporate bits of Scripture into their objects.

If an object is supposed to bring good luck, rather than ward off evil, it is called a talisman. The books of magic provide elaborate designs for talismans of all sorts, but most people do not realize that, to be considered effective, talismans have to be made of the appropriate materials, at the astrologically ideal times, and with considerable ritual. By the way, makers of these magical objects must receive no fee for their services.

INCANTATIONS

"The chill serpent in the meadow is burst asunder by incantations," wrote Vergil, himself suspected of being a magician. But magic says it can do more than influence the physical world. It claims to have power over the invisible world, and in the hands of those who associate themselves with The Devil, persons the old rabbinical authorities called *hartummin*, it can deceive humans and call up devils and demons. As with everything else in magic, it is a matter of will.

Incantations must be done perfectly or the magician will fail, perhaps suffer. With all the complicated names of devils and demons involved, and the beating their names have taken as they have been handed down over the centuries and from one language to another, this is no easy matter. One thinks of Scoprell, a character in English literature, who picks up a book and reads as its title "An Easy of Huming Understanding, by John Lookye."

THE INFERNAL MISSAL

One Sylvain Nevillon (tried at Orléans in 1614 for witchcraft) confessed to attending a Black Mass at which the celebrant was dressed in a black chasuble decorated with broken crosses—others claim the Black Mass was celebrated in a black cope without crosses—and mumbling from a missal with red and black leaves. Another witch of Orléans, Gentien le Clerc, said the missal he saw was bound in some hairy hide, such as a wolf's skin. The pages of the missal were said to be red, black, and white. Some say magic books had red letters, which hurt the eyes. The defrocked priest, the Abbé Boullan, in nineteenth-century France said Black Mass following the traditions of blasphemy set up by the confessions of such witches and used a similar missal. We'll hear of him later.

SUPERSTITIOUS PRACTICES AND PRETENDED MAGIC

A decree by the king of France in 1682 restored witchcraft to the much earlier crime of mere superstition and pretense. In the modern world a witch is more likely to be sued for fraud (for not having practiced real witchcraft) than prosecuted for having done so, as I have said. Burning at the stake, or slow roasting (as was done with Jacques de Molay of The Templars) is no longer acceptable. Although the Witchcraft Act was repealed in England in 1736, those who claimed to be able to perform witchcraft could be punished, but not severely.

WITCHES AT THE DOOR

Put an iron object under your doormat. Do not leave a broom outside the door at night. Plant red flowers in a row along the path to your front door. Put a hex sign prominently on the front of the house.

CALLING THE ANGEL AXIR TO "ENTER THE PATHWAY OF EVIL"

From Israel Regardie's *The Golden Dawn*:
 Bind and veil Sigil with white cord and black cloth. Place it without [outside] *the Circle at the West, and say*: Hail unto ye, Lords of the Land of Life, hear ye these my words for I am made as ye are, who are

formers of the soul. With the divine aid, I now purpose to call for this day and hour from the dark depths of my sphere of sensation the Angel Axir of the Lesser Earthly Angel of the Northern Quadrangle, whose magical seal I now bind...to obtain from that Angel the true knowledge of Earth....*Draw the pentacle into the Circle with the front of the sword....Consecrate immediately with Fire and with Water at the West of the Circle*. Creature of Sigils, purified and made consecrate, enter thou the Pathway of Evil.

BASQUE MAGICAL OINTMENTS

The flying ointment of Basque witches (according to information obtained by torturing one of them, Maria of Ituren) involved skinning toads alive and mixing the dried, powdered flesh with *usainbelar* (water plantain). Other witch ointments included one made of "toads' blood and babies' hearts."

FRENCH WITCHCRAFT

In the century after the executions of Joan of Arc and a marshal of France (Gilles de Rais) on charges of witchcraft, the persecution of witches increased. The first secular trial for witchcraft in France was held in Paris in 1390. Henceforward witchcraft would be a criminal offense as well as heresy. By the mid-fifteenth century, when the first French work on witchcraft was published (*La Vauderye de Lyonois*, 1460), the witchcraft scare was growing rapidly. A witch at Provins (near Paris) testified in 1452 that there were only 50 or 60 of her sisters in all of France. A few years later there were serious witch hunts at Metz (one authority explaining that unusually bad weather had spoiled the crops and witches were blamed) and 30 years later a too-cold summer was blamed on witches and 25 more witches were burned at Metz. The poet Martin le Franc was convinced that there were "Witch Woodstocks" with many thousands in attendance and a witch hunt began in earnest in Briançon. It was dangerous to speak of the possibility that witchcraft was fraud or that any suspect might be innocent. By the 1580s, Nicholas Remy, a judge with an intense personal hatred of witches, was condemning 900 to the stake in a decade in Lorraine, and books on the terrors of witchcraft poured forth from the likes of Jean Bodin (1580), Pierre Le Loyer (1586), Pierre Crespet (1590), Martin Antoine Del Rio (1599), and others. The seventeenth century saw thousands of people burned at the stake in France and something of an epidemic of possessed nuns. We discuss some of these phenomena elsewhere in this book.

THE WIFE AND THE *INCUBUS*

When Saint Bernard was visiting Nantes in 1135, a woman sought him out and confessed to him that she had had sex with an *incubus* for six years but that eventually her husband found out about it and left her. Now the *incubus* could not be shaken off. Saint Bernard gave her his staff to take to be with her, and the *incubus* was driven off. It is not recorded how she used the staff.

NUDITY

Some covens like to perform naked. This reminds us to note that nudity (or a mask with nothing else) is a feature of certain magical operations. Sexual energy is thereby increased and the work rendered more powerful, in theory. There are witchcraft covens that operate naked, though flowing robes and heavy jewelry are more popular. In fact, some ceremonial magic demands elaborate robes of appropriate colors. The Black Mass uses a naked figure (preferable a virgin, later devirginated), male or female, depending on your sexual tastes, as the altar. Demons and other apports are said to appear naked on occasion.

It has always puzzled me that the dead, buried naked, wrapped in a shroud, appear in period costume which does not look the worse for having spent centuries in the tomb. Eliphas Lévi, however, produced Apollonius of Tyana in a shroud, but he could not engage him in conversation. Someone produced an Elizabethan ghost for me but I noticed that his shoes were modern. (Shoes for right and left feet were not introduced until well after the sixteenth century.) A shroud and bare feet would have solved this problem.

FULL MOON

There has always been a belief that devils and demons and spirits in general and evil forces of all kinds, supernatural and human, are perked up by the full moon. One astronomer says the full moon may affect the inner ear. People used to say the moon created lunatics. In the Middle Ages people believed that moonbeams striking their heads at the full moon would addle their brains. Bartenders now all know that the crazies drink more at ·

the full moon. Policemen say crime goes up and the offenses are crazier at the full moon.

Twenty years ago, the then president of the New Jersey Psychological Society (Dr. Virginia Bennett) told the press (*New York Sunday News*, 28 February 1975, 52):

> Most of the things attributed to the moon entering its full phase could be classified as deviant behavior, and people prone to such behavior are far more profoundly influenced by seemingly unrelated and unimportant facts...far more likely to be superstitious and susceptible to suggestion....[and] may believe the moon is having an influence on them and act accordingly.

This conception of the importance of legend and self-fulfilling prophecies is not unconnected to the history of the deviant behavior of witchcraft or to the public perception that witchcraft is a real and present danger.

ABRACADABRA, HOCUS-POCUS, MUMBO JUMBO

Abracadabra comes from a pagan god (Abraxas), *hocus-pocus* from the "*Hoc est Corpus*" ("This is My Body") of transubstantiation in the Latin Mass, and *mumbo jumbo* from a grotesque African idol of that name. The use of the first and the last might possibly signify in demonology and the middle one may strike some as blasphemy.

Conjurors' use of *presto* (fast) is not really part of a charm or spell. In *The Arabian Nights, open sesame* is a magical phrase; in the comic books *shazzam* is similar. When the name of a devil or demon or The Devil himself is used, we have demonology.

It is remarkable that some black magicians include the names of God and the angels and saints in their invocations. To anagrammatize these, or to use them backwards in disrespect and rejection, is one thing; to use them "straight" looks very odd.

THE RIGHT WORDS

It is a firm belief in magic that if one does not say the incantation exactly right—it's an incantation, not an invocation—there will be no result. One must get the *hocus-pocus* right. That term is a Protestant insult to the Roman Catholic Mass.

Those who still would like to cling to the Latin Mass—which the Roman Church did say at the sixteenth-century Council of Trent was forever, an idea they dropped after a Vatican council in our century—argue that the words of consecration don't work in other languages, making the Mass more like a Protestant memorial of the Last Supper than a Roman Catholic miracle of transubstantiation on the altar.

In the history of magic there are reports that the single word *Agla*, if said in the right way, produced extraordinary results. It is also said that merely by pronouncing seven names correctly (*Adonai, Perai, Tetragrammaton, Anexhexeton, Inessensatoal, Pathumaton,* and *Itemon*) King Solomon was able to bring all demons under his personal control. The name *Primematum* holds power over the whole host of Heaven. The name of God commands the hosts of Hell. You open the Gates of Hell by chanting *Zazas, Zazas, Nasantanada, Zazas.* Closing them is considerably more difficult. You know of the story with "Open, Sesame!" What was the password for closing?

TELL IT TO THE JUDGE

If you ever have to go to court, you may be able to win over the judge if you carry a talisman in your pocket. Just write this on a piece of paper you keep hidden on your person:

A L M A N A H

L

M A R E

A A L B E H A

N

A R E H A I L

H   A

There is apparently no way you can guess which way an American jury is going to decide. If they go against you, you could set Adramalech on them. When setting any demons on people, however, consider the magical law by which evil can be returned to the one who looses it.

THE SOURCES OF WORDS

If you look very closely at words, you will find that etymologies (their origins) reveal a great deal. For instance, did you ever notice that the first people to *arrive* must have been Frenchmen coming to the shore (*á rive*) of Britain? Or that Britons must have got German toilet water through

French intermediaries, which is why we don't use a German name for it but call it *eau de Cologne*?

Look at *dæmon*, which Greek word first meant "spirit" and gave us *demon* (bad spirit). Look at Greek *diabolos* which meant "(false) accuser"

¶ The Apprehenſion ·and confeſsion
of three notorious Witches.

Arreigned and by Iuſtice condemned and
executed at *Chelmes-forde,* in the Countye of
Eſſex, *the 5. day of Iulye, laſt paſt.*
1 5 8 9.
¶ With the manner of their diueliſh practices and keeping of their
ſpirits, whoſe fourmes are heerein truelye
proportioned.

IOAN PRENTIS
& hir Bid

JACKE

GILL

A publication on the Chelmsford Witches (1589) shows them and their familiars.

and eventually produced *diabolical*. Consider that *witch* originally meant "poisoner." That *sorcerer* first dealt in casting lots. That *devil-may-care* is elliptical for "The Devil may care (but I don't)". That *fascination* was first accomplished through the eyes? That the original *magi* were Persian. That it was three magicians/astrologers and not three kings who first came to adore the Christ Child in Bethlehem and to offer magical sacrifices of gold, frankincense and myrrh. You knew they came because of astrological predictions, right? They were following that new star in the heavens. Did you know that *thaumaturgy* is the working of wonders? That workers of spells and curers of ills were at first merely knowledgeable, able to see what was otherwise hidden (*occult*), wise, as in *wise woman* and *wizard*?

A CHARM FOR WINNING AT GAMBLING

On the first Thursday of the new moon, at the hour of Jupiter, before sunrise, write on virgin parchment: *Non licet ponare in egarbona quia pretia sanguinis*. Place the head of a viper in the middle of the page, fold the corners in, and when you are going to gamble tie the parchment with the writing and the head to your left arm, under your clothes, with a red ribbon. They say this works—but I wouldn't bet on it.

DEMONOMANCY

You can burn branches and leaves to get answers (that's botanomancy) or throw arrows up in the air and see how they fall (that's bellomancy) or ask spirits (that's sciomancy) or demons (that's demonomancy). Astrology, palmistry, or numerology, even reading tea leaves seems safer than any of those.

ACE IT

It's easy. When shuffling a deck of cards, secretly say to yourself the magic word *Pilatus*. That way you will get an ace.

BURN OUT

A candle that is left to burn itself out is not only a fire hazard. It could cause a death in the household.

Bodegas sell all sorts of "blessed" candles of various colors and dedicated to various saints and purposes. Pick the one that suits your intention. Of course, it's superstition.

Whether lighting candles or votive lights in church is piety or super-stition is an argument I do not wish to engage in, but my own preference instead of lighting a candle is to give a beggar enough to make her or his eyes light up. I don't do it often but when I do it makes me feel good for a while. And it's less fattening than an overpriced Dove Bar.

BLOOD AND TEARS

You would think that being in the grip of devils and demons a witch might weep. Witches (says an ancient tradition) can weep only three drops at a time. And not salt tears, either.

If you can draw even one drop of a witch's blood, her spell is broken.

RECIPES FOR THE HOME

In another book, I gave Reginald Scot's recipe for the flying ointment of *bacularia*. Applied to the body liberally and to a broom handle (often with a broom handle being used for masturbation in the witch's excited state) it was widely believed, accepted as evidence in both ecclesiastical and civil courts, that witches flew to the *Sabbat*. (The witches said so themselves. The evidence of the possessed, however, was unacceptable; French judges decided that "demons lie.") Scot, a debunker of witchcraft, says sex-starved old women simply got high on the drugs contained in flying ointments, having hyped themselves up with the thrills of blasphemy. I agree with Scot.

Though the editors or printers mangled my text at that point, there was enough information, without going back to Scot's late sixteenth-century *Discoverie of Witchcraft*, to convince some people who wrote to me to complain that I was encouraging the manufacture of formulae containing psychotropic drugs or (worse) "the fat of young children." That's as bad as "finger of birth-strangled babe" called for by the witches in *Macbeth*. Human blood is shed in selling yourself to The Devil and it is used in many recipes such as the stew of snakes and other demons creatures that one prepares to change into an animal form. It is essential for certain dire curses.

I hope anyone foolish enough to be concocting a flying ointment used another recipe I gave, from an old Betty Crocker of witchcraft: 100 grams of lard, 5 grams of hashish, and a pinch each of hellebore root and crushed sunflower seeds, to which one adds "flowers, hemp, and poppy" and sim-mers covered "over water" for two hours. There are enough drugs in that to make it both illegal and mind-bending.

These are the two states witches seem to favor the most, and to seek.

SEX AND DRUGS

Some magicians believe their powers are drained by sex but increased by drugs. Some believe their powers are increased by sex but diminished by drugs. Some use both stimulants. Both are powerful reasons magic works.

MAGIC WORKS

Magic takes action in a world of fears and oppressions. It undertakes to change things, miraculously if necessary, typically "an attempt to help that makes a botch" (according to Daniel Lawrence O'Keefe's social theory of magic in *Stolen Lightning*), but boldly, drastically, often personally, asserting the individual against society and its most revered institutions. It quarrels with its sibling (or parent?), religion. Theoretically it can be thaumaturgy (white magic) by witch doctors or wise women or the more masculine and focused art of sorcery (black magic), but the distinctions and involvements and motives blur. French has only one word *(sorcier)* for both witch (or wizard) and sorcerer.

You were supposed to kiss a lady's hand, a bishop's ring, the pope's shoe, and The Devil's rear end.

Oddly, there were more letters from cat lovers objecting to the recipe I gave for a love potion (taken from the writings of the poet William Butler Yeats) that called for making tea (in a black teapot) from the desiccated liver of a black cat. I omitted the recipe for flying ointment using a cat's brain, but that was not taken into account when my love-philter potion was discussed. If you do not wish to kill a cat just to get a lover, you can take what I think of as the vegetarian approach: crush vervain, southernwood, and orris root between sandstones and make a sachet in a green silk bag, worn pinned to your underwear. Or try one of the highly advertised perfumes, especially those containing musk. Or add pheronomes to them.

Speaking of smells, magic is full of recipes to attract or repel humans and demons. Aleister Crowley put together a hair pomade so sexually arousing that horses reared in the street as he passed by, but that seems to have been more scientific than magical. Here's a magical incense formula: by weight 40 percent frankincense, 30 percent sandalwood, 10 percent myrrh, 10 percent cinnamon, 5 percent patchouli leaf, and 5 percent orris root, all powdered, and throw in a dash of saltpeter. When burned with incantations, it is said to bring devils and demons to do your will.

Whatever recipes you use, it is best to get them out of a *grimoire*, and remember that these cannot be bought or sold or printed. They must be in manuscript and in red ink. It is said that the red letters burn the eyes if looked at too unblinkingly. *Grimoires* are usually bound in black, though there are rumors about human skin being used, and they must be given to you as part of a witch's legacy, as must such items of magical paraphernalia as the chalice you use in ceremonies. Money being involved cancels all powers. The ones to get, if possible, are the *Veritable Grimoire* of the French magicians and *The Key of Solomon*, attributed to that wise king (but obviously much later in compilation). Each is often undiscriminatingly called *The Black Book*, from its cover.

I saw a genuine *grimoire*, handwritten but bound, among a load of generally worthless books at Tepper's auction in New York one time, but I did not have the courage to buy it. Friends say I ought to have bought it (when it then would have been useless to me but I might have given it to someone who could use it). I believe that would have been unconscionable, and if by some weird means it did work I would think myself guilty of all the malefaction the recipient of the book might do. That, in fact, is why witches hand on their recipes. Those who use them after the deceased in some way keep the powers of the deceased active in the world, perpetuate in some way the malice and revenge that usually prompted the original turn to witchcraft.

The advice of the Chinese is probably best; be in awe of supernatural beings but have nothing to do with them.

HIGH-TECH COMMUNICATION BY WITCHCRAFT

The witch pricked all the letters of the alphabet on the arms of two lovers who were separated. When one wanted to communicate to the other, she or he sucked the blood from whatever letters spelled the message. The other's wounds would bleed and convey the message.

MAGIC AND THE BIBLE

The Bible forbids magic, although Moses used his brother Aaron's staff as a magic rod to impress the Egyptians. The Witch of Endor called up the dead to speak to King Saul. Christ raised the dead and cast out devils. And so on. *Exodus* XXII:26 says you must not let the magician live. *Leviticus* IX and XX in various ways condemn magic, soothsaying, raising ghosts and spirits, etc. *Deuteronomy* XVIII likewise condemns soothsayers, necromancers, passing a person through fire by sorcery, and uttering prophecies "in the name of other gods." *I Samuel* denounces witchcraft (though, as noted, *II Samuel* shows the Witch of Endor in action). *II Kings* denounces Jezebel as a sorceress and Manassas for passing his child through fire, while praising Josiah for clearing out all the idol worshiping and "all who call up ghosts and spirits." *Isaiah* denounces necromancy and says Babylon fell because of superstition, divination and spells. And yet the Bible itself has been used for divination—open it blindfolded at random for a message. It is also used in exorcism by "bell, book, and candle." (The "book,"I have said, is the Bible.) The Bible is desecrated in the Black Mass and also, some say, in the Mass of Saint Secaire and similar blasphemies.

No observing Jew or devoted Christian can play with the black arts. Christians are said to put thereby their souls in danger of being damned. Jews are in danger of being stoned to death by the orthodox, for *Leviticus*, while not denying the power of necromancers to raise the dead, demands that the holy people "shall stone them; their blood shall be on their heads."

It is arguable that spiritualists and mediums who converse with the dead also are anathema and ought to be stoned. That is, if they really do raise "ghosts and spirits."

On the other hand, Eliphas Lévi (Alphonse-Louise Constant), in my view the greatest ritual magician of the nineteenth century, though the magazine he edited with Jules Michelet and others was banned by French authorities and he was much feared and often condemned, is shown in his deathbed photograph laid out clutching the cross like a devout Roman Catholic.

I could describe magic in a number of familiar and unfamiliar traditions but, because I happen to be interested in cabalistic studies, let me give you a page or so on Jewish magic. It has an unusual attraction for us non-Jews.

JEWISH MAGIC

The Laws which govern every aspect of orthodox Jewish life are nothing if not clear, and it is patent that Jewish Law forbids all connection with the occult, despite the fact that the Jewish world is peopled (if that is the word) by innumerable evil forces, from Satan to the demons that make it unsafe for an unmarried man to live alone.

Not everyone, not even in The Books of Moses, has always steered clear of magic and witchcraft, however. There were all sorts of ways in which the future was foretold, even by the High Priest wearing the jeweled breastplate which incorporated devices for divination. Love philters and necromancy were expressly forbidden, and yet Jewish lore is full of them, as well as of curses. The father of the priest Melchisedech, the first to offer bread and wine rather than animal sacrifice (it is said), was believed to have been a sylph. The Witch of Endor calling up the dead seems to have been tolerated. Christ brought back Lazarus from the dead (but out of charity, not just to chat, as Cagliostro is said to have done) and drove out devils and performed some lesser miracles (such as water into wine) that were standard with magicians. He used saliva, the laying on of hands, and other gestures common among magicians, though even the Sadducees and the Pharisees dared not accuse Him of magic.

It is seldom if ever remarked that the darkening of the sky at the Crucifixion and the dead rising from their graves and appearing to many are effects often attributed to merely human witches and wizards who summon magical powers. The Resurrection, of course, is something no magician has ever accomplished, though some have boldly claimed to be reincarnations of earlier magicians. There is no intention here of outraging any believer in either the Old or the New Testament. The point is simply that what we ourselves believe we tend to call religion and what others believe we often dismiss as superstition, mythology, heresy, blasphemy, and lies.

As in most religions, amulets and talismans have often been used by Jews, especially against the evil eye. Objects had great powers in their eyes. It was said that to touch the Ark of the Covenant meant death, and the story is told of someone dropping dead after reaching out a hand helpfully to steady it when it was carried in procession. Moses performed both magical tricks and real magic, most famously the parting of the Red Sea, followed by the killing of many Egyptian enemies. The Jewish Simon Magus (The Magician) was converted to Christianity but was criticized for wanting to buy magical powers greater than his own. (He appeared one day in a fiery chariot in the sky, like the Prophet Elijah, but Saint Peter grounded him.) The Apostles were given what some would define as magical powers. On Pentecost, for instance, they received the gift of tongues, a sure sign, traditionally, of magical powers when it is not a sign of demonic possession. The saints were often spoken of as superior to the ancient Jews and the heathens in that they could perform greater miracles. It is said that their faith could move mountains.

The letters of the Hebrew alphabet having been associated with numbers, numerology inevitably played a big part in Jewish superstition. This was taken over into Christian culture, and numerology is practiced today by many who have no idea that their religions absolutely forbid it.

In orthodox Jewish religion the magical power of names, closely related to numbers, especially the secret name of God, which servants of The Temple shouted to drown out on the few occasions that the High Priest was obliged to pronounce it, was of vast significance. God refused to give Moses His name. "I Am" is all He thought was needed, and with His name power was involved. God is traditionally in Hebrew referred to by substitutes for His name, such as "Lord," and "The Most High." Christians searched the Cabala for the secret name of God to anagrammatize and use in black magic. It is *Emeth*, and not being Jewish I do not think I shall bring the world to its end by writing that name here. Given wit enough, you might have guessed it, where no one could have guessed the nonsense syllables of *Rumpelstiltskin* in the informative fairy tale. *Emeth* is essentially "Truth." Truth is surely the creative power of all the world's religions. Or love.

Jewish folklore includes stories of magicians and of Rabbi Loew of Prague, the man credited with creating (by using the knowledge of Eleazar of Worms and the secret name *Emeth*) the dreaded Golem, a Frankenstein monster. It is said that others were able to create Golems but no one was powerful enough to control them. That superstition is gone today but others are common now in Jewish, as in all other, communities. Gentiles find it odd that Jews will not only avoid writing the secret name of God (which most of them do not know) but write "G-d" and even, if very ignorant, "the g-ds of the Greeks."

In the Middle Ages, Jews were often considered to be magicians and astrologers, and there is testimony that the likes of Zedekias, a cabalist, convinced many important unbelievers with their magical displays. What the cabalists brought most significantly, however, was the mystical interpretation of Scripture to the West, especially to such centers of magical studies as Toledo. There Arabs, Jews, and Christians met and there a large and beautiful synagogue still stands despite the expulsion of the Jews by decree of the Catholic kings. When the Jews were given notice that they must become Christians or leave Spain and Portugal, many become *conversos*, and from that group a fair number of learned men, some lifelong students of the Cabala, were recruited into Christian religious orders, especially the Dominicans. These zealous new converts brought special knowledge to the Holy Inquisition. De Spina the demonologist and Nostradamus the prognosticator (whose boldly Christian surname looks a bit like over-correction) both came from Jewish families. Someone ought to research the families of Jakob Spengler and Heinrich Kramer, author of the "hammer of witches" famous as the *Malleus Malificarum* (1486).

Humanists such as Pico della Mirandola (who regarded magic as a natural science), scientists such as Paracelsus (who was interested not only in medicine but in magic potions, not only in mining but weird creatures who lived in the bowels of the earth), magicians such as Cornelius Agrippa (whose very name became synonymous with a book of spells) and others all studied Hebrew texts. All of them learned much from their study of the Cabala. Even when magical books were faked they might be given Hebrew provenances. It made them seem more reliable.

Around serious scholars of the Cabala a lot of superstitions arose. The savants were said to be seeking the Philosopher's Stone in alchemy, or pursuing immortality through sexual connections with elemental spirits, or trying to make demons do their bidding. In an age when theology and philosophy were confused, and magic and science indistinguishable, cabalists were misunderstood and often feared. Charlatans played upon those fears, both inside and outside the ghettos to which the Jews were confined. At the same time, a knowledge of the Cabala was regarded as a great gift and a marketable commodity. Even the popes were widely believed to deal in cabalistic studies and to consult not only Jewish lawyers and doctors but Jewish magicians and astrologers. In some few cases this was fact.

BRIEF BIBLIOGRAPHY OF JEWS AND MAGIC

Bamberger, B. J. *Fallen Angels.*
Guinzburg, C. D. *The Kabbalah.*
Kohut, A. *Jüdische Angelologie und Dæmonologie.*
Scholem, G. G. *Major Trends in Jewish Mysticism.*
Stehelin, J. P. *Traditions of the Jews.*

Trachtenberg, J. *The Devil and the Jews.*
————*Jewish Magic and Superstition.*
Weber, T. v. *Jüdische Theologie.*
Westcott, W. W., trans. *Sephir Yetzirah.*

SUPER ILLIUS SPECULA

Like all pronouncements from the Throne of Peter, this papal bull (from the *bulla* or seal that made it official), is named for its opening words. It opened a Pandora's Box of evil. It dates from 1326 and Pope John XXII. It marks the change in the Roman Catholic Church from denying the very existence of witches to declaring sorcery a crime. By the time several hundred years later the church and its Dominican "dogs" finished hunting down witches, hundreds of thousands of people in Europe had been tortured or put to death in the most horrible fashion.

THE HOLY INQUISITION

The large number of individuals who suffered under The Holy Inquisition raises the question in some minds that can be briefly put thus: If witches and magicians had devils and demons at their command, how is it that they could not defeat the prying church authorities?

Casanova had an answer. He said it was because the church officials commanded more devils and demons than anyone else.

GO HANG

When they tried to hang Sir Robert Tressilian, Chief Justice of the King's Bench, at Tyburn, for treason, in 1388, they first had to take away from him the lists of devils and demons and the talismans with which he had equipped himself.

A HOT TIME IN THE OLD TOWN

In Geneva, in three months in 1515 some five hundred people were burned at the stake for witchcraft.

EXECUTION OF WITCHES

In England and America, witches were hanged or pressed to death. In France and Germany, the witch was strangled first (usually), then burned. In Sweden, the witch was strangled and burned or beheaded. In Italy and Spain, the witch was burned alive. Jacques de Molay, Grand Master of the Templars, we have already seen, was slow roasted on a spit. Uncooperative witches might be burned with green wood, which was slower to kill them. The American writer George Lincoln Burr estimated that at least 100,000 witches were burned in Germany alone. C. L'Estrange Ewen estimates that the German total is 100 times as many as were executed in England. Rossell Hope Robbins guesses at 200,000 for the whole of Europe 1450–1750.

THE BARBARITY OF SEVILLE

The tribunal of Seville on 15 October 1818 (the *Encyclopedia of Witchcraft and Demonology* tells us) "sentenced Ana Barbero, for superstition, blasphemy, and a pact with the Devil, to two hundred lashes and six years' exile" (later remitted to eight years in a penitentiary for prostitutes).

DEBUNKING FRAUDS

A number of professional magicians have tried to alert the public to fakery. The Amazing Randi is in a long line that stretches back to Houdini

Witches hanged in Scotland, Sir George Mackenzie's *Law and Customs of Scotland in Matters Criminal* (1678).

and before, and scholars (Guy Lambert of The Royal Society for Psychical Research in London devoted his spare time for life to exposing fraudulent mediums) have attempted to police those who claim occult powers.

But The Amazing Randi's exposure of the spoon bender Uri Geller or the notorious Peter Popoff (who was receiving broadcast messages in his hearing aids) has done little to rid us of New Age quackery and self-promoting gurus and expensive "psychic readings" over the telephone. The Amazing Randi's relentless campaign to get an airline to drop horoscopes from its in-flight magazine has never succeeded. You can still find someone in any town to read your palm, your tea leaves, or your Tarot, though phrenology—the "science" of reading the bumps on your head, which flourished in America in the nineteenth century—seems to have disappeared.

Psychics are no longer connected with devils and demons in the public mind and even the laws that threaten to fine or imprison fortune-tellers are not enforced. However, the "professional psychics" on television and the gypsy "readers" in storefront "parlors" in the medieval age would have been accused of dealing with The Devil and promptly done away with. We are now in what you might call a media-evil age as far as these fakes are concerned. Avoid all Indian mystics, Baba Ganou and all self-appointed gurus, black singers down on their luck pushing Psychic Masters, table-rappers and all other rappers for the pop cult. Your mind, if not your soul, is in danger. Avoid pseudo-psychic friends.

THE POWER IS WITHIN YOU

I've said that the usefulness of The Tarot and such is not that they draw powers to us but that they reach down into us for something latent there. Phineas Quimby, who is responsible for Christian Science because he taught Mrs. Mary Baker Eddy whatever she knew, emphasized that power to heal is inherent. Occultists often say all people have extra-sensory perception (ESP) and similar gifts and that some few are more in touch with their talents than others. When you call upon angels or devils to help you, you may tap resources not outside but within, for better or worse. Be careful of your depths!

THE PROBLEM OF THE OCCULT

This vexing question can be easily solved if you will take time to ponder what Walt Whitman said of the great American painter Thomas Eakins

(1844–1916): "I never knew of but one [visual] artist and that's Tom Eakins who could resist the temptation to see what they thought ought to be rather than what is."

WHITE MAGIC

If magic is used to help people, then it is called "white." If it involves communication with devils and demons, I call it "black." On the subject, there are a number of herbals (with truly useful medicines) and books on folklore which touch on the subject, such as *Magical Medicine* by the distinguished American folklorist, Wayland P. Hand. There are many other books such as Gareth Knight's *History of White Magic* (1978) and D. G. Phillips' *White Magic* (1981). See Brian Inglis' *Fringe Medicine* (1964) and C. Grant Loomis' *White Magic* (1948).

RITUAL MAGIC

Butler, Eliza Marian. *Ritual Magic* (1949).
Cazeneuve, Jean. *Sociologie du rite* (1971).
"Conway, David". *Ritual Magic* (1972).
King, Francis. *Ritual Magic in England* (1970).
Waite, A. E. *The Book of Ceremonial Magic* (1961).

MAGIC CIRCLE

Performing magical rituals within a circle protects you—if the circle is properly drawn and inscribed—from whatever demons you might call up. In Jewish weddings it used to be the custom for the guests to circle the bride and groom seven times, bearing lighted candles. This dove away demons, spirits of darkness.

Ritual magicians warn that some demons are devilishly clever in devising ways to get you to put a foot outside the circle. Those particularly horrible in appearance (or stinking, for there is a distinct odor of evil just as there is an odor of sanctity, it is said) might tempt you to flee. Stay within the circle, whatever happens.

Witches were supposed to wind up their spells by dancing in a circle. Because Satan is The Adversary, in black magic things are reversed (as in the Black Mass). So they danced widdershins, which is to say counterclockwise.

Superstition looked at rings in the turf formed by underground fungi and imagined these were Fairy Circles, the little people's dancing places.

Circular depressions in fields of grain these days get all sorts of imaginative responses. But if a circle is more or less than nine feet in diameter, it is not a magic circle, and for magical purposes it must be drawn with the tip of a magical sword, so a very wide diameter is impossible.

SOME MAGICAL ORDERS

The following are said still to exist in Europe: *Ordo Templi Orientis* or *OTO* (founded by Theodor Reuss, 1902) and one or more imitations or offshoots of it, *Les Fréres du Sieur de Pasqually* (founded in the eighteenth century by Le Sieur de Pasqually, 1715–1779), *Ordre des Inconnus Silensieux* (founded by "Papus," Gérard Encausse, 1865–1921), and various pseudo-magical groups pretending to worship Baphomet, to continue the tradition of The Rosy Cross (including one branch of the Masons). In addition there are societies for psychical research and various semi-religious groups (under which rubric may come The Theosophical Society founded by Mme. Blavatsky and others in 1875 and much altered since).

THE REWARDS OF MAGIC

The chief reward must be the assertion of the self, but one might expect that successful magicians would be able to reap huge social and financial rewards, charming people, foretelling stock market fluctuations, and so on. History shows, however, that The Devil never pays. If you want to get rich as a magician, try stage illusion. In 1994, someone who started with a Jewish name but who (as a Brooklyn student of mine said) "made the name David Copperfield famous," was paid 24 million dollars.

ARTICLES IN THE LEARNED
JOURNALS AND POPULAR MAGAZINES

In the little guides to further reading which I have sprinkled through this book, not wishing to bother you with footnotes and massive bibliography, I have in the name of concision confined myself to references to books. Standard guides to periodicals, however, will lead the interested reader to many worthwhile contributions there. Some, in fact, deal authoritatively with matters that have never been explored in books. Your local librarian will help you, provided you do not sail up to the reference desk as Montague Summers used to enter the staid Reading Room of The British Museum—with a large portfolio emblazoned with VAMPIRES in scarlet letters.

Advanced scholars will also want to investigate *Dissertation Abstracts* to locate such doctoral studies as K. Galicia's "*La Femme diabolique dans le prose français du dix-neuvième siècle*" (City University of New York, 1994) and Charles Stewart's "Demons and the Devil: Representations of the Supernatural in Modern Greece..." (Oxford University, 1992).

PSYCHICAL RESEARCH

I once edited (writing an introduction) two volumes of papers of The Society for Psychical Research called *Phantasms of the Living*. It was by Myers, Gurney, and Podmore. I recommend it and these works:

Hall, H. Trevor. *The Strange Case of Edmund Gurney.*
Myers, F. W. H. *Human Personality and Its Survival of Bodily Death.*
Podmore, Frank. *Modern Spiritualism.*

If a ghost appears to you unbidden, you are not involved in the black arts. However, if you attempt to raise a ghost or participate in a séance at which one appears you are involved in necromancy and, according to most religions, in danger of damnation.

Unbidden is the key word. You cannot be faulted for having premonitions or precognition of any kind or "second sight" or powers of telepathy or even telekinesis, or for veridical dreams, unwished-for apparitions, or similar psychic experiences. Presumably you ought to be careful that in clairvoyance or clairaudience or automatic writing or trance-state experiences and so on you are not in contact with devils or demons or, by means unapproved, even with your Guardian Angel—something that many magicians strive mightily to achieve—or even with saints.

I look forward to the day when real science is applied to the examination of powers within us, and when reproducible experiments with objectively examined and honestly reported results make parapsychology at least as much of a true science as is psychology. People are working on it.

WHITE MAGIC, AGAIN

Many of those who tell me they are witches say they never practice the black arts, that they perform only curative, positive, *white* magic. If they are Christians I usually let them in on the fact that for a thousand years even white magic has been absolutely forbidden by the church. If white magicians are Catholic, they have excommunicated themselves even by planning to do good this way. In some jurisdictions they may go to jail if they are detected. If people tell you to take this or that herb because it will do you good, OK—but if they tell you to take it with a little charm to recite, or just to take it at a certain hour or phase of the moon, then they are practicing magic. To use the Ouija board is necromancy. To use the *I Ching* or The Tarot I think of as plumbing the unconscious—but if you keep your Tarot cards wrapped in silk when you are not using them, to retain their power, you are practicing magic.

THE MARK OF THE DEVIL

Perhaps as strange as the moles that investigators insist on finding on children who are "identified" as reincarnations of the Dalai Lama—the moles are supposed to represent the extra arms this super-powerful character once had, like the extra arms on heathen idols—are the marks that The Devil is supposed to put on witches.

The anonymous pamphlet called *Newes from Scotland declaring the Damnable Life and death of Doctor Fian, a notable Sorcerer who was burned at Edenbrough in January last* (1591) tells us (spelling in the quotations that follow is modernized) that "the Devil doth generally mark [witches] with a privy mark...and generally so long as the mark is not seen by those which search them...[witches] will never confess." Witches were also supposed to have insensitive spots. You stuck them with long needles until you found a spot where they did not feel pain. That was taken as proof that they were witches. (You could fake this with a needle that retracted into a handle.)

Newes from Scotland reports that, after a "poor peddler" brought the witches to the attention of King James, Geillis Duncane was found to have The Devil's mark on her throat; that Agnis Sampson had to be shaved before The Devil's mark was found on her genitals; and that John Cunningham (also known as "Doctor Fian") had no mark anyone could find (but was condemned anyway). King James had half a mind to disbelieve the confessions wrung from these people, but Agnes Simpson (as her name would probably be rendered today) said to the king that she could tell him the secret words he whispered to his queen on their wedding night, words which no one else could possibly know. (They were probably a confession by James himself—that he was gay.)

So King James believed the story told him that two hundred witches or so used to meet off the coast of North Berwick in Lothian, with Geillis Duncane playing the "Jew's trump," which the King called her before him to demonstrate. King James believed that witches were trying to keep him from consummating his marriage. He believed that Agnes derived poison from a black toad and hoped to get some scrap of the King's clothes to work magic on him if she could not kill him by poison.

All the "accustomed pain" of hideous torture is suffered by "Doctor Fian" and his tongue can utter no confession, but finally two witches' pins are found to be holding his tongue and, those removed, he confesses his evil, that he has bewitched a man who was his rival for the love of a girl in Saltpans (and made the man suffer fits every twenty-four hours) and tried to use three pubic hairs of the girl to make magic to seduce her. (He has been given, however, three hairs from a cow. The cow tries then to have sex with "Doctor Fian"!) In prison "Doctor Fian" attempts to "lead the life of a Christian" and return to God, but Satan appears and threatens

An old woodcut shows The Devil and a vain woman who sees his behind in her mirror.

him. "Doctor Fian" then is once again of The Devil's party and he stays so, even when the torturers pull out his nails one by one to insert pins, even when they put him to the excruciating torture of "the boots." He declares his previous confession false, "only done and said for fear of pains." He declares he was lying under torture. And so they put him to death, afraid of him, amazed at his unrepentant stance even as he is strangled. Then they burn the body, a body that enraged them because they never were able to find the mark of The Devil.

King James went on to write his demonology book (1597), of which there is more in another place. King James, convinced of the reality of witchcraft, fearful of the "sperm-stealing" witches can do to render males impotent, writes of how witches are recruited because they want wealth or power or revenge, how they celebrate their evil ceremonies and how they work. He says that if the witches "missed one iota of all their rites; or if any of their feet once slid over the [magic] circle through terror of his fearful apparition, [Satan]...carries them with him body and soul" to Hell. King James goes on to explain how The Devil appears in various animal and human shapes and performs his mischief in the world and makes his devotees kiss what King James calls "his hinder parts." As Moses could look at God Himself only from the back because of His glory, so one can kiss only the "hinder part" of The Prince of Darkness. King James has a peculiar passage in which he suggests that the mark of The Devil is put in a sensual place—and that The Devil uses his tongue to make the mark.

WHY WOMEN RATHER THAN MEN ARE MOST OFTEN WITCHES

The Dominicans who wrote the *Malleus maleficarum* derived *femina* from "*Fe* and *Minus*" because women are, in their opinion, deceitful and imperfect (made from a bent rib), and most of all "ever weaker to hold and preserve the faith" than men are.

These monks were, of course, celibate. The not-celibate but homosexual King James in his *Dæmonologie* says that women are "frailer" and more easily duped by The Devil. Eliphas Lévi, the celibate priest who left the priesthood, says women are better at sorcery because "they are more easily transported by excess of passion." A modern woman in The Craft tells me that it is because The Devil has sex with his followers and "The Devil is heterosexual."

I hope that *The Complete Book of Devils and Demons* will reach not only practicing witches (most of whom are women) but all feminists (ditto), for the history of witchcraft is intricately bound up with the misogyny of both ecclesiastical and secular institutions down the ages. Those who persecuted witches were trying their damnedest to put their male monotheism in the place of The Goddess and the goddesses of polytheism. And they feared and perhaps envied the powers of women, creative, intuitive, and more. Witchcraft is a chapter in the history of the oppression of women and perhaps can be part of the history of women's liberation.

THE RESPONSE OF A GERMAN WITCH TO "KINDLY QUESTIONING" (AND TORTURE) IN 1587

From *Fugger News-Letters* edited by Victor von Klarwell and translated (1924) by P. de Chary:

> The herein mentioned, malefic and miserable woman, Walpurga Hausmännin, now imprisoned and in chains, has, upon kindly questioning and also torture, following on persistent and fully justified accusations, confessed her witchcraft and admitted the following. When one-and-thirty years ago she had become a widow, she cut corn for Hans Schlumperger, of this place, together with his former servant, Bis im Pfarrhof by name. Him she enticed with lewd speeches and gestures, and they convened that they should, on an appointed night, meet in her, Walpurga's, dwelling, there to indulge in lustful intercourse. So when Walpurga in expectation of this sat awaiting him at night in her chamber, meditating upon evil and fleshly thoughts, it was not the said bondsman who appeared unto her, but the Evil One in the latter's guise and raiment and indulged in fornication with her. Thereupon he presented her with a piece of money, in the semblance of half a thaler, but no one could take it from her, for it was a bad coin and like lead. For this reason she had thrown it away. After the act of fornication she saw and felt the cloven foot of her whoremonger, and that his hand was not natural, but as if made of wood. She was greatly affrighted thereat

Thumbscrews.

and called upon the name of Jesus, whereupon the Devil left her and vanished.

On the ensuing night the Evil Spirit visited her again in the same shape and whored with her. He made her many promises to help her in her poverty and need, wherefore she surrendered herself to him body and soul. Thereafter the Evil One inflicted upon her a scratch below the left shoulder, demanding that she should sell her soul to him with the blood that had flowed therefrom. To this end he gave her a quill and, whereas she could not write, the Evil One guided her hand. She believes that nothing offensive was written, for the Evil One only swept with her hand across the paper. The script the Devil took with him, and whenever she piously thought of God Almighty, or wished to go to church, the Devil reminded her of it.

Further, the above-mentioned Walpurga confesses that she oft and much rode on a pitchfork by night with her paramour, but not far, on account of her duties. At such devilish trysts she met a big man with a grey beard, who sat in a chair, like a great prince, and was richly attired. That was the Great Devil to whom she had once more dedicated and promised herself body and soul. Him she worshiped and before him she knelt, and unto him she rendered other suchlike honours. But she pretends not to know with what words and in which fashion she prayed. She only knows that once she heedlessly pronounced the name of Jesus. Then the above-mentioned Great Devil struck her in the face and Walpurga had to disown (which is terrible to relate) God in heaven, the Christian name and belief, the blessed saints and the Holy Sacraments, also to renounce the heavenly hosts and the whole of Christendom. Thereupon the Great Devil baptized her afresh, naming her Höfelin, but her paramour-devil, Federlin. . . .

Since her surrender to the Devil, she had seemingly oft received the Blessed Sacrament of the true Body and Blood of Jesus Christ, apparently by the mouth, but had not partaken of it, but (which once more is terrible to relate) had always taken it out of her mouth again and delivered it up to Federlin, her paramour. At their nightly gatherings she had oft with her other playfellows trodden underfoot the Holy and Blessed Sacrament and the image of the Holy Cross. The said Walpurga states that during suchlike frightful and loathsome blasphemies she at times truly did espy drops of blood upon the said Holy Sacrament, whereat she herself was greatly horrified . . . .She confesses, also, that her paramour gave her a salve in a little box with which to injure people and animals, and even the precious fruit of the field. He also compelled her to do away with and to kill young infants at birth, even before they had been taken to Holy Baptism. This she did, whenever possible. . . .

She rubbed with her salve and brought about the death of Lienhart Geilen's three cows, of Bruchbauer's horse, two years ago of Max Petzel's cow, three years ago of Duri Striegel's cow, two years ago of Hans Striegel's cow, of the cow of the governor's wife, of a cow of Frau Schötterin, and two years ago of a cow of Michel Klingler, on the village green. In short, she confesses that she destroyed a large number of cattle over and above this. A year ago she found bleached linen on the common and rubbed it with her salve, so that the pigs and geese ran over it and perished shortly thereafter. Walpurga confesses further that every year since she has sold herself to the Devil she has on St. Leonard's Day exhumed at least one or two innocent children. With her devil-paramour and other playfellows she has eaten these and used their hair and their little bones for witchcraft.

She was unable to exhume the other children she had slain at birth, although she attempted it, because they had been baptized before God.

She had used the said little bones to manufacture hail; this she was wont to do once or twice a year. Once this spring, from Siechenhausen, downwards across the fields. She likewise manufactured hail last Whitsun, and when she and others were accused of having held a witches' revel, she had actually held one near the upper gate by the garden of Peter Schmidt. At that time her playfellows began to quarrel and struck one another, because some wanted to cause it to hail over Dillingen Meadows, others below it. At last the hail was sent over the marsh towards Weissingen, doing great damage. She admits that she would have caused still more and greater evils and damage if the Almighty had not graciously prevented and turned them away.

After all this, the Judges and Jury of the Court of this Town of Dillingen, by virtue of the Imperial and Royal Prerogative and Rights of his Right Reverence, Herr Marquard, bishop of Augsburg, and provost of the Cathedral, our most gracious prince and lord, at last unanimously gave the verdict that the aforesaid

Walpurga Hausmännin be punished and dispatched from life to death by burning at the stake as being a maleficent and well-known witch and sorceress, convicted according to the context of Common Law and the Criminal Code of the Emperor Charles V and the Holy Roman Empire. All her goods and chattels and estate left after her to go to the Treasury of our most high prince and lord. The aforesaid Walpurga to be led, seated on a cart, to which she is tied, to the place of her execution, and her body first to be torn five times with red-hot irons. The first time outside the town hall in the left breast and the right arm, the second time at the lower gate in the right breast, the third time at the mill brook outside the hospital gate in the left arm, the fourth time at the place of execution in the left hand. But since for nineteen years she was licensed and pledged midwife of the city of Dillingen, yet has acted so vilely, her right hand with which she did such knavish tricks is to be cut off at the place of execution. Neither are her ashes after the burning to remain lying on the ground, but are thereafter to be carried to the nearest flowing water and thrown thereinto. Thus a venerable jury have entrusted the executioner of this city with the actual execution and all connected therewith.

FROM ISAAC D'ISRAELI'S
THE CURIOSITIES OF LITERATURE

Benjamin Disraeli's father published this in 1866 as part of "Dreams at the Dawn of Philosophy," suggesting connections between pseudoscience and superstition and science itself:

Albertus Magnus, for thirty years, had never ceased working at a man of brass, and cast together the qualities of his materials under certain constellations, which threw such a spirit into his man of brass, that it was reported his growth was visible; his feet, legs, thighs, shoulders, neck, and head, expanded, and made the city of Cologne uneasy; at possessing one citizen too mighty for them all. This man of brass, when he reached his maturity, was so loquacious, that Albert's master, the great scholastic Thomas Aquinas, one day, tired of his babble, and declaring it was a devil, or devilish, with his staff knocked the head off; and, what was extraordinary, this brazen man, like any human being thus effectually silenced, "word never spake more." This incident is equally historical and authentic; though whether heads of brass can speak, and even prophesy, was indeed a subject of profound inquiry, even at a later period. Naudé, who never questioned their vocal powers, yet was puzzled concerning the nature of this new species of animal, has most judiciously stated the question, whether these speaking brazen heads had a sensitive and reasoning nature, or whether demons spoke in them? But brass has not the faculty of providing its own nourishment, as we see in plants, and therefore they were not sensitive; and as for the act of reasoning, these brazen heads presumed to know nothing but the future: with the past and the present they seemed totally unacquainted, so that their memory and their observation were very limited; and as for the future, that is always doubtful and obscure—even to heads of brass! This learned man then infers, that "These brazen heads could have no reasoning faculties, for nothing altered their nature; they said what they had to say, which no one could contradict; and having said their say, you might have broken the head for anything more that you could have got out of it. Had they had any life in them, would they not have moved, as well as spoken? Life itself is but motion, but they had no lungs, no spleen; and, in fact, though they spoke, they had no tongue. Was a devil in them? I think not. Yet why should men have taken all this trouble to make, not a man, but a trumpet?"

Our profound philosopher was right not to agitate the question whether these brazen heads had ever spoken? Why should not a man of brass speak, since a doll can whisper, a statue play chess, and brass ducks have performed the whole process of digestion? Another magical invention has been ridiculed with equal reason. A magician was annoyed, as philosophers still are, by passengers in the street; and he, particularly, by having horses led to drink under his window. He made a magical horse of wood, according to one of the books of Hermes, which perfectly answered its purpose, by frightening away the horses, or rather the grooms! the wooden horse, no doubt, gave some palpable kick. The same magical story might have been told of Dr. Franklin, who finding that under his window the passengers had discovered a sport which they made too convenient for themselves, he charged it with his newly-discovered electrical fire. After a few remarkable incidents had occurred, which at a former period had lodged the great discoverer of electricity at the Inquisition, the modern magician succeeded just as well as the ancient, who had the advantage of conning over the books of Hermes. instead of ridiculing these works of magic, let us rather become magicians ourselves!

The works of the ancient alchemists have afforded numberless discoveries to modern chemists; nor is even their grand operation despaired of. If they have of late not been so renowned, this has arisen from a want of what Ashmole calls "apertness;" a qualification early inculcated among these illuminated sages. We find authentic accounts of some who have lived three centuries, with tolerable complexions, possessed of nothing but a crucible and a bellows! but they were so unnecessarily mysterious, that whenever such a person was discovered, he was sure in an instant to disappear, and was never afterwards heard of.

In the "Liber Patris Sapientiæ" this selfish cautiousness is all along impressed on the student, for the accomplishment of the great mystery. In the commentary on this precious work of the alchemist Norton, who counsels,

"Be thou in a place secret, by thyself alone,

That no man see or hear what thou shalt say or done.

Trust not thy friend too much whereso'er thou go,

For he thou trustest best, sometyme may be thy foe,"

Ashmole observes, that "Norton gives exceeding good advice to the student in this science where he bids him be secret in the carrying on of his studies and operations, and not to let any one know of his undertakings but his good angel and himself: and such a close and retired breast had Norton's master, who,

"When men disputed of *colours of the rose,*

He would not speak, but kept himself full close!"

We regret, that by each leaving all his knowledge to "his good angel and himself," it has happened that "the good angels" have kept it all to themselves!

It cannot, however, be denied, that if they could not always extract gold out of lead, they sometimes succeeded in washing away the pimples on ladies' faces, notwithstanding that Sir Kenelm Digby poisoned his most beautiful lady, because, as Sancho would have said, he was one of those who would. "have his bread whiter than the finest wheaten." Van Helmont, who could not succeed in discovering the true elixir of life, however hit on the spirit of hartshorn, which for a good while he considered was the wonderful elixir itself, restoring to life persons who seemed to have lost it.

And though this delightful enthusiast could not raise a ghost, yet he thought he had; for he raised something aërial from spa-water, which mistaking for a ghost, he gave it that very name; and which we still retain in *gas*, from the German *geist*, or ghost! Doubtless we have lost some inconceivable secrets by some unexpected occurrences, which the secret itself should have prevented taking place. When a philosopher had discovered the art of prolonging life to an indefinite period, it is most provoking to find that he should have allowed himself to die at an early age! We have a very authentic history from Sir Kenelm Digby himself, that when he went in disguise to visit Descartes at his retirement at Egmond, lamenting the brevity of life, which hindered philosophers getting on in their studies, the French philosopher assured him that "he had considered that matter; to render a man immortal was what he could not promise, but that he was very sure it was possible to lengthen out his life to the period of the patriarchs." And when he death was announced to the world, the abbé Picot, an ardent disciple, for a long time would not believe it possible; and at length insisted, that if it had occurred, it must have been owing to some mistake of the philosopher's.

Paracelsus has revealed to us one of the grandest secrets of nature. When the world began to dispute on the very existence of the elementary folk, it was then he boldly offered to give birth to a fairy, and has sent down to posterity the recipe. He describes the impurity which is to be transmuted into such purity, the gross elements of a delicate fairy, which, fixed in a phial in fuming dung, will in due time settle into a full-grown fairy, bursting through its vitreous prison—on the vivifying principle by which the ancient Egyptians hatched their eggs in ovens. I recollect at Dr. Farmer's sale the leaf which preserved this recipe for making a fairy, forcibly folded down by the learned commentator; from which we must infer the credit he gave to the experiment. There was a greatness of mind in Paracelsus, who, having furnished a recipe to make a fairy, had the delicacy to refrain from its creation. Even Baptista Porta, one of the most enlightened philosophers, does not deny the possibility of engendering creatures, which "at their full growth shall not exceed the size of a mouse:" but he adds that "they are only pretty little dogs to play with." Were these akin to the fairies of Paracelsus?

They were well convinced of the existence of such elemental beings; frequent accidents in mines showed the potency of the metallic spirits; which so tormented the workmen in some of the German mines, by blindness, giddiness, and sudden sickness, that they have been obliged to abandon mines well known to be rich in silver. A metallic spirit at one sweep annihilated twelve miners, who were all found dead together. The fact was unquestionable; and the safety-lamp was undiscovered!

Never was a philosophical imagination more beautiful than that exquisite *Palingentesis*, as it has been termed from the Greek, or a regeneration; or rather, the apparitions of animals and plants. Schott, Kircher, Gaffarel, Borelli, Digby, and the whole of that admirable school, discovered in the ashes of plants their primitive forms, which were again raised up by the force of heat. Nothing, they say, perishes in nature; all is but a continuation, or a revival. The semina of resurrection are concealed in the extinct bodies, as in the blood of man; the ashes of roses will again revive into roses, though smaller and paler than if they had been planted; unsubstantial and unodoriferous, they are not roses which grew on rose-trees, but their delicate apparitions; and, like apparitions, they are seen but for a moment! The process of the *Palingenesis*, this picture of immortality, is described. These philosophers having burnt a flower, by calcination disengaged the salts from its ashes, and deposited them in a glass phial; a chemical mixture acted on it, till in the fermentation they assumed a bluish and spectral hue. This dust, thus excited by heat, shoots upwards into its primitive forms; by sympathy the parts unite, and while each is returning to its destined place, we see distinctly the stalk, the leaves, and the flower, arise: it is the pale spectre of a flower coming slowly forth from its ashes. The heat passes away, the magical scene declines, till the whole matter again precipitates itself into the chaos at the bottom. This vegetable phoenix lies thus concealed in its cold ashes, till the presence of heat produced this resurrection—as in its absence it returns to its death. Thus the dead naturally revive; and a corpse may give out its shadowy reanimation, when not too deeply buried in the earth. Bodies corrupted in their graves have risen, particularly the murdered; for murderers are apt to bury their victims in a slight and hasty manner. Their salts, exhaled in vapour by means of their fermentation, have arranged themselves on the surface of the earth, and formed those phantoms, which at night have often terrified the passing spectator, as authentic history witnesses. They have opened the graves of the phantom, and discovered the bleeding corpse beneath; hence it is astonishing how many ghosts may be seen at night, after a recent battle, standing over their corpses! On the same principle, my old philosopher Gaffarel conjectures on the raining of frogs; but these frogs, we must conceive, can only be the ghosts of frogs; and Gaffarel himself has modestly opened this fact by a "peradventure." A more satisfactory origin of ghosts modern philosophy has not afforded.

And who does not believe in the existence of ghosts? for, as Dr. More forcibly says, "That there should be so universal a *fame* and *fear* of that which never was, nor is, nor can be ever in the world, is to me the greatest miracle of all. If there had not been, at some time or other, true miracles, it had not been so easy to impose on the people by false....

THE HEIGHT OF THE WITCH PERSECUTIONS

In Britain, Scotland and East Anglia were most affected; in Switzerland, the persecutions were centered in Bern and Basle; in France, it was Lorraine and Vaudois and other areas that were affected; and in Germany, principally the Rhineland was the region of witch persecutions. There was some activity in the Basque Country, in Spain, in Italy, in Sweden....The persecutions tended to flare up and die down and stretched from 1484, in some cases, into the eighteenth century but, in most countries, ended with the seventeenth century.

The Devil dances with his followers (1608).

Simon Magus tries to buy magical powers from the Apostles. Vercelli Roll, thirteenth century.

5
Some Major People

INTRODUCING SOME INTERESTING PEOPLE

It would be impossible to present in a few pages a complete or even representative selection of people of the sort who, on one side or the other, have been involved in the centuries of history of devil worship, black magic, witchcraft, and the suppression of the black arts.

Here I give you a few varied personalities, hoping to suggest to you—and throughout this book of bits and pieces the items and their juxtapositions are meant to suggest comparisons, contrasts, and conclusions for you to reach for yourself with this do-it-yourself kit—some of the kinds of people who have been part of the long story of witchcraft, forbidden by King Saul over a thousand years before Christ, still with us two thousand years after Him. In fact, representations of figures dressed for magic in animal skins and antlers occur on the walls of prehistoric caves in Europe four thousand years old or older.

MEET APOLLONIUS OF TYANA

The French ritual magician who called himself "Eliphas Lévi" was a member in the middle of the last century of an occult circle clustered around Lord Lytton (Edward Bulwer-Lytton, author of *The Lyons Mail* and *The Last Days of Pompeii*). Lytton gathered around him in his semi-fake old mansion a coterie of magical adepts. Lévi was expelled from the group when he published his book on *Transcendental Magic* the fact that he had attempted to raise an ancient philosopher, Apollonius of Tyana, from the dead.

First, Lévi fasted for three weeks, the number 21 being significant. Then he prepared a room in London with an altar with a white marble top. It rested on a new white lambskin and was surrounded by four mirrors and a magic circle of magnetized iron chain. Dressed in a white robe (to indicate the purity of his intentions) and crowned with vervain (to protect him against demons), Lévi took up his text for the ritual and commenced to burn twigs in chafing dishes and to recite the incantation.

He says he felt the earth shake and glimpsed a figure of a man in the smoke, a corpselike man dressed in a shroud. He was frightened at this ghost and unable to make it stay or speak. When his arm was touched, it went numb. He fainted. For days later it stayed numb, and Lévi was sure that, although he had not raised Apollonius of Tyana, he had summoned someone, even if the apparition said nothing. Two words seemed to have got into Lévi's tortured imagination. They were *death* and *dead*. He warned those who might try the same thing that it was a perilous experiment. It seems to have accomplished little, but it frightened Lévi a lot. And publicizing it got him thrown out of Lytton's little circle.

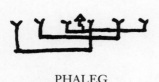

PHALEG

GILLES DE RAIS WAS *NOT* BURNED AT THE STAKE

Rank (as they say in the armed forces still) has its privileges. Though he confessed "voluntarily and freely" (albeit after extreme torture) to murdering and sodomizing a whole host of little boys in the service of The Devil, and was found guilty of dealing with The Devil, of apostasy, of heresy, of sodomy, and murder, he was not burned alive. He was strangled at the place of execution (because he had proved cooperative and had not revoked his forced confession) on 26 October 1440 and his body placed on the pyre with two of his fellow criminals. But his relatives were allowed to take it off the pyre before the flames got to it. Though excommunicated, Gilles de Rais, "Blue Beard" of the fairy stories, was buried in a Carmelite convent church. And a terrible priest, Prelati, the one who led the Marshal of France astray and participated in all his monstrous deeds, walked away unscathed after a few short months in prison.

Blue Beard: The notorious Gilles de Rais.

CORNELIUS AGRIPPA

(Heinrich) Cornelius Agrippa (von Nettlesheim) was a scientist and philosopher, cabalist and diplomat, who lived 1486–1535. He can serve as a fine example of an intellectual of his time who combined scientific observation with occult speculation. He fell afoul of the Holy Inquisition for defending a woman accused of witchcraft. He incurred the wrath of the clergy in general for lecturing on the philosophy of Reuchlin, a student of Hebrew and the cabalistic writings in an age when the destruction of all Jewish books (save the *tananbk* or Old Testament) was seriously suggested in German lands.

Agrippa was a lawyer, a university professor of philosophy and theology, a spy, an ambassador, a royal physician, a city orator (of Metz), a theologian of the Lutheran Reformation, three times married, famous in a number of European countries (royal patrons in Germany, Italy, France, and The Netherlands all tended not to pay him his salary and he died poor), and a considerable scientist. But all people could talk about was a big black dog that went everywhere with him—it was called Monsieur—and was suspected of being a demon in disguise. When Agrippa died in Grenoble, and Monsieur and his companion Mademoiselle instantly and mysteriously disappeared, people were certain that Cornelius Agrippa had been a black magician all along. A friend testified that he had often walked Monsieur and it was a dog, not a familiar spirit. No one believed him. Was there not Agrippa's own book *De occulta philosophia*?

Agrippa's relevant works have been translated and reprinted: *Three Books of Occult Philosophy or Magic* (1971), *Agrippa: His Fourth Book of Occult Philosophy* (1978), and *The Philosophy of Natural Magic* (1974). Henry Morley wrote his biography in 1856, but we need a modern one. Perhaps his *De Nobilitate et præcellentia feminiei sexus* (published 1532, written much earlier) would get him modern attention if feminists could read Latin.

On Occult Philosophy (not printed until decades later than 1510, when it was composed) in which he dismisses devils and demons and concentrates on inherent psychic powers, arguing that "imagination on its own, according to the various passions, first of all changes the physical body with a transmutation that can be felt, by altering the accidents in the body and by moving the spirit up or down, inward or outward" and that it is due to inherent psychic powers that we are able to perform what we erroneously think of as caused by outside forces. He eventually abjured the occult and said that only theology was worth study. Theology, he argued, was unfortunate because it put one in the company of the most despicable group of people imaginable, the clergy.

MARTIN LUTHER AND THE DEVIL

You've heard that Roman Catholics spread a rumor that the father of Martin Luther was The Devil himself. Protestants told the story of Luther and The Devil at the Wartburg, a castle at Eisenach in which Frederick III of Saxony gave the Reformer protection during the period of nearly a year in which he translated the Bible into German. The story is that The Devil bothered Luther frequently, trying to put him off this task, and once Luther grew so angry he flung his ink bottle at The Devil.

In Henri D'Aubigné's *History of the Reformation*:
The keeper of the Wartburg is still careful to call the traveler's attention to the spots made by Luther's inkstand.

George W. Stimpson quotes this in *Why Do Some Shoes Squeak?* and comments:
Such is the case at the present time [1984], and there is reason to believe that fresh ink is occasionally applied to the spot for the benefit of visitors to the Wartburg.

Less dramatic, but also from Martin Luther: "As I found he [The Devil] was about to begin again, I gathered together my books and got into bed. Another time in the night I heard him above my cell walking in the cloister, but as I knew it was the devil I paid no attention to him and went to sleep."

MOTHER SHIPTON AND NOSTRADAMUS

Mother Shipton claimed to be a prophetess. Not the most notable of British women of this stripe—that would have to be Mother Ann Lee (1736–1784), who came to America and founded The Shakers, 1776, declaring herself to be The Messiah and a worker of miracles—still Mother Shipton is said to have prophesied the death of Cardinal Wolsey and others. In the seventeenth century she became a subject of popular literature. Richard Head put out an unreliable *Life and Death of Mother Shipton* (1667). In this and in subsequent publications such as the *Wonderful History* (1686) you have a good example of the growth of such a legend. In Charles Hindley's *Life of Mother Shipton* (1862) she is credited with having predicted the invention of the steam engine and the telegraph. She has now been forgotten, but such seers as Nostradamus continue to be popular. In every catalogue of remaindered books I see one or more editions of his prophecies and yet more and more books of them keep coming out. Presumably this will not cease until, with one result or another, the time in the twenty-first century arrives for which he prophesied the end of the world.

Whether such prophesying is claimed to be with or without the aid of devils and demons, it is condemned by ecclesiastical authorities and embraced by the general public. The desire to know the future, even though by the nature of the problem the future cannot be changed, is one of the principal motivations of witchcraft and dealing with demons.

ROBERT FLUDD

Robert Fludd (1574–1637) published in defense of the Rosicrucians under his own name and some improbable aliases. He is more important in the history of the Rosicrucian movement (which has little or nothing to do with Californian sun-baked, half-baked Rosicrucians, especially the AMORC founded by H. Spenser Lewis in 1915) than in the history of demonology, but he was a magician.

Old Mother Shipton calls up demons, and two other witches fly in this seventeenth-century woodcut.

ONE THEORY OF WHERE "DR. FAUSTUS" ORIGINATED

From Isaac D'Israeli's *The Curiosities of Literature* (1866), p. 29:

The tradition of the Devil and Dr. Faustus was derived from the odd circumstance in which the Bibles of the first printer, Fust, appeared to the world. When he had discovered this new art, and printed off a considerable number of copies of the Bible, to imitate those which were commonly sold as MSS., he undertook the sale of them at Paris. It was his interest to conceal this discovery, and to pass off his printed copies for MSS. But as he was enabled to sell his Bibles at sixty crowns, while the other scribes demanded five hundred, this raised universal astonishment; and, still more when he produced copies as fast as they were wanted, and even lowered his price. The uniformity of the copies increased wonder. Informations were given in to the magistrates against him as a magician; and in searching his lodgings a great number of copies were found. The red ink, and Fust's red ink is peculiarly brilliant, which embellished his copies, was said to be his blood; and it was solemnly adjudged that he was in league with the devil. Fust was at length obliged, to save himself from a bonfire, to reveal his art to the Parliament of Paris, who discharged him from all prosecution in consideration of this useful invention.

PETRUS POMPONATIUS

Because their names appeared most often on the title pages of works published in the international language of scholarship in their time, early modern writers often have Latin pseudonyms such as that of the Italian Pietro Pomponazzi (1462–1525). As a student of Aristotle, he shared the Greek master's views that the soul was mortal and that demons did not exist, although he admitted belief in astrology and magic. His ideas made his work unpopular in his time, for they went against Renaissance belief.

MARK TWAIN

Samuel L. Clemens [Mark Twain] (1835–1910) liked to shock people with comments like this:

We may not pay Satan reverence, for that would be indiscrete, but we can at least respect his talents. A person who has for untold centuries maintained the impossible position of spiritual head of four-fifths of the human race, and political head of the whole of it, must be granted the possession of executive abilities of the highest order.

THE SCREWTAPE LETTERS

C. S. Lewis, in the preface to his book of this title, a delightful collection of business communications between a minor devil called Screwtape and his boss, says:

There are two equal and opposite errors into which our race can fall about the devils. One is to disbelieve in their existence. The other is to believe, and to feel an excessive and unhealthy interest in them. They themselves are equally pleased by both errors and hail a materialist or a magician with the same delight.

MONSIGNOR RONALD KNOX

"It is stupid of modern civilization to have given up believing in the devil, when he is the only explanation of it."

FYODOR MIKHAYLOVICH DOSTOYEVSKY

In *The Brothers Karamazov* (c. 1880):

"If the devil doesn't exist, but man has created him, he has created him in his own image and likeness."

VERGIL

Publius Vergilius Maro (70–19 B.C.) studied the *Iliad* and the *Odyssey* of Homer and wrote the great Latin epic of the *Aeneid*, giving Rome a glorious pseudo-historical background and an inspiring hero. Vergil died on a trip to Greece to authenticate some of his epic of the tale of Troy. His achievement in the *Aeneid* and other works made him the supreme master of Latin literature, a position he retained when the classics were revived in Europe and Latin became the basic subject of study by all learned men.

It is not as an epic poet or ethical philosopher, however, that Vergil is relevant here, but as a magician. Somehow his books came to be used for divination and somehow rumors sprang up about his magical powers. He was said to have created a fly which ate all the other flies of Naples and to have conversed with the dead. Like Roger Bacon, Albertus Magnus, and many other erudite men. Vergil was assumed to know "more than heaven permits" as well as to be extremely well versed in permitted subjects of study. The incredible magical tales fathered on Vergil were first collected in *Les Faicts merveilleux de Virgille* in the sixteenth century. Modern studies such as J. W. Spargo's *Virgil the Necromancer* (1934) discuss his alleged connections with the black arts.

REGINO OF PRÜM

His is an odd name that deserves to be better remembered, for it was this ecclesiastic who reported (c. 906) a paragraph which he said derived from the Synod of Ancyra in the fourth century. In it witches fly by night—in their evil imaginations—in service of the moon goddess, Diana. Regino wanted to stress that this was all fantasy, that only God, not some pagan goddess, could perform such miracles, and that these witches were lying or more likely deluded, their purposes evil, their claims false. In this skeptical attitude toward witches flying, and in fact in being able to harm any Christian protected by the name of Jesus and the armor of righteousness, Regino was in perfect harmony with the teachings of the early fathers of the church.

Actually, this information Regino reports may have come not from the early source he claims but from a much later, much different source, perhaps some Frankish writer. But Regino's comment came to be known as a *canon episcopi* and became part of the Canon Law when the Benedictine monk Gratian included it in the compilation called *Decretum Gratiani* put together 1139–1142. The *canon episcopi* led clerics to condemn witchcraft as mere superstition and at the very same time, preaching vehemently and repeatedly against witchcraft, they put into the minds of the peasantry and even the prelates that if there is a lot of smoke there must be some fire. In the long run the fires of persecution were lit all across Europe as the "reality" of witchcraft, the church said, could no longer be doubted. Witchcraft, in the words of a British parliamentarian in quite another context, had increased, was increasing, and ought to be diminished.

And so Regino's sober judgment was swept aside in favor of zealous eradication of the heresy of Satanism.

"I'M INNOCENT"

The first pope of this name reigned in the early fifth century and did so much good for the church he became Saint Innocent. Innocent VIII reigned in the late fifteenth century, a little over a thousand years later, and was far less effective or even sensible. It was the bull *Summis desiderantes affectibus* of 1484 that launched the height of the witchcraft persecutions. He's the one to blame.

True, Innocent had received reports in Rome that in Germany the witchcraft trials, more severe perhaps than those in France in the previous century, were turning up confessions of the most horrendous sorts from those accused of (and tortured to get evidence out of regarding) witchcraft. It was clear to him that, if what he heard was true, the heresy of Satanism was epidemic. He determined to find out. After deploring the way in which witches were spreading disease and death, blighting crops and ruining lives (particularly in rendering good Christian men impotent or sterile), in his papal pronouncement he appointed two Dominicans to go to Germany and to report what they found. The result was the book that Catholics and later Protestants were to use to send hundreds of thousands to their death, the *Malleus maleficarum* of 1486. Its authors, two Dominican monks, were taken by judges as supreme authorities. Their book was on the bench at every witchcraft trial. Jacob Sprenger and Heinrich Kramer, the authors of this "hammer of witches," thus were responsible for the torture and judicial murder of thousands upon thousands of people. They wrote the most evil German book published before *Mein Kampf*.

"THE ENGLISH HIPPOCRATES"

Thomas Sydenham (1624–1689) holds a high place in the history of medicine in England and was a hard-headed scientist, a friend of Boyle and Locke, who trusted in reason and the avouch of his own eyes. He was widely renowned in his own time and is recalled in medical terminology as well as medical history. I particularly like some of the remedies he recommended. I do not need his advice on gout (from which he suffered painfully and on which he wrote extensively) or on hysteria (which he insisted was a distinct disease) but I am attracted, as many men of my age may be, to the good doctor's idea that the cure for aging is to put the patient in bed with a young person.

When it came to the vexing problem of witchcraft, Sydenham was far ahead of most of the medical men of his time. When Sir Kenelm Digby

(or Sir Gilbert Talbot, who appears to be the real inventor of it) was peddling his magical Powder of Sympathy (which could cure at a distance and
was on a par with Tarot readings or "psychic" analyses by telephone), Sydenham was saying that witchcraft was all delusion, stupid superstition, and that
the idea that insane people were possessed of devils was itself insane.

"COUNT CAGLIOSTRO"

A whole book could be devoted to the fakes and frauds who abound in the
history of the occult, but for a single striking example let us introduce
"Count Alessandro di Cagliostro," who was really a Sicilian of low parent-
age, named Giuseppi Balsamo (1743–1795). For years this charlatan daz-
zled the courts of Europe and peddled an elixir of youth; dabbled in
confidence games and seductions and "Egyptian" freemasonry (which eventually got him imprisoned in Italy for the last years of his life—the sentence reduced from death, which is what the Holy Inquisition had
recommended); and built up a wholly fraudent facade as a magician. In his
involvement with a phony "Egyptian" rite, he has a place in the history of
freemasonry. In his involvement with the affair of the Diamond Necklace
at the French court in 1785, he has a place in the history of France (and
briefly had a home in The Bastille). In his reputation as a necromancer,
using black magic to bring up the ghosts of the past, he belongs here.

JOAN OF ARC

Joan of Arc (1412–1431) is probably the most eminent woman ever burned
at the stake for witchcraft. She is a saint (since 1920) and was either divinely
inspired or certifiably insane. Just about puberty, she began to hear voices
(she said): Saint Michael the Archangel, Saint Catherine, and Saint Margaret, all told her (in French) that it was her mission to get the English inter-
lopers out of France. They were no longer, at that time, in her native area
on the borders of Lorraine and Champagne, but the Battle of Agincourt
had wished them on the French and the Paris area was thick with them.

Her determination made the wimpy Dauphin, King of France in 1429
and then he declined to push on against the English. She did, was captured,
and was sold to the English by one of their allies, John of Luxembourg.
She was tried before an ecclesiastical court (the bishop of Beauvais presiding) for sorcery. She was convicted. Just as she was going to be burned
at St.-Ôuen on 24 May 1431, she recanted. Soon after, she switched her
story again and declared her voices were authentic. It really didn't matter

much to her judges, who were at least as politically motivated as worried about witchcraft. They burned her at the stake in Rouen on 30 May 1431.

It seems impossible to believe now that she was a witch. Schizophrenic maybe, not Satanist. If she really did hear divine voices, she is not to be blamed, for she practiced no black magic; they came, if they came, unbidden. Dealing with Saint Michael, an archangel, is not dealing with the dead, any more than hearing the Blessed Virgin speak to you would be (the doctrine of the Assumption of the Blessed Virgin requires you to believe that she never died, so there is no necromancy in that, even if you solicit her). Dealing with Saint Catherine and Saint Margaret would have been necromancy if Saint Joan had initiated it, I suppose, although we are told we can pray to the saints. When they respond, that's when we get into difficulties.

Another great woman, Saint Teresa, said it all: Be careful of what you ask for because most of the misery in the world comes from answered prayers. Saint Joan prayed, it seems, to help her nation and to be famous for doing so. Look at what it got her. She is the only saint ever to be convicted of sorcery.

ALAIN-RENÉ LESAGE

The first French writer to live by his writing (1668–1747), Lesage wrote a fantasy, based on a Spanish novel, called *Le Diable boiteux* (1707), translated by J. Thomas as *Asmodeus* (1924).

MAGIC INTO SCIENCE

That is the title of H. M. Pachter's 1951 study of Theophrastus Bombastus von Hohenheim (1493–1541) who considered himself better than the great physician Celsus and called himself Paracelsus. Rejecting Aristotle and Galen, he pushed medicine out of the Middle Ages and, boastful and self-willed, he pushed himself out of one university appointment after another. He wrote in lively German and was among the first if not the first notable professor to lecture in that language.

Where Galen said the world was made up of four elements (fire, water, earth, air) and that the human being had four corresponding humours (or liquids) in him, ideally in balance, Paracelsus taught that the macrocosm of the world and the microcosm that is the human being were comprised of three elements (salt, sulphur, mercury) and were physical, spiritual, and divine. He was metallurgist and magician, physician and Neo-Platonist and pansophist, astrologer and scientist. He named some minor spirits. He was a mystic and alchemist as well as a student of natural science. See A. Koyre's *Mystiques, spirituels, alchémistes* (1955) and N. Guterman's translations (1951) of selected works from his long bibliography. He represents the mixture of the occult and observation that constituted science in the Renaissance, when many medical men were accused of being magicians and, in fact, some were, and when alchemy and chemistry were the same study, as were astrology and astronomy.

See Manly Palmer Hall's *The Mystical and Medical Philosophy of Paracelsus* (1965). Years ago a "paracelsus" organization in Los Angeles sold base-metal-to-gold courses in alchemy. They have been replaced by newer scams.

STRABO

This abbot of Reichenau lived in the first half of the ninth century, was a student of Rabanus Maurus, and was long credited with the principal exegesis of the Bible, the *Glosa ordinaria*. His long poem *De Visionibus Wettini* (On the Visions of Wettin, one of his teachers) presents a delirious trip through hell, purgatory, and paradise, anticipating the descriptions of the sufferings of the damned and the rewards of the elect that were to come in Dante's *Divine Comedy*. For a long time after its composition, Western Europe's view of hell was shaped by Strabo's ideas.

AN AMATEUR OF WITCHCRAFT AND DEVILDOM

William Beckford (1759–1844) was the dilettante son of a father of the same name who was twice Lord Mayor of London and held other important offices in his livery company (The Ironmongers) and The City. Unlike his grandfather (who had been Governor of Jamaica) and his father, the young Beckford took little interest in politics, though he was a Member of Parliament for many years. His interests lay rather in exotic sex and in exotic literature. He wrote (in French) the oriental romance *Vathek* and he translated the oriental tale *Al Raoui*.

At his weird country house of Fonthill Abbey he lived with an Italian dwarf and other servants and even the king was not able to get an invitation to come within the twelve-foot walls surrounding the estate. Beckford assiduously collected fantastic curios and art on his European tours. His extravagance forced him eventually to sell the house. It is said that the very next day after the sale the tower fell and crushed the building. He was very lucky in all matters. Even sex scandals could not ruin a wealthy man in his position. Lord Byron, no prude himself, called Beckford "The Apostle of Paederasty." J. G. Lockhart called him "a male Horace Walpole," referring to the principal figure in the Gothic genre to which *Vathek* partly belonged. Beckford may have been one of those aesthetic, wealthy homosexuals in Britain who sometimes gravitate toward even more dangerous adventures in the occult. There is a long list of such people, but we choose a name far enough back in history not to embarrass anyone today.

When Beckford's library was auctioned in the 1880's, Guy Chapman noted that in one book Beckford had written: "A book of singular rarity and particularly amusing to amateurs of witchcraft and devildom in general." Montague Summers identified the book as *Commonefactio de angelicis et pythonicis adparitionibus* ("A Grave and Moral Discourse upon the Appearances of Good and Evil Spirits," 1630). It had been a sermon preached at Strengnas by its bishop in 1629, Laurentius Paulinus, afterwards archbishop of Uppsala. Summers added, citing no other evidence, that: "Beckford assuredly carried his researches into the dark sciences much further than good Archbishop Paulinus would have allowed or approved."

Now that remark by J. G. Lockhart about "a male Horace Walpole." You may recall that it was the effete Walpole, at his "Gothick" country house at Strawberry Hill, who launched the great vogue of the Gothic novel with *The Castle of Ortranto* in the eighteenth century. Beckford was happy not to be blamed for the Gothic Revival: "I have enough sins to answer for," he is reported to have said, "without having that laid to my charge." Summers may well have been gay and a magician himself, but was probably a priest who was what is now termed "closeted."

Beckford's sins may not have included dealing with devils and demons. Anyone as rich and as eccentric as he was, anyone so reclusive as he was, might well have had rumors of the diabolical circulated about him. That was not a demon who opened the thirty-foot-high gate to Fonthill Abbey (which had a high wall all around it) or even refused to let King George IV inside. It was Beckford's pet Italian dwarf. What Beckford's chief sin was appears from a comment of Lord Byron. Lord Byron tried to see Beckford when they both happened to be at an inn together overnight but "the great Apostle of Paederasty Beckford," Byron recorded, made himself scarce.

W. P. Frith (1819–1909) in his autobiography tells of a "distant connection" who managed to get into Fonthill Abbey, closed to the public and fiercely guarded, and ran into a gardener who kindly showed him both the gardens and the house full of spectacular treasures of art. Then the gardener revealed that he, in fact, was the owner, William Beckford, and invited the visitor to stay for dinner.

They had a wonderful meal and chat and at eleven o'clock Beckford rose and left the room without a word. A servant informed the guest that, as he had found his own way in, he could find his own way out. Mr. Beckford? He had gone to bed. And—by the way—the visitor was warned to "look out for the bloodhounds that are let loose in the garden every night." The visitor spent the night in a tree near the house and the next morning managed to escape unscathed from Fonthill Abbey.

EUGÉNE VINTRAS

In 1839 Pierre-Michel-Eugène Vintras gave up his job in a French cardboard box factory to devote himself to anti-Roman Catholic activity. He said he had received a letter—a more modern version of the mystical vision?—from Saint Michael the Archangel. Later he had standard visions of the Blessed Virgin and Saint Joseph (who is rarely reported to make personal appearances, unlike his wife) that convinced Vintras that he was the reincarnation of the prophet Elijah. This much alone would qualify him to represent the wilder shores of sorcery, but there was to be more.

He founded an organization called The Work of Mercy and combined magic with political action to place a German con man named Karl Wilhelm Naundorf, who claimed to be the son of Louis XVI and Marie Antoinette, on the nonexistent throne of France as Louis XVII. Vintras enters our sphere of interest here when he begins to celebrate black masses, which he termed Provictimal Sacrifices of Mary, in vestments with the holy cross inverted. He was reported to be able to produce by magical means chalices overflowing with blood, blood-stained hosts, and more. This drew a small but dedicated circle of semi-Satanists.

In 1841 he had a mystical vision of hell, The Devil and a host of demons urging him to join them. Vintras declined, but it did not deter him from blasphemous activities. He went on to set up The Church of Carmel and continued even after the pope condemned it. Black masses were certainly celebrated and homosexuality was allegedly practiced in connection with them, such a charge going back in French history at least as far as The Templars. Vintras claimed he was a white, not a black, magician and that the orgies in which he and his followers engaged were righting by sex magic the wrongs done by Adam and Eve to mankind. Others spoke of black magic and *incubi*, *succubi*, demon worship.

Vintras died in 1857 and his work and church (which suffered a schism) were taken up by a sex-crazed acolyte, the defrocked priest known as the Abbé Joseph-Antoine Boullan. He was convinced he was the reincarnation of Saint John the Baptist and we deal with him in connection with J. K. Huysmans. Huysmans believed at one time that the Abbé Boullan was engaged in battles not only with competing sorcerers (whom he had taught some murderous spells and who turned on him and were trying to kill him by magical means) but also with what Huysmans called "evil demons."

Vintras was also a great influence on a wide spectrum of magicians in France (such as St.-Yves d'Alveydre), Poland (such as Hoene Wronski), and in our century in the United States (such as homosexual worshipers of Baphomet). Vintras' chief magical enemy was the drug addict Marquis de Guaita, major follower of Eliphas Lévi and (with Oswald Wirth) founder of a Rosicrucian sect in Paris. The marquis was only twenty-seven when he died of debauchery after publishing a book against Satanism and dabbling in black magic himself. He accomplished a lot in his brief life. The Rosicrucians infiltrated rival sects and learned their secrets, after which they denounced Vintras. The marquis described Vintras as a dangerous dealer in the perverse and he railed against Boullan as "a priest of infamy, a base idol of mystical Sodom, a magician of the worst type, a wretched criminal and an evil sorcerer." There were many who believed that by telepathy and spells Guaita in Paris killed Vintras in Lyons. Colin Wilson in *The Occult*, however, doubts that the marquis had the "nervous vitality to project malice telepathically."

ITE, MISSA EST

Joris-Karl Huysmans' study in Satanism, *Là Bas*, includes a terrifying description of a Black Mass of the sort he probably actually attended in Paris, and here is the end of it, set in "the chapel of an old Ursuline convent." We omit the "torrent of blasphemies and insults" and obscenities that preceded the consecration. (The translation is by Keene Wallis, 1958.)

Docre contemplated the Christ surmounting the tabernacle, and with arms spread wide apart he spewed forth frightful insults, and, at the end of his forces, muttered the billingsgate of a drunken cabman. One of the choir boys [actually, acolytes] knelt before him with his back toward the altar. A shudder ran along the priest's spine. In a solemn but jerky voice he said, "*Hoc est enim corpus meum*," then, instead of kneeling, after the consecration, before the precious Body, he faced the congregation, and appeared tumefied, haggard, dripping with sweat. He staggered between the two choir boys, who, raising the chasuble, displayed his naked belly. Docre made a few passes and the host sailed, tainted and soiled, over the steps.

Durtal felt himself shudder. A whirlwind of hysteria shook the room. While the choir boys sprinkled holy water on the pontiff's nakedness, women rushed upon the Eucharist and, grovelling in front of the altar, clawed from the bread humid particles and drank and ate divine ordure.

Another woman, curled up over a crucifix, emitted a rending laugh, then cried to Docre, "Father, father!" A crone tore her hair, leapt, whirled around and around as on a pivot and fell over beside a young girl who, huddled to the wall, was writhing in convulsions, frothing at the mouth, weeping, and spitting out frightful blasphemies. And Durtal, terrified, saw through the fog the red horns of Docre['s headdress] who, seated now, frothing with rage, was chewing up sacramental wafers, taking them out of his mouth, wiping himself with them, and distributing them to the women, who ground them underfoot, howling, or fell over each other struggling to get hold of them and violate them.

The place was simply a madhouse, a monstrous pandemonium of prostitutes and maniacs. How, while the choir boys gave themselves to the men, a little girl, who hitherto had not budged, suddenly bent over forward and howled, howled like a dog. Overcome with disgust, nearly asphyxiated, Durtal wanted to flee. He looked for Hyacinthe. She was no longer at his side. He finally caught sight of her close to the canon [Docre] and, stepping over the writhing bodies on the floor, he went to her. With quivering nostrils she was inhaling the effluvia of the [burning] perfumes and of the couples.

"The sabbatic odour!" she said to him between clenched teeth, in a strangled voice.

"Here, let's get out of this!"

They go to a room over a nearby bar and Hyacinthe says "I want you" and drags him into bed and "obscenities of whose existence he had never dreamed." Then he discovers that the bed is "strewn with fragments of hosts." Disgusted, he decides to terminate his affair with this married lady who likes Black Masses.

THE BLACK MASS EXPLAINED

Jules Michelet in his *Satanism and Witchcraft* traces the blasphemies of the Black Mass to the revolt of the peasantry against the strictures of the church and the perverse sexuality of the ritual's orgies to the dreadful social conditions under which the peasants lived. Encouraged by the church to increase and multiply, the peasants could not feed the mouths they had. Forbidden by the Church to marry close relatives, they were forbidden by their feudal lords to marry strangers lest they become the serf of the wife's lord. Only the eldest son inherited his father's few holdings, his power in the family, and the right to marry. Brothers and sisters mated with each other out of wedlock and the mother committed incest with the eldest son, who now exercised all his dead father's rights. In unholy unions which Michelet finds reminiscent of "the Jews and the Greeks" of old, the Black Mass's excess found their start. The blasphemous rituals offered psychological and physical release for the peasants, an outlet for anger and resentment, a time of festivity and feasting and sexual abandon. While the chatelaines of great castles indulged themselves in the vilest excesses (which their privileged positions permitted) with slaves and cicisbios and lovesick knights and even on occasion their noble husbands, the poor in their dreary lives had the escape valve of the Sabbat, of the Black Mass.

JORIS-KARL HUYSMANS

This French novelist of the decadence (born and died in Paris, 1848–1907) was of Dutch ancestry and his real names were Georges and Charles. After a beginning in Naturalism, he published *À rebours* (1884) and *Là bas* (1891), among other works. In the first, his hero somewhat resembles the Marquis Stanislas de Guaita and the other sensation-seeking drug addicts dedicated to decadence and inhabiting the fringes of the occult world in Paris. In the second, his autobiographical hero records his involvement with Satanism. Huysmans' hero, Durtal, like himself, gradually makes his way to Roman Catholic piety, though Durtal goes well beyond his author in becoming an oblate in a Benedictine monastery. In real life some magicians such as Eliphas Lévi retired into the arms of the church in later life.

This fashionable and somewhat fey flirtation with evil appealed to such English writers as Oscar Wilde. Wilde's Dorian Gray is given a "poisonous book" by the sinister Lord Henry Wotton in *The Importance of Dorian Gray*. It was likely a Huysmans novel. Well after both Huysmans in real life and Dorian Gray in fiction, some Englishmen tried to combine the study of the occult with the *frissons* of immorality. Aleister Crowley and some of his homosexual hangers-on look like Huysmans characters. In real life, the Abbé Boullan and some others *were* Huysmans' Black Mass in *Là bas* has gay acolytes that would do the self-proclaimed homosexual prelates of a New York "Old Catholic" church proud. Other persons and incidents somewhat resemble Huysmans' literary creations in all but the final concessions to respectability.

The appeal of sorcery to feckless sensation seekers with larger incomes than brains deserves a book of its own. A more serious study would connect modern gay witches with the long tradition of homosexual shamans, common in many cultures.

REINCARNATION OF SAINT NICHOLAS

The Italian saint whose feast is celebrated each year on 13 November in every Roman Catholic church was Pope Nicholas I. (858–867) He was called Nicholas the Great. The Prussian military genius, Field Marshal Helmuth, Graf von Moltke (1800–1891) was much involved in the occult and was connected with people seeking the Holy Grail in the style of Parsifal and Sir Gawain. The Holy Grail was thought to have reached Niedermünster in Germany in the ninth century. Moltke considered himself to be the reincarnation of Pope Nicholas the Great. He was sure of it.

A MODERN SYBIL

She was called by a forename that means "divinely wise," but when I met the self-advertised witch Sybil Leek she seemed more charming than clever enough to create charms. She was dressed in a purple frock which was unfortunate for a woman of her excessive width, and from her neck hung a "jewel" that was no more than the largest glass pendant from the bottom of one of the chandeliers she may have been peddling in her part-time antique business. Her British accent was not, shall we say, upper class, and her magical connections hardly seemed to qualify her as the queen of the witches of the world (which she estimated in the 1960s at 20,000 or more).

Sybil Leek was a nice lady but I didn't believe her when she asserted that she came from an unbroken line of English witches that stretched back to the twelfth century and I didn't think she really believed it either. I was under the impression that she thought that, first, she did have some psychic powers, and second, she could never get to use them at all unless she convinced a lot of people she had much more on the ball than she really had.

I mention her as a nice example of witches one is likely to run into in America, women who are a mixture of charlatanism and something else and who are desperately seeking celebrity. Sybil Leek wound up, as far as I know, in Florida, but not after some fame on television as a witch, ghost-hunting in supposedly haunted houses, lecturing on horoscopes and graphology and whatever else came long, and as the author of a number of books on almost all the pseudo-sciences from astrology to palmistry.

After she prophesied in a *Playboy* interview in 1969 that the Russians would be the first to land men on the moon, and soon, her star faded. She taught a number of "occult" people a number of useful things, among which was to avoid predictions or to couch them in language vague enough so that you cannot be discredited when you guess wrong. Alternately, you can take the Jeanne Dixon route and be right enough often enough that you can get away from the occasional gaffe. Nobody's perfect, not even the occult experts that Nancy Reagan consulted in the White House in a tradition that goes back to the wives of much earlier presidents than "The Great Communicator." Finally, Americans are too leery of devils and demons for occult experts here to make much of being in touch with infernal powers.

THE COUNT OF ST.-GERMAIN

The Secret Brotherhood, a group of masters of the universe, was supposed in the eighteenth century to have sent to earth as one of its representatives the odd duck who turned up in Paris calling himself a count and boasting that he had discovered the Philosopher's Stone, so that he could make gold, or the elixir of life (which is just tea made from senna leaves), or just about anything else one could wish. My own recipe for the elixir calls for alcohol and a lot of snakes.

St.-Germain casually claimed to be thousands of years old. That could be neither proved nor disproved (like his alleged death in Germany in 1784) but it certainly was true that he had learned many languages and had an array of talents in the arts and especially in the art of conning the public. Mme. de Pompadour swore by his "water of rejuvenation," a kind of gerovital tonic, apparently. *Tout* Paris lionized him.

His most impressive trick was to appear at several places at exactly the same time. Whether this was witchcraft or not is still debated.

I met a handsome old gentleman in California once who confided to me that he was the famous count. I doubted his story. I began by asking him about Lord Lytton's baronial hall, which I happen to have seen. The count was supposed to have visited there but could not recall it. Then I discovered he could not speak French.

That may do for San Diego but I don't think it will work even in northern California.

Like so much in the occult field, promises of things we really would like to believe—that people can live for centuries, for instance, or that even if they die they are reincarnated or at least there is what one so-called expert called a "persistence of personality"—seduce those all too ready to believe. Yes, Paracelsus was right: Too much reliance on mere rationality blinds us to what intuition or other subtle powers can reveal. But some stories are just too hard to swallow, even with a glass of senna tea.

GERALD GARDNER

The author of the influential *Witchcraft Today* was a colonial official who was pensioned off in Britain and started a new career as a defender of witchcraft. He founded a witchcraft museum in an ancient house on the Isle of Man and, once the ban on witchcraft in Britain was lifted (1951), went public, setting up covens. He died in 1964 but Gardnerian witches still survive in Britain. He never claimed to be in league with The Devil. Rather he attached himself and his followers to *wicca* (wisdom) of the Old Religion.

ROYAL FAMILY DESCENDED FROM A DEMON

I have met someone who claims direct descent from Vlad Tepès (The Impaler), but truly impressive occult genealogy is in the Plantagenet line. William the Conqueror (who married Matilda, a descendant of Alfred the Great) was the illegitimate son of Robert "The Devil," Duke of Normandy. One of William's sons followed him on the English throne (1087–1100) as William *Rufus* and was said to be a black magician, ritually murdered in the forest. William *Rufus* (so-called from his red hair) had no children and was succeeded by his brother, Henry I, called *Beauclerc* because he could write. Henry I married Matilda, daughter of the king of Scotland, and their daughter, also Matilda, married first the Emperor Henry V and then Geoffrey V, Count of Maine and Anjou. Here's where the demon lineage came in. The counts of Anjou went back to Count Fulke in about the tenth century, and Count Fulke was married to Melusine, a demon.

Melusine and he had four children, but the count noticed something odd about her. She would never remain in church for the consecration and elevation of the host. So one time he instructed his knights to keep her there. When the climax of the Mass arrived she could not stand it and, seizing her children, she flew out of the church, back to her demon relatives. From connections of the House of Anjou came such stalwarts as Richard *Coeur de Lion*, Edward I and II and III, and the Richard, Duke of York, who was the first to use the surname Plantagenet. Elizabeth II's lineage includes the Plantagenet kings.

King Charles II, a Stuart, was widely reported to have been a changeling. His unusually swarthy appearance lent color to the rumor.

THE MASTER OF DEVILS AND DEMONS

Edward George Earle Lytton Bulwer-Lytton, first Baron Lytton (1803–1873), who was active in politics but essentially was a writer determined to succeed in all kinds of genres from historical novels to science fiction (*The Coming Race*, published anonymously, deserves more attention), considered himself to be a sorcerer. It was rumored he turned to black magic to kill his wife. She, Rosina Wheeler, separated from him after less than ten years of marriage and hounded him for the rest of her life, even making him the villain of her novel *Cheveley; or, The Man of Honour*. A better explanation of the interest in the occult is that this ambitious socialite mixed in circles in London and Paris where sorcery and even Satanism were in the very air in the first half of the nineteenth century.

Bulwer-Lytton was a man of many talents. For example, when actor friends of his wanted vehicles, he dashed off hit plays for them, only briefly interrupting his steady stream of novels and periodical essays. He decided to study sorcery and turned his talents to that. He gathered like minds at his family house called Knebworth, but he was never very good at the black arts. We have seen that Eliphas Lévi visited him.

He describes the ideal sorcerer in his book *The Haunted and the Haunters*:
If you could fancy some mighty serpent transformed into man, preserving in the human lineaments the old serpent type, you would have a better idea; the width and flatness of frontal, the tapering elegance of contour disguising the strength of the deadly jaw—the long, large, terrible eye, glittering and green as the emerald—and withal a certain ruthless calm, as if from the consciousness of immense power.

That is the sort of hero needed to take on the devils and demons and wrest them to his service. While witches seek the assistance of devils and demons, sorcerers defy them, seek to command the surly and dangerous spirits. They need both the slyness and the wisdom attributed to the serpent, a symbol since the days of Adam and Eve, if not before, of the cold, calculating, clever intelligence. The serpent even in pre-Jewish religions, however, has usually been regarded as evil, as in the case of Ahriman (the devil of the Zoroastrians) and perhaps the *seraphim* the Hebrews borrowed from their neighbors.

Is the sorcerer evil when he seeks to command devils and demons and make them obey his will? Perhaps, if he becomes their god and puts them to work that God Himself has not dictated for them.

Edmund Wilson ticked off Lord Lytton by calling him "a half-trashy novelist, who writes badly, but is patronized by half-serious readers, who do not care much about writing." Lord Lytton was also a half-serious magician, with half-serious followers.

Lord Lytton's chief contribution to the world of mystery must be the opening line he composed for one of his popular fictions; it is used now for retelling ghost stories: "It was a dark and stormy night...."

Lord Lytton appears as a character, Desbrow, in Lady Blessington's novel *The Two Friends* (1835); as Lord de Clifford in Lady Lytton's novel *Cheveley; or, The Man of Honour* (1839); as Bertie Tremaine in his friend Benjamin Disraeli's novel *Endymion* (1880); and as Lord Surbiton in his friend W. H. Mallock's *A Romance of the Nineteenth Century* (1881). But nowhere is he discussed in terms of his diabolical dandyism, which might have been a very colorful subject.

Matthew Hopkins, seventeenth century, Witch-Finder-General, was hoisted by his own petard: He was executed for witchcraft himself.

A CLERGYMAN TAKES ON THE SKEPTICS

Joseph Glanvill (1636–1680) pointed out the dangers of witchcraft in *Sadducismus triumphatus* (1681). He was groundbreaking on psychics and mediumship and, because he was the king's chaplain and a captivating storyteller, he was very influential.

Protestantism looked askance at relics and miracles of saints and papist practices. The Reformation announced that all before had been superstition, that the age of miracles was long over. Where, then, to find evidence of the supernatural? In witchcraft and demonology. Joseph Glanvill set out as a member of The Royal Society to convince the scientists of the reality of the Other World, "to regain a parcel of Ground which bold Infidelity hath invaded." "Those who dare not say," he wrote in what came to be known as *Sadducismus triumphatus*, "There is no GOD, content themselves (for a fair step and Introduction) to deny that there are Spirits and Witches." Thus once again heresy and magic were connected and the enemies of society became the enemies of God Almighty. Convinced that The Devil and his "Dark Kingdom" would triumph if no one believed what The Enemy of Mankind was up to, Glanvill undertook to present arguments from both scripture and reason and to catch and convince with a "choice collection of modern relations." He offered these stories as proof that The Devil was alive and active even in an Age of Reason.

Glanvill's aim was to give Protestants not only a sense of sin but a sense of the spiritual through an emphasis on the supernatural. After all, the Bible was the cornerstone of the Protestant religion, and did not scriptures as well as tradition demand a belief in the supernatural, in The Devil and all his works and pomps?

Soberly Glanvill undertook to answer half a dozen objections to the existence of witches: "that the notion of 'spirit' is itself an absurdity," "that the actions attributed to Witches are absurd or impossible," "that 'tis very improbable that the Devil...should be at the beck [and call] of a poor Hag," that to believe the stories of children victimized is "to accuse Providence" of not protecting innocence, that though the reasonable man must "scorn the *ordinary tales of Prodigies*" the appearances of angels (especially bad angels) are undeniable and not uncommon, that there can be diabolical as well as divine miracles.

He coined the phrase "the climate of opinion." If the climate of opinion in his time was turning from God as it turned toward science, he was going to turn it back, even at the cost of launching a crusade against The Devil in which many of his fellow Britons would die.

In a time when science threatened faith, not unlike the nineteenth century (when Darwin elaborated Glanvill's recognition that things in nature evolve gradually), this divine was anxious that man not lose sight of the supernatural as he strove to understand and control the natural world. His compatriots were hardly less superstitious than when Bishop Hall fulminated (in a passage I quote in the "Superstition" section of my book *Elizabethan Popular Culture*, 1988) against

> godlesse religion, devoute impietie. The superstitious is loud [bold]
> in observation, servile in feare....This man dares not stirre forthe
> till his breast be crossed, and his face sprinkled [with holy water]:
> if but an hare crosse him the way, he returnes, or if his journey
> began unawares on the dismall day; or if he stumble at the thresh-
> old. If he sees a snake unkilled, he feares a mischiefe; if the salt
> fall towards him, he looks pale and red, and is not quiet until one
> of the waiters have powred wine on his lappe; and when he
> sneezeth, thinks them not his friends that uncover not [do not take

off their hats]. In the morning he listens whether the Crow crieth even or odd, and by that very token presages of the weather. If he heare but a Raven croke from the next roofe, he makes his will, or if a Bittour flie over his head by night: but if his troubled fancie shall second his thoughts with the dreame of a fairie garden, or greene rushes, or the salutation of a dead friend, he takes leave of the world, and says he cannot live. He will never set to sea but on a Sunday; neither ever goes without an Erra Pater [almanac with lucky days, etc., marked] in his pocket....Old wives and starres are his counsellors; his night-spell is his guard, and charmes his Physicians. He weares Paracelsian Characters [written charms} for the toothache, and a little hallowed waxe is his Antidote for all evils....Some wayes he will not goe, and some he dares not; either there are bugges [frightful creatures] or he faineth them....

MORE THAN THIRTY INTERESTING PERSONALITIES OF BRITISH DEMONOLOGY

The history of British witchcraft has been written by C. L'Estrange Ewen, Christina Hole, and many others. From the mass of colorful characters emerge some we have noted in this book with entries of their own. Now here are some that can be given briefer attention:

AGNES, wife of Ode, freed (1209) after passing the red-hot-iron test for witchcraft. She carried a red-hot bar of iron and was not seared.

SIR JAMES ALTHAM, one of the judges who condemned nineteen witches at a stroke at Assizes at the Castle of Lancaster, August 1612.

ROGER BACON (1214–1294) was scientist and occultist. He was confined by his Franciscan order 1257–1267 and 1278–1292 for magic and heresy. Centuries later he was still so alive in folklore that one of the University wits of Shakespeare's time (Robert Greene) put him on the stage in *Friar Bacon and Friar Bungay*. He introduced the Arab gown Academe.

AGNES BROWNE, MARY BARBER, JOAN VAUGHN, HELEN JENKENSON, AND ARTHUR BILL, all executed at Northampton in July 1612 as "the Northamptonshire Witches."

JANE CLARKE of Wigston (Leicestershire) and her son and daughter were "swum" for witchcraft in Leicester in 1717, but the grand jury threw out the indictment that followed and the twenty-five witnesses ready to testify.

ELEANOR COBHAM, DUCHESS OF GLOUCESTER (d. 1446?), was accused of treason and being his accomplice in black magic by one Roger Bolingbroke and was imprisoned for about the last five years of her life.

MARGARET COOPER of Somerset (1594) was dispossessed of a demon in the form of a bear with no head.

NATHANIEL CROUCH (1632–1728) wrote *The Kingdom of Darkness* (1688) under a pseudonym, dealing with demons and witches.

JOHN DARREL (*fl.* 1562–1602) was an unpopular exorcist who caused the Anglican Church to forbid exorcism under Cannon 72 (1603).

ANNIS DELL and her son GEORGE DELL were executed at Hartford on 4 August 1606 for "cruel and bloody murther" by witchcraft of "a childe called Anthony James."

JOYCE DEVEY was "possest with the devill" at Bewdley, near Worcester, in 1647.

GILES FENDERLYN confessed to having "made a covenant with the devil for fourteen years" and he "afterwards killed his wife," London c. 1652.

SIR ROBERT FILLMER (d. 1653) introduced some sense into witchhunts with his *Warning to the English Judges concerning Sorceresses*. A lawyer and shrewd politician, he found the flaws in the "proofs" of William Perkins.

ALICE GOODRICH died in prison at Derby after she was falsely accused by a boy called Thomas Darling of being a witch. Samuel Harsnett (*q.v.*) discussed the fraud in a book (1603). Shakespeare consulted the book for names of demons in *King Lear*.

JOHN HAMMOND published *A Most Certain Strange and True Discovery of a Witch, Being Overtaken by Some of the Parliament Forces* (1643). She was shot by a soldier who saw her surfing on the river at Newbury, using a "plank."

ARCHBISHOP SAMUEL HARSNETT (1561–1631) studied the exorcisms of John Darrel (*q.v.*) and wrote an exposé of him (1599) and *A Declaration of Egregious Popish Impostures* on the subject of freeing people of bewitchments (1603).

MARY HICKS and her daughter ELIZABETH HICKS (aged nine) were executed for witchcraft at Huntingdon, July 1716. Executing children was rare.

BISHOP FRANCIS HUTCHINSON (1660–1739 wrote *An Historical Essay concerning Witchcraft* (1718) which introduced more responsible methods into witchcraft inquiries.

ABRAHAM JOINER a teenager living in Shadwell who, having spent all his money on a woman, said he didn't know where he could get any more unless The Devil gave him some, which The Devil appeared and did, etc. (1721).

ALICE KYTELER was accused (1324) by an Irish bishop, Richard of Ledrede, of witchcraft, murder of three husbands, and sex with demons, but she escaped to England. Several of her accomplices were caught and punished in Ireland.

JOHN LAMB (d. 1628), an astrologer suspected of dealing with demons, was killed by a mob which identified him as "the Duke (of Buckingham)'s Devil."

ANDREW MACKIE of Ring Croft, Stocking, Scotland, had a house with "an apparition, expressions and actings, of a spirit" haunting it (1696).

MARY, QUEEN OF SCOTS (1542–1587) did not, as was rumored, agree to supporters' attempting to kill her rival Elizabeth by witchcraft. Indeed, Mary made witchcraft a capital offense in Scotland (1563, repealed 1736). Her son was a strong opponent of witchcraft (James VI of Scotland, James I of the United Kingdom).

MERLIN of the Matter of Britain was the legendary magician of the King Arthur stories. Wales recognizes two Merlins, *Myrddin Emrys* (Merlin Ambrosius, who persuaded Aurelius to bring Stonehenge from Ireland and used magic to effect that) and *Myrddin Wyllt* (Merlin Silvester, who after the Battle of Aderydd in 573 A.D. retired to the woods).

PATRICK MORTON a boy who lied about witchcraft as Pittenween in Scotland, and three people died before he confessed. Beatrice Laing, whom he identified as bewitching him, was released.

THE OSBORNES, husband and wife of Tring, were lynched by the mob that accused them of witchcraft (1751).

WILLIAM PERKINS (1555–1602), Puritan divine, author of a *Discourse of the Damned Art of Witchcraft* (1608) discussing The Devil's Mark, deals with demons, proofs of witchcraft, etc. Considered authoritative in its time.

JOAN PETERSON was tried for poisoning Lady Powel(l) at Chelsea and for witchcraft (1652).

MICHAEL SCOTT (1175?–1234?), whose supposed descendant Sir Walter Scott also wrote about witchcraft, served royal personages as physician and magician on The Continent. He was credited with a demon horse, a demon ship, and various miracles. He was astrologer, alchemist, scholar of Aristotle and Avicenna, medical expert, much more.

JANE WENHAM "the Wise Woman of Wakerene," was exonerated in Hertfordshire in what has often been said to be the last witchcraft trial in England (1712).

CHRISTINA WILSON was convicted and executed as a witch (Dailkeith, 1551) when she failed a crucial test: When she touched the corpse, it bled, proving her guilt as a witch.

FRANCIS MOORE

Francis Moore (1657–1715?) dropped out of sight and no one knows what happened to him, but *Old Moore's Almanac* (which first appeared as *Vox Stellarum*, The Voice of the Stars, 1700) still publishes astrological predictions. It is said to have predicted, among other things, World War II and the atomic bomb which ended it in the Pacific.

PRIME MINISTER BALFOUR

Arthur James Balfour (1848–1930) was leader of the Conservatives and from 1902–1905 prime minister of Great Britain. He was awarded the most coveted honor, the Order of Merit, in 1916 and in 1922 was created first Earl of Balfour. He was profoundly curious about spiritualism.

Guy Lambert, C.B., who had been Lord Balfour's parliamentary secretary, told me in the 1950s when he was advising me as I wrote the introduction to collected papers on psychical research of Myers, Gurney, and Podmore (all of whom he also knew) as *Phantasms of the Living*, many stories about Lord Balfour's profound interest in psychical research and deep beliefs in spiritualism and other matters. Lord Balfour gave séances quite a boost by his distinction, for he held the highest offices: First Lord of the Treasury, First Lord of the Admiralty, Foreign Secretary, Lord President of the Council, Prime Minister, President of the British Association, Chancellor of Cambridge University, etc. He was certainly one of the most learned and philosophically minded of politicians and most dedicated of students of the occult. And open-minded. "We are none of us infallible," he said, "not even the youngest of us."

JAMES STEPHENS

James Stephens (1882–1950) rose from the slums of Dublin to international fame as a writer of both poetry and prose, but we note him here for his collection of *Irish Fairy Tales* (1920) and the mysticism in his own work. D. C. Browning's *Everyman's Dictionary of Literary Biography* says this anthology was "appropriately made." Stephens was "sometimes compared to a lep-rechaun." He was less than five feet tall and a little bit mischievous.

ARTHUR MACHEN

A short piece of fiction on *The Angel of Mons* in World War I gained this hard-working journalist the distinction of having his fiction taken as fact. *The Angel* became a legend and he included it in his *The Bowmen and Other Legends of the War* (1915). For some forty years he wrote fine novels of the supernatural and he had some interest in the occult.

VICTOR NEUBURG

Neuberg (1883–1940) was closely associated, in bed and in magic, with Aleister Crowley, who delighted in treating him sadistically, humiliating him, mocking him, and using him for magical and sexual purposes. He can serve as an example of masochists who are drawn to sex magic and who appear in various Personal Ad solicitations in (generally homosexual, such as *Drummer*) way-out magazines. From these exploited persons some magicians claim to derive a sense of power. See Crowley's own works and Jean Overton Fuller's *The Magical Dilemma of Victor Neuburg* (1965). Crowley's curse on his erstwhile "top" is said to have caused Neuberg a couple of years of "nervous breakdown."

ALEISTER CROWLEY

Crowley (1875–1947) has received far more attention than he is worth. He was not a noble soul, like Scott of the Antarctic, to whom, said Herbert Ponting, "it was human endeavour that mattered, not mere ambition to achieve." Crowley was that most unfortunate of people, the charlatan with a little something real obscured by all the self-promotion and stupidity that playing to the gallery encourages. The true Revelation is that Crowley was not The Best—just an Englishman with the wrong accent and worse morals. Nevertheless, Crowley, regrettably, must get a mention; this book would be incomplete without him because he did at least attempt to deal in devils and demons as well as in what he insisted was white (and sex) "Magick" and personal publicity. In my view he was not a black magician, but he would have been one if he could have pulled it off. He certainly had the ego the master magician requires and almost succeeded in attaining wisdom in the way that William Blake suggested: the fool persisting in his folly until he becomes wise. He never grasped the basic fact that if you want to do magic to *impress and astound* people, even a bench of bishops, you ought to go in for conjuring. What he called "Magick" is not driven by the reactions of others and is not publicized to shock. It is a private, personal, powerful application of the will, not the whim.

Crowley was into everything. He tried to dominate any organization he joined, designed a set of unnecessarily ugly Tarot cards, managed to get thrown out of Italy by Benito Mussolini, had some unintentionally hilarious photographs taken and intellectual poses reported, and surrounded himself with some extraordinary individuals and an aura of menace. John Symonds, a far more interesting character, has done much to establish Crowley's reputation in *The Great Beast* (1951) and *The Magic of Aleister Crowley* (1958). His former colleague in The Order of the Golden Dawn, Israel Regardie, gives fascinating glimpses into Crowley's "Work" in *The Eye in the Triangle* (1970, a symbol from Masonry which Americans will note appears in an adaptation on the back of every dollar bill courtesy of Master Mason George Washington and his friends).

In his autobiography, *The Confessions of Aleister Crowley* (edited by John Symonds and Kenneth Granta, 1971), he says something of Victor Neuberg mentioned above:

> I soon saw that Neuberg with his shambling gait and erratic gestures, his hangdog look and his lunatic laugh, would damage me in the estimation of the natives. So I turned the liability into an asset by shaving his head except for two tufts on the temples, which I twisted up into horns. I was thus able to pass him off as a demon that I had tamed and trained to serve me as a familiar spirit. This greatly enhanced my eminence. The more eccentric and horrible Neuberg appeared, the more insanely and grotesquely he behaved, the more he inspired the inhabitants with respect for the Magician who had mastered so fantastic and fearful a genie.

Crowley published the results of *Paris Workings* of sex magic with Neuburg in which Crowley took the passive sexual role but appears to have directed the proceedings. Crowley was a busybody in many ways.

ROBERT CALEF'S LEGACY

Robert Calef (1648–1719) was born in Boston and was successful there as a merchant but he did not share the views of all of his fellows. He deserves more attention than he has received for his *More Wonders of the Invisible World*, printed in London in 1700 after no Boston publisher would take it. Calef's book is a reply to the famous Congregational minister Cotton Mather, author of *The Wonders of the Invisible World* (1693). Selections from Cotton Mather's works were edited by Kenneth B. Murdock (1926) and T. J. Holmes published *The Mather Literature* (1927), but Calef's book remains obscure. It deserves better.

It needs to be emphasized that the witchcraft persecutions of New England were simply pious people putting principles into practice. The Puritans are notorious for narrow-mindedness. H. L. Mencken went so far as to define a Puritan as someone who is afraid that someone else, somewhere, is having a good time. Nonetheless, Puritans must be seen as good Christians with the sincere desire to do right insofar as God gives them the ability to see it. While their ethos prevailed, America was more intolerant of difference but more dedicated to principles. America went so far in the other direction, and with such disastrous results, that the Christian Right is now making a comeback.

Do not expect it to be tolerant. Tolerance is difficult for Christians, despite Christ's commandment to love one another and to do unto others as we should wish them to do unto us and forgive those who trespass against us. For Christ also said: "Those who are not with Me are against Me." A Puritan doing her or his duty is always a fearsome sight. A Puritan with a chip on the shoulder or (worse) a legitimate gripe is a terror.

Witchcraft being feared and prosecuted in New England arose from the beliefs and the dedication to those beliefs of the members of a strait-laced but by their lights law-abiding group of people themselves twisted out of shape by earlier persecution. Today we have Pat Robertson (to name but one religious leader) and an army of evangelicals, charismatics, Pentecostals, fundamentalists, and the more concerned than comfortable in the traditional Christian churches convinced that these are the Last Days, the days in which (as *Genesis* I:28 suggests to them) the faithful are by right to seize dominion over all and enforce by whatever means necessary the biblical laws until The Messiah comes again. Their rule *demands* what today's jargon would call "zero tolerance" toward witches and witchcraft. It insists further (say some who read the Bible strictly) the death penalty for sorcerers.

In this climate of completing ideologies, the arguments between Increase and Cotton Mather on the one side and Robert Calef and some others even more skeptical than he was on the other look surprisingly modern. The Born Again are out to get the Born to Be Bad. Orthodoxy (as the ancient joke used to go) is my doxy; heterodoxy is your doxy. I am right (or Right) and you are wrong—and must not be allowed to continue in error even if I have to kill you to save your soul or (if God has already damned you) simply in hope of making of you an example to deter those who can still be brought onto the correct path. History shows us the horrific results of Christians who have turned from worrying about saving their own souls and improving their personal conduct to saving the souls of others and waging campaigns of correction. Piety armed is dangerous.

America may be looking forward again to *Deuteronomy versus* Democracy. The battle will be fiercer than in our colonial theocracy in Massachusetts, with zealots on both sides, and much at stake. Most certainly it is going to challenge materialist America for the better or the worse and involve events far bloodier and far more bloody-minded than ever happened in New England. It may reach out beyond the blasphemers and the infidels to attempt to straighten out the homosexuals, for instance, and absolutely everyone else perceived by the self-identified devout to be dangerously deviant from the dictates of the Bible, even the Jews for whose guidance the Old Testament was revealed. It's identify the Enemy time, from The Enemy of Man and his devotees to anyone else not Born Again in the way you are. The so-called Glorious Mosaic is throwing rocks.

I am not the only one to expect a clash as Christian coalitions of various sorts confront Rainbow mentalities, as Moses meets Multiculturalism. For example, Harvey Cox reports "Warring Visions of the Religious Right" in the *Atlantic* (November 1995) and says Rousas John Rushdooney's 1,124-page *The Roots of Reconstruction* "includes a proposal that the death penalty be enforced today for adulterers, homosexuals, blasphemers, astrologers, witches, and teachers of false doctrine." Cox declares: "The thought of Rushdooney's disciples gaining government power qualifies as the real nightmare scenario presented by the religious right."

JOHN DEE

Dr. Dee (1527–1608) was astrologer and alchemist, scientist and occultist, diviner and necromancer, and as a young man at St. John's College (Cambridge) he introduced into a performance of a play by Aristophanes such stupendous effects that ever after he was regarded as a magician. He did, in fact, amass an amazing library, and many occult books (which he was said to have destroyed in old age, like Shakespeare's Prospero) were among them.

He was hauled before the Star Chamber (a powerful court, so-called from the decoration of its ceiling) on the charge of trying to kill "Bloody" Mary by sorcery; he was acquitted. In the reign of Elizabeth he was a favorite and in 1575 he demonstrated for her the "magic mirror" of basalt that he had obtained from Mexico and which he used for scrying. You can see it too. It is in The British Museum now. He also told fortunes with the use of crystals and practiced this with the Count Palatine Albert Laski of Siradz when that worthy visited England in 1584. Dee formed an inner circle of alchemists seeking the philosopher's stone (disbanded 1589). Ben Johnson (according to the gossipy John Aubrey) got the idea of *The Alchemist* from Dr. Dee and was amused by Dee's distilling egg shells.

Dee said he talked with angels and called up spirits. He got involved with a somewhat sleazy medium called Edward Kelley, who one day in Prague astounded him by having reams of documents rain down on his head while they walked outdoors. With Kelley he tried to raise the dead by necromancy. He wrote a treatise on the Rosicrucians and a great deal of geographical and mathematical work. Everyone said he dealt with demons and some said he could make gold and did so for Queen Elizabeth and perhaps for Emperor Rudolf and Stephen, King of Poland. He was just the imposing figure to bring excitement to what a Prince of Wales once dismissed as "some small proud German court where there is nothing to do."

In 1604, without success, he petitioned the new king, James I, to remove from him the imputation of being a magician.

RUDOLF STEINER

Steiner (1861–1925) laid the groundwork for German occultism in the twentieth century, including the superstitions of Hitler and his gang. Steiner was a significant contributor to the study of mind and of mental disease and he believed in paranormal powers. He was a Theosophist before he invented "anthroposophicism" (or "anthroposophistry"?) in Switzerland. A scientist, he did not believe in devils and demons but his writings about an astral world were seized upon and distorted by those who do believe in and even attempt to contact evil powers.

THE SAD END OF "THE *ILLUMINATUS* OF LEIPZIG"

Johann Georg Schröpfer (1750–1774) was a magician who is said to have dispatched a demon to vex one of his enemies. The demon, angered that when he arrived at the target's home, the target gentleman was already dead, returned to bother this master, and Schröpfer was driven to madness and suicide. This is an interesting variation on the old ideas that a curse can boomerang and hurt the sender or that when magic is done wrong it can destroy the magician rather than the intended victim.

THE GREATEST MEDIUM OF VICTORIAN ENGLAND

Daniel Dunglas Home (pronounced "Hume," as in the surname of the earls to whom he was distantly related) lived 1833–1886. From an early age he said he was aware of psychic powers. He had a premonition of his mother's death, was so accompanied by spirit rappings that his aunt made him move out of her house, and his séances were a feature of America's burgeoning interest in spiritualism. They were attended and praised by William Cullen Bryant and other famous people, some of whom swore Home could levitate. This was supposed to be a concomitant of spiritual ecstasy. When St. Ignatius Loyola said Mass, they say, he had to be held down by acolytes, and Joseph of Cupertino is reported to have given a demonstration of flying at The Vatican, to the delight of the pope. When Joseph was dying, his abbot told him to cease levitating but he could not stop. Later, in England, Home's levitations impressed the earls of Dunraven and Crawford and other important persons.

He went to England in 1855 and was an immediate success as a medium. Sir David Brewster, an expert on optics, swore there was no trickery. Lord Lytton and others interested in the occult flocked to Home's séances. In Italy he performed for many, including Robert Browning and his wife. In Rome he was converted to Catholicism, though later (1864) he was to be expelled from Rome as a black magician.

Well before that, in London, at the homes of Thomas Milner-Gibson (president of the Board of Trade) and other socially prominent persons, he held séances to which people were thrilled to be invited. He performed before crowned heads all over the Continent. When doubts grew about his authenticity, for salons were packed with fraudulent mediums of all sorts), he gave a demonstration without the closed cabinets, dim lights, or darkness that usually shrouded the production of ectoplasm (made of gauze), trumpets suspended in the air, ghostly hands, and the rest. When he won over Sir William Crookes, a Fellow of the Royal Society, a highly respected scientist who vouched that there was no deception, the whole business of mediumship took on a new color in the eyes of many people.

Home's autobiographies and *Lights and Shadows of Spiritualism* (which he wrote with William Howitt, author of *A Popular History of Priestcraft* and a convinced spiritualist, 1877) give his views on the subject of mediumship, but no one who did not see him in person can truly understand the tremendous effect he had in his time. Those who claimed he was in league with The Devil and those who considered he was nothing at all but an ordinary trickster were both wrong. Whatever you explanation, D. D. Home was extraordinary.

People still suspected fraud and for that or more personal reasons they battled against him and the vogue of spiritualism. For instance, from the diary of William Allingham (1824–1889), the poet (published 1906):

Sludge [in a work by Robert Browning] is [a satirical attack on] Home whom Browning told me today a great deal that was very amusing. Having witnessed a séance of Home's, at the house of a friend of Browning's, Browning was openly called upon to give his frank opinion on what had passed, upon which he declared with emphasis that so impudent a piece of imposture he never saw before in all his life, and so took his leave. Next day Browning's servant came into his room with a visitor's card, and close behind him followed the visitor himself—no other than Mr. Home, who advanced with a cordial smile and right hand outstretched in amity. He bore no ill will—not he! Browning looked sternly at him (as he is very capable of doing) and pointing to the open door, not far from which is a rather steep staircase, said, "If you are not out of that door in half a minute I'll fling you down the stairs." Home attempted some expostulation, but Browning moved towards him, and the Medium disappeared with as much grace as he could manage.

Other people took D. D. Home much more seriously. Some swore they saw him float up to the ceiling in broad daylight. He was very likely the most popular medium of his time. Some rumor went around that Robert Browning had disliked Home ever since Browning and Elizabeth Barrett Browning, his famous wife, attended a Home séance in Florence and Home produced a wreath of flowers from the spirit world for Mrs. B but nothing for Robert Browning himself. Browning was jealous.

THREE INFLUENTIAL WRITERS
OF THE LAST THREE CENTURIES

Joseph Glanvill (1636–1680) was a scientist, one of the founding members of The Royal Society, but most of all he was a clergyman and in his "philosophical considerations touching witches and witchcraft" known as *Sadducismus triumphatus* (1666) he argued the existence of and danger from witchcraft, his high reputation as a thinker giving this insidious volume a long and influential life.

Francis Barrett in *The Magus* (1801) pulled together into what he thought of as a "complete system" all the old manuals of witchcraft and privately inducted some leading personages into the occult mysteries, being one of the few authors of magic books to try to make a business out of his knowledge.

W. E. Butler based his textbook on *Magic: Its Power, Ritual, and Purpose* (1961) on his personal practices and it was a leader among hand-on or what the British call DIY (do-it-yourself) books. He offered instructions by mail on cabalistic matters. At least he did not pretend to be in touch with Venusians, as did several Londoners of his time who announced they were adepts in the occult. James I of the United Kingdom signed a strict statute against sorcery in the second year of his reign (1604) but it gradually fell into disuse until the Puritans triumphed in the Civil War. It was not repealed, however, until the reign of George II (1736). Clergymen such as the Reverend Mr. Glanvill had a lot to do with keeping the statute from being scrapped over this long period. Its repeal opened the way to the publication of books by magicians. These came thick and fast despite the fact that one of the greatest appeals of the occult is the thrill of being involved in secret societies and enjoying a sense of superiority that comes from considering oneself a member of a favored and mysterious elite.

In this old woodcut (1608) the witch rides on a goat.

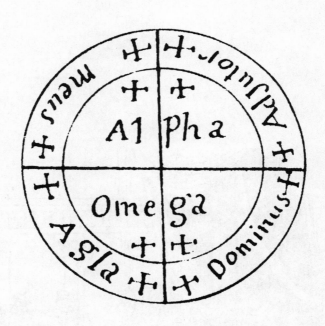

A scene from a fairy tale in a nineteenth-century illustration by
George Cruikshank.

6
Some Minor Spirits

JOHN HENRY, CARDINAL NEWMAN ON MINOR SPIRITS

Also besides the hosts of evil spirits I considered there is a middle race, neither in heaven nor in hell, partially fallen, capricious, wayward, noble or crafty, benevolent or malicious as the case might be.—*Apologia pro vita sua*.

CHILDREN TAUGHT TO FEAR BUGBEARS

From Reginald Scot's famous *Discouerie of Witches* (1584):
Our mother's maids have so frayed us with Bull-beggars, Spirits, Witches, Urchins, Elves, Hags, Faeries, Satyrs, Pans, Faunes, Sylens, Kit-wi-the-Can[dle]stick, Tritons, Centaurs, Gyants, Impes, Calcars, Conjurors, Nymphs, Changelings, Incubus, Robin Goodfellow, the Spoorn, the Mare, the Man-in-the-Oak, the Hell-wain, the Firedrake, the Puckle, Tom-thombe, Hobgoblin, Tom-tumbler, Boneless, and such other Bug[bear]s, that we are afraid of our shadow.

Some of these words can stand commentary here. *Bull-beggars* seem to use the word *bogle* in both parts of the construct: a *bull-beggar* is some sort of bugbear that boggles the mind. *Urchins* are not street arabs but actually hedgehogs, an animal form that spirits were said to adopt on occasion; on the dedication page of this book is a sixteenth-century hedgehog from the very first printed picture of a witch's familiar in any English book. Spirits, Witches, Elves, Hags, Fairies, Satyrs, Pans, Faunes—these are all pretty recognizable, but *Sylens* were "Syleham lamps," from a village in Suffolk where drainage was poor, misleading swamp lights that lead the traveler astray and perhaps into danger. In *The Anatomy of Melancholy*, Robert Burton cites "those which Mizaldus called *Ambulatores*, that walk about midnight, on heaths and desert places, which draw men out of the way and lead them all night a by-way, or quite barre them of their way; these have several names in several places; we commonly call them pucks." If the *ignis fatuis* looked more like a candle, it was said to be carried by Kit (a nickname for Christopher) "o' the Canstick."

Tritons and Centaurs came from classical mythology, and Giants were common in all myths. (Ghosts of *Gyants* were called *Spriggans* and they could cause much sorrow, stealing goods or even children.) *Imps* (or *Pugs*) were tiny devils more mischievous (like pixies) than malicious. *Calcars* are really *calkers*, an old name for diviners or conjurors. *Robin Goodfellow* is a "sportive or capricious elf," according to the dictionary, and his forename is a short version of *Robert*, in British folklore associated with The Devil. The "goodfellow" part is supposed to disarm enmity through euphemism. The same fear of offending is seen in the names used in English for the fairies ("the good neighbors"), the Scottish for them ("the Fair Folk"), the French for the Fates that preside over a child's birth (*les bonne dames*, "the good ladies"), and so on.

The *Spoorn* is a spectre or phantom, the *Mare* more familiar in the word *nightmare*. *The Man in the Oak* seems to be a holdover from the oak as sacred to the Druids and spirits as dwelling in trees (which is why we still have Christmas trees at Yuletide). The old rhyme I learned as a child told how to protect yourself from attacks by fairies:

> Turn your cloak,
> For fairy folk
> Are in the oak.

The *Hell-wain* was a phantom wagon seen in the night sky, the *Fire-drake* a fearsome dragon. A *Puckle* as a *puckrel* is a witch's familiar or as a *pukehold* is the creature dwelling the ground like a *puke* (the Icelandic word for "devil"). He can get you into a pickle, like the Irish *pooka* or the Welsh *pwca* or the Cornish *bucca* or Puck of Shakespeare's countryside and Ben Johnson's Puck-hairy (suggesting Old Harry, The Devil).

Tom Thumb is best known to Americans as the name adopted for the midget that P. T. Barnum made famous; it was earlier a name for any tiny (often mischievous) fellow, an imp, etc. *Tom Tumbler* appears to be of the same sort. *Boneless* was a bogeyman rather like The Blob of B-movie fame.

Well after Elizabeth and Scot's time came "Boney" Bonaparte, used as a bugbear to frighten children. "Old Boney" was said to come and get them if they were bad. One scholar derived *elf* and *goblin* from Guelph and Ghibeline in Italian politics.

The same psychology that creates monsters in the kiddies' closets, and monsters the parents threaten to sic onto the disobedient offspring, functions in the creation of all these devils and demons and things that go bump in the night.

THREE KINDS OF FAIRIES

Webster's Third defines a fairy as "a mythical being of folklore and romance usually having diminutive human form and magic powers and dwelling on earth in close relationship with man." But fairies are not only tiny; they also come in medium (brownies) and full sizes (beautiful human-sized fairies) or fairies who could cast a "glamour" of deceit to make things look as they were not and who may just have *looked* gorgeous, were often said to captivate men, sometimes marrying into mankind and producing children half fairy and half human, just as certain angels were said to have bred with the sons of men.

A simpler division is into two categories: good fairies (such as fairy godmothers, etc.) and bad fairies (such as those who put curses on people, especially infants). Bad fairies are hard to distinguish from malevolent spirits, devils, demons. Isobel Gowdie, arraigned as a witch in Scotland in 1662, told the court under oath that both witches and fairies can ride on straws carried in the wind by simply chanting "Horse and hattock [a small hat], in The Devil's name!" In this they both resemble the spirits of the air which Paracelsus named *sylphs*.

VIRGINS ARE SAFE FROM SUPERNATURAL HARM

As reported by John Milton:

> Some say no evil thing that walks by night
> In fog, or fire, by lake or moorish fen,
> Blue meager hag, or stubborn unlaid ghost,
> That breaks his magic chain at curfew time,
> No goblin, or swart fairy of the mine,
> Hath hurtful power o'er true virginity.

GOOD SPIRITS AND BAD ONES OF THE NORTHLAND

Norwegians used to believe in "Seventh Father of the House." This was a spirit, seven generations old, that lived in a horn hanging on the wall. It was supposed to whisper valuable advice and help the family.

Now, such a creature could in no way be called a devil or a demon. I mention it to bring up the fact that many sprites and such creatures are not devilish and may, in fact, have some connection to stories told of real people of ancient times, people who seemed to have strange powers, but humans nonetheless.

In this category, I believe, fall a great many of the creatures of Scandinavian superstition. Take undergrounders, for instance. Ola J. Holten wrote in the folklore journal *Du mitt Nordmore* in 1975 of these *diskar* and recounted tales he had heard as a boy in Surnadal from an old storyteller (b. 1874) named Sivert Fiske. This tale makes clear, however, that these undergrounders have supernatural powers and are not simply human beings strange in appearance, residence, and ways. In Holten's and my translation:

> Up in the Svealia you can find a big tree named Stuppul and under this big old tree there is hidden a treasure in gold, guarded by the undergrounders.

> Once there were two young fellows from Moen Farm who climbed up to Stuppul to dig for the buried treasure. It was the middle of the night, because you cannot find a troll treasure by the light of day. Nor may you utter one word while you are searching for it.

> They dug under Stuppul and after a while they heard a sound of iron struck. There appeared to be a container there. One of the men bent down to grab ahold of the container but it was very heavy and he hurt his fingers. The pain was so great he cried out: "Ah!"

> The word had been spoken. Instantly the container vanished and from the hole cold water gushed out, streaming down Sveahill. The young man was transfixed, forgetting the pain in his fingers. Then a little old man jumped out from behind Stuppul, and laughed. The treasure hunters lost their courage and ran.

> From that day to this no one has dared to dig for gold under Stuppul and ever since then, from the hole under the tree, the water has flowed, producing the little stream we can see for ourselves coming down Sveahill.

And still the undergrounders guard the treasure under Stuppul.

Guarding their treasures from human predators, these undergrounders cannot be said to be evil. Elves, on the other hand, are often said to be malicious or even downright evil and thereby come closer (if not close enough) to being classified as minor devils and demons.

Their name suggests that elves may come from the *white* mists, perhaps from the Alps. They are active in the folklore of all European countries. In Scandinavia they are said to give the sheep *alved* (elves' fire) and humans such diseases as *elveblest* (caused by an elf breathing on you). You may say allergies; the Norwegians say elves. In The Faroes if you get a sudden twinge you are said to have been shot with an elf's arrow (*alvaskot*). When the tryranny of Harold *Haarfager* drove some Norwegians into exile in Iceland (A.D. 874), they took with them the doorposts of their homes, on which they had carved representations of elves for protection, and they brought to Iceland the ancient custom of the *alf-blot* (sacrifice to the elf) which Christianity was unable to eradicate (though in later times it might be disguised as dedicated to some saint).

Beaming down to earth on moonbeams, the elves, like fairies, dance by moonlight in circles. Don't step inside one of the circles, say the Scandinavians, or you will die. In the old poem of *Master Olof at the Elves' Dance* (in our translation):

Master Olof rode out at the dawn of the day
And came where the elf-folk were dancing at play.
The dance is so merry, so merry in the greenwood.

And the very next morning ere daylight was red
In the house of our Olof were three people dead.
The dance is so merry, so merry in the greenwood.

Master Olof himself and his lovely young bride
And Master Olof's old mother (from sorrow she died).
The dance is so merry, so merry in the greenwood.

In contrast, in British folklore stepping inside a fairy circle is said to give one power. The elves and fairies of British folklore are usually benign; the dwarfs tend to be ill-tempered and vengeful. Even in Iceland, where dwarfs are no longer part of the folklore, you can see by such place-names as *Dvergastein* and *Dvergol* that they were once prominent in the folk imagination.

Dwarfs and gnomes and other creatures were supposed to live underground. In The Faroes and The Orkneys and Denmark and many other places they are said to be common in stones, in mountains, under the earth. Hadding (a mythic king of Denmark) and the historical Gorm the Old (who founded the royal house of Denmark, still reigning after a thousand years) were both said to have visited underground kingdoms. Saxo Grammaticus says that Gorm the Old met a woman who, in depth of winter, was carrying a green branch in her hand. She led him to the winterless underground region where heroes fought and loved and feasted, but to eat or drink or love there meant one could never return to the surface of the earth and was doomed to being enthralled.

One way to recover someone lost to the undergrounders, they say in Sweden, is to ring the church bells. The undergrounders hate the sound and will release their captive to stop it. German undergrounders may help in the mines, take time out to help you cobble shoes, or perform other useful tasks, but evil dwarfs are also common in German folklore. Dwarfs, like Rumplestiltskin, are likely to demand full payment for services rendered and to be extremely angry when foiled. They may be devilish, but they are really not devils—unless you believe the story in Giraldus Cambrensis that they are like elves and fairies "angels that fell with Lucifer," the worst going to hell and the rest pent up under the earth.

FAIRY TALES

Among the best known adapters of fairylore to literature are these, all of whom (oddly) would probably have thought their other writings to be more likely to last:

CHARLES PERRAULT (1628–1703), a historian now remembered only for his *Histoires ou Contes du temps passé*, which gave us "Bluebeard," "Little Red Riding Hood," "The Sleeping Beauty," and more. Badly translated from the French, his "slipper of fur" in "Cinderella" became a "glass slipper." His *Contes de ma Mere l'oye* was the source of our *Mother Goose's Tales*.

JAKOB LUDWIG KARL GRIMM (1785–1863) and WILHELM KARL GRIMM (1786–1859), famous linguists (Grimm's Law) and founders of comparative myth and folklore now remembered best for *Kinder-und Hausmarchen* (1812–1822), full of rather frightening fairy tales which may have damaged young psyches for nearly two centuries. Modern witches hate the Brothers Grimm for the bad publicity. Their fairy tales were translated into English in 1823.

THOMAS CROFTON CROKER (1798–1854), antiquary and employee of The Admiralty, was the first writer in English to regard folk tales and fairy tales as literature. His *Fairy Legends and Traditions in the South of Ireland* (1825–1828) was highly regarded by Sir Walter Scott, another lover of old stories and customs.

HANS CHRISTIAN ANDERSEN (1805–1875), arguably the best loved "gay" writer of all time, is known not for his poems and satirical sketches or boasting autobiography but for "The Emperor's New Clothes," "The Tinder Box," "The Little Mermaid" and other fairy tales. His stories were translated into English the year they first appeared in Danish, 1835.

ANDREW LANG (1844–1912), historian, anthropologist, classicist, philosopher, journalist, is probably most lovingly recalled for his fairy tale books known by the various colors of their covers: *The Yellow Fairy Book*, etc. Other British authors of fairy tales of Lang's time include John Ruskin, Charles Kingsley, Robert Louis Stevenson, Oscar Wilde, and Rudyard Kipling. These writers are all more famous for work other than fairy tales.

THE GOOD NEIGHBORS

Briggs, Katherine. *An Encyclopedia of Fairies, Hobgoblins, Brownies, Bogies, and Other Supernatural Creatures* (1976).
Evans-Wentz, W. Y. *The Fairy Faith in Celtic Countries* (1911).
Fodor, Nandor. *Between Two Worlds* (1964).
Hole, Christina. *Haunted England* (1940).
Jones, Ernest. *On the Nightmare* (1949).
Kirk, Robert. *The Secret Commonwealth of Elves, Fauns, and Fairies* (1691).
Leach, Maria and Jerome Fried (eds). *Funk & Wagnall's Standard Dictionary of Folklore, Mythology and Legend* (1979).
Underwood, Peter. *This Haunted Isle* (1984).
Whitaker, Terence. *Haunted England* (1987).
Yeats, William Butler. *Fairy and Folk Tales of the Irish Peasantry* (1888).

THE SECRET COMMONWEALTH

Sir Walter Scott, much interested in the folklore and fairy tales of olden times, published in a limited edition in 1815 a seventeenth-century manuscript left incomplete on the death of a Reverend Mr. Kirk in 1692, spirited away into the realm of Faerie, it was alleged. The work was called *The*

Secret Commonwealth of Elves, Fauns and Fairies. Kirk and many others appears to have believed implicitly in these ordinarily gentle little creatures of Celtic superstition. There was a lot of discussion of fairies, believe it or not, at the trial of Joan of Arc.

There are many traditions of fairy dancing (in a ring), fairy music, fairy glens and homes in Irish raths, good and bad fairies, enchantments and spells, demon lovers, and so on. Rue (the "herb of grace") will drive fairies off, holly attracts them. Some people say they have wings, others that they pass among humans unnoticed. They are to be treated well if you wish good from them and to be called "good neighbors" or "people of peace." The presentation of fairies in stories for children has done much to spark juvenile imagination and to make children less afraid of, more believing in, a nonthreatening world of the supernatural from which beautiful and delicate creatures come to mix in human affairs.

But at least some fairies can be threatening. Gervais of Tilbury (*fl.* 1211) in *Otia imperialie* (dedicated to the Emperor Otto IV and regarded as authoritative in its time) has a chapter on night demons called *De Lamiis et nocturnis larvis*. In it he says as fact that fairy maidens are normal in size, if unusually beautiful, and can mate with human beings but can be dangerous if made jealous, exacting fatal revenge. These *fadas* represent an unusual identification of fairies with demons of the night. Usually fairies, though they are said to live underground and be shy, are not defined as demons but rather as friendly, helpful spirits, more like the useful brownies than the sometimes naughty leprechauns of folklore.

Because our focus here is devils and demons, these generally friendly minor spirits cannot receive all the attention we might like to give them. Another book, another time. Interested readers should look at the works of Thomas Keightley, Andrew Lang, Douglas Hyde, and Katherine Briggs.

SOME NASTIES WITH OBSOLETE NAMES

Cacodemon, afrite, gin, deev, bogle, nis, urchin, dwerger, pigwidgeon, flibbertygibbet.

SOME MINOR SUPERNATURAL SPIRITS

Among these are bogeys, boggarts, buccas, bugaboos, bugberas, dobbies, goblins, kelpies, knockers, *larvæ*, *lemures*, pucks, radiant boys, revenants, trolls, and windigoes.

GENIUS LOCI

Primitive people believed each place had, as the Latin puts it, a "spirit of the place." Evil spirits are said to be especially fond of dreary and deserted places (wild heaths, barren moors, echoing chasms), places of violence (gallows, scenes of murders), and crossroads. So you can have a Fairy Glen near Blarney Castle or a Devil's Mountain. As noted elsewhere, The Devil is well represented among American place-names, for our pioneers were plain speakers: Death Valley, Last Chance, Hardscrabble, Lickskillet, Despair.

THE FAERIE QUEENES

Here are some famous fairies from European myth:

AEVAL, fairy queen of Munster (Ireland). When the men of the district were said to be failing to satisfy their women, Aeval held a fairy court. The women invited discussed the issues and decided that men needed to be more open and inventive about sex.

BANSHEES are fairies that warn of approaching death but one banshee leader in the second century is said to have arrived at Samhain (about Halloween) and taken Fingin MacLuchta, King of Munster, to see the fairies' hoard of treasure.

NOS BONNES MÈRES (Our Good Mothers) are the fairies on the east coast of Brittany.

THE CORRIGAN are said to be Druids who were turned into fairies and swap fairy children for human ones. Many people believed in changelings until fairly recently. We still speak of a "bad seed."

MELUSINE was the daughter of a water goddess (Pressina) who turned Melusine into a serpent for attacking her father. Melusine is shown with a serpent's tail on the gingerbread cakes stamped with her image still sold by the bakers of cakes for the May Fair held near Lusignan (near Poitiers, France).

FAIRY FOLK AND THE LITTLE PEOPLE

The malevolent spirits in Ireland are more or less limited to the pre-Christian survivals rather than to Christian heresies. Prominent in Irish folklore are the fairies, some of whom are said to have married humans and some of whom are reported as being much smaller. Also smaller were the leprechauns or "little people," who may in fact enshrine memories of the earliest inhabitants encountered by Iron Age people. These small and secretive people are said to live in remote places, in caves or underground. They are traditionally supposed to be afraid of iron in any form. Like trolls in Scandinavia, they can be mollified by gifts and occasionally, if unreliably, they can be recruited to help humans.

FATA MORGANA

This is an enchantress we know from Arthurian legend as Morgan LeFay (The Fairy). She is first mentioned in our literature in a Latin life of Merlin the magician by the chronicler Geoffrey of Monmouth (c. 1150), principal contributor of the legends of King Arthur to what became known as the Matter of Britain. However, Morgan Le Fay, sister of The Once and Future King, goes back much farther. She has some obscure connections with Celtic goddesses not of magic but of war and the sea. Her connection with fairy enchantments, much feared in the Middle Ages, gradually changed Morgan Le Fay from a beautiful and helpful woman into a personification of malevolent witchcraft. The whole story is in L. A. Paton's *Studies in the Fairy Mythology of Arthurian Romance* (1903), but the undying popularity of the Arthurian legends has guaranteed that as much has been written about her in the rest of this century as in any other century. She and Arthur and Guinevere and Lancelot and Merlin and the rest have been featured in a novel by T. H. White, a musical that added the name *Camelot* to the common vocabulary, a novel by Walker Percy, a Walt Disney film or two, and much more. While Merlin, from whom she was said to have learned her magic, remained a good magician, Morgan Le Fay became a kind of *femme fatale* and an evil magician.

GUIDES TO RESEARCH ON FAIRY TALES

Eastman, Mary H. *Index to Fairy Tales, Myths and Legends* (2nd ed. 1926, plus supplements).

Ireland, Norma O. *Index to Fairy Tales, 1949–1972 (1973,* plus supplements).

Lüthi, Max. *Once upon a Time* (trans. L. Chadeayne and P. Gottwald, 1970).

Ward, Donald (ed. and trans.). *German Legends of the Brothers Grimm* (2 vols., 1981).

THE ELF OF THE ROSE

This is one of the lesser-known stories of the great Hans Christian Andersen (1805–1875). Often he created his stories out of his own vivid imagination, but sometimes he used materials he was told in his Danish youth, and this story actually goes back at least as far as an Italian master storyteller, Giovanni Boccaccio, who died exactly five hundred years before Andersen did. Boccaccio also furnished materials for Chaucer and Shakespeare, Dryden and Keats, Tennyson and Longfellow, Swinburne and "George Eliot," and many other writers.

In the midst of a garden grew a rose-tree, in full blossom, and in the prettiest of all the roses lived an elf. He was such a little wee thing, that no human eye could see him. Behind each leaf of the rose he had a sleeping chamber. He was as well formed and as beautiful as a little child could be, and had wings that reached from his shoulders to his feet. Oh, what sweet fragrance there was in his chambers! and how clean and beautiful were the walls! for they were the blushing leaves of the rose.

During the whole day he enjoyed himself in the warm sunshine, flew from flower to flower, and danced on the wings of the flying butterflies. Then he took it into his head to measure how many steps he would have to go through the roads and cross-roads that are on the leaf of a linden-tree. What we call the veins of a leaf, he took for roads; ay, and very long roads they were for him; for before he had half finished his task, the sun went down: he had commenced his work too late. It became very cold, the dew fell, and the wind blew; so he thought the best thing he could do would be to return home. He hurried himself as much as he could; but he found the roses all closed up, and he could not get in; not a single rose stood open. The poor little elf was very much frightened. He had never before been out at night, but had always slumbered secretly behind the warm rose-leaves. Oh, this would certainly be his death. At the other end of the garden, he knew there was an arbor, overgrown with beautiful honey-suckles. The blossoms looked like large painted horns; and he thought to himself, he would go and sleep in one of these till the morning. He flew thither; but "hush!" two people were in the arbor,—a handsome young man and a beautiful lady. They sat side by side, and wished that they might never be obliged to part. They loved each other much more than the best child can love its father and mother.

"But we must part," said the young man; "your brother does not like our engagement, and therefore he sends me so far away on business, over mountains and seas. Farewell, my sweet bride; for so you are to me."

And then they kissed each other, and the girl wept, and gave him a rose; but before she did so, she pressed a kiss upon it so fervently that the flower opened. Then the little elf flew in, and leaned his head on the delicate, fragrant walls. Here he could plainly hear them say, "Farewell, farewell;" and he felt that the rose had been placed on the young man's breast. Oh, how his heart did beat! The little elf could not go to sleep, it thumped so loudly. The young man took it out as he walked through the dark wood alone, and kissed the flower so often and so violently, that the lit-

tle elf was almost crushed. He could feel through the leaf how hot the lips of the young man were, and the rose had opened, as if from the heat of the noonday sun.

There came another man, who looked gloomy and wicked. He was the wicked brother of the beautiful maiden. He drew out a sharp knife, and while the other was kissing the rose, the wicked man stabbed him to death; then he cut off his head, and buried it with the body in the soft earth under the linden-tree.

"Now he is gone, and will soon be forgotten," thought the wicked brother, "he will never come back again. He was going on a long journey over mountains and seas; it is easy for a man to lose his life in such a journey. My sister will suppose he is dead; for he cannot come back, and she will not dare to question me about him."

Then he scattered the dry leaves over the light earth with his foot, and went home through the darkness; but he went not alone, as he thought—the little elf accompanied him. He sat in a dry rolled-up linden-leaf, which had fallen from the tree on to the wicked man's head, as he was digging the grave. The hat was on the head now, which made it very dark, and the little elf shuddered with fright and indignation at the wicked deed.

It was the dawn of morning before the wicked man reached home; he took off his hat, and went into his sister's room. There lay the beautiful, blooming girl, dreaming of him whom she loved so, and who was now, she supposed, travelling far away over mountain and sea. Her wicked brother stooped over her, and laughed hideously, as fiends only can laugh. The dry leaf fell out of his hair upon the counterpane; but he did not notice it, and went to get a little sleep during the early morning hours. But the elf slipped out of the withered leaf, placed himself by the ear of the sleeping girl, and told her, as in a dream, of the horrid murder; described the place where her brother had slain her lover, and buried his body; and told her of the linden-tree, in full blossom, that stood close by.

"That you may not think this is only a dream that I have told you," he said, "you will find on your bed a withered leaf."

Then she awoke, and found it there. Oh, what bitter tears she shed! and she could not open her heart to any one for relief.

The window stood open the whole day, and the little elf could easily have reached the roses, or any of the flowers; but he could not find it in his heart to leave one so afflicted. In the window stood a bush bearing monthly roses. He seated himself in one of the flowers, and gazed on the poor girl. Her brother often came into the room, and would be quite cheerful, in spite of his base conduct; so she dare not say a word to him of her heart's grief.

As soon as night came on, she slipped out of the house, and went into the wood, to the spot where the linden-tree stood; and after removing the leaves from the earth, she turned it up, and there found him who had been murdered. Oh, how she wept and prayed that she also might die! Gladly would she have taken the body home with her; but that was impossible; so she took up the poor head with the closed eyes, kissed the cold lips, and shook the mould out of the beautiful hair.

"I will keep this," said she; and as soon as she had covered the body again with the earth and leaves, she took the head and a little sprig of jasmine that bloomed in the wood, near the spot where he was buried, and carried them home with her. As soon as she was in her room, she took the largest flower-pot she could find, and in this she placed the head of the dead man, covered it up with earth, and planted the twig of jasmine in it.

"Farewell, farewell," whispered the little elf. He could not any longer endure to witness all this agony of grief; he therefore flew away to his own rose in the garden. But the rose was faded; only a few dry leaves still clung to the green hedge behind it.

"Alas! how soon all that good and beautiful passes away," sighed the elf.

After a while he found another rose, which became his home, for among its delicate fragrant leaves he could dwell in safety. Every morning he flew to the window of the poor girl, and always found her weeping by the flower-pot. The bitter tears fell upon the jasmine twig, and each day, as she became paler and paler, the sprig appeared to grow greener and fresher. One shoot after another sprouted forth, and little white buds blossomed, which the poor girl fondly kissed. But her wicked brother scolded her, and asked her if she was going mad. He could not imagine why she was weeping over that flower-pot, and it annoyed him. He did not know whose closed eyes were there, nor what red lips were fading beneath the earth.

And one day she sat and leaned her head against the flower-pot, and the little elf of the rose found her asleep. Then he seated himself by her ear, talked to her of that evening in the arbor, of the sweet perfume of the rose, and the loves of elves. Sweetly she dreamed, and while she dreamt, her life passed away calmly and gently, and her spirit was with him whom she loved, in heaven. And the jasmine opened its large white bells, and spread forth its sweet fragrance; it had no other way of showing its grief for the dead. But the wicked brother considered the beautiful blooming plant as his own property, left to him by his sister, and he placed it in his sleeping room, close by his bed, for it was very lonely in appearance, and the fragrance sweet and delightful.

The little elf of the rose followed it, and flew from flower to flower, telling each little spirit that dwelt in them the story of the murdered young man, whose head now formed part of the earth beneath them, and of the wicked brother and the poor sister. "We know it," said each little spirit in the flowers, "we know it, for have we not sprung from the eyes and lips of the murdered one. We know it, we know it," and the flowers nodded with their heads in a peculiar manner. The elf of the rose could not understand how they could rest so quietly in the matter, so he flew to the bees, who were gathering honey, and told them of the wicked brother. And the bees told it to their queen, who commanded that the next morning they should go and kill the murderer.

But during the night, the first after the sister's death, while the brother was sleeping in his bed, close to where he had placed the fragrant jasmine, every flower cup opened, and invisibly the little spirits stole out, armed with poisonous spears. They placed themselves by the ear of the sleeper, told him dreadful dreams and then flew across his lips, and pricked his tongue with their poisoned spears. "Now have we revenged the dead," said they, and flew back into the white bells of the jasmine flowers. When the morning came, and as soon as the window was opened, the rose elf, with the queen bee, and the whole swarm of bees, rushed in to kill him. But he was already dead. People were standing round the bed, and saying that the scent of the jasmine had killed him.

Then the elf of the rose understood the revenge of the flowers, and explained it to the queen bee, and she, with the whole swarm, buzzed about the flower-pot. The bees could not be driven away. Then a man took it up to remove it, and one of the bees stung him in the hand, so that he let the flower-pot fall, and it was broken to pieces. Then every one saw the whitened skull, and they knew the dead man in the bed was a murderer. And the queen bee hummed in the air, and sang of the revenge of the flowers, and of the elf of the rose, and said that behind the smallest leaf dwells One, who can discover evil deeds, and punish them also.

GREMLINS

These caused unaccountable problems for RAF pilots; they bolloxed up flying in World War II. They were still around when I was a Flying Officer (flying a desk) in the RCAF in the fifties. Douglas Marshall and F.V.R. Royce, authors of *Griff on the Gremlins* (1943), wrote:

When one lives perpetually on the edge of distinctly unpleasant finality there must be *something* to combat any insidious effects, and hence the Gremlins. Blame 'em for every confounded thing that goes off the rails, extract every once of humour from their hypothetical adventures, cling to the myth for all you are worth.

These pesky creatures can be compared and contrasted with devils and demons, on whom much also has been blamed.

HARLEQUIN

This colorful figure is familiar from the *commedia dell'arte* and pantomime but, if you look closely at his traditional costume, you may see some hint that he was once Hellquin and led a Wild Hunt of fellow demons. The Norse superstition went from Norway to Normandy to Britain and in time we had The Devil and his Dandy Dogs or damned souls rushing through the skies. He devolved also into a demon form of King Herla (in Walter Map's chronicle), into Samuel Harsnett's demon Hellwain (in a book Shakespeare knew and quoted), and into Herne the Hunter, whom Shakespeare talks of haunting Windsor Forest (in *The Merry Wives of Windsor*). His antics onstage often remind us of the vice of medieval drama.

ELVES AND THE LIKE

The Devil is not a big part of the belief systems of the Far North or Europe. He represents one Christian concept that never quite caught on fully. In most places, except perhaps for Denmark (closest to German superstitions), The Devil is a Scandinavian joke. When he occurs in folk literature it is usually as a fool.

But the farther north one goes, the more one hears about little people. "Paul Christian" says in *The History and Practice of Magic* that there "the belief in elves and the like increases and spreads." His editors suggest that Christian's book needs to be supplemented by Thomas Keightley's *Fairy Mythology*, the Grimms' *Teutonic Mythology*, and Craigie's *Scandinavian Folk-lore*, but Christian writes of elves:

The Norwegians imagine them as little naked men with blue skins who take up their abode underneath the hills, trees and houses. They sometimes attack a poor peasant and lead him miles out of his way, so far indeed that he never comes back. Nevertheless some of their victims have been seen again who, during their long absence, have lost their reason and cannot give any information about the mysterious creature who had led them astray. When an elf had taken possession of a tree or a house, woe betide anyone who would try to uproot or destroy it to plant or build something else in its place. They have been seen, it is said, to carry for considerable distances churches whose neighbourhood they felt to be unsuitable. Icelanders accuse them of sometimes stealing new-born children who have not yet been baptised and of putting one of their own in its place; but mothers and nurses take every precaution and these accidents are very rare. This type of elemental inhabits rocks, hills and often brooks, rivers and sea. It is said that their sisters and daughters who, in spite of their azure complexion, are of an enchanting loveliness, sometimes prefer the inhabitants of earth to their subterranean lovers. Tales are told of Icelandic families who owe their origin to this mysterious kind of union. They are believed to have no soul, or at least no immortal soul; but, as the children born of an elf and a man share the natures of both father and mother, they only have to be baptised by total immersion in holy water to obtain an immortal soul. Certain traditions speak of these marriages as examples of enduring affection; but it appears that however happy they may be at first these unions always have a tragic end.

Elves are invisible and only very rarely reveal themselves to the eye of man. Nevertheless, they can sometimes be seen gambolling in rays of sunshine, enjoying the gentle heat which they lack in their subterranean dwellings. They also like to walk the earth and especially to gather at crossroads [always much haunted places in early beliefs] during the first night of the New Year. At this period magicians walk abroad in the countryside, wait to see the genies go by and, by pronouncing certain magic words, compel them to reveal the future. Icelanders advise their children and their servants never to do anything which might offend these invisible hosts who might at any time visit their homes. Others, even more solicitous, open doors and windows, serve a meal of milk and fruit and leave a lamp lit on the table all night in order to show their sympathy towards any elves who may happen to pass that way.

In the Faroe Isles the elves, who otherwise resemble those of Iceland, wear a grey costume and a black hat. Their invisible herds pasture with those of the inhabitants; but sometimes the shepherds glimpse the shadowy image of a heifer or a dog that does not belong to our world and they consider this vision as a sign of the protection afforded them by the elves.

In Sweden these spirits are famed for their dancing and melodious singing. Often they gather in hollowed rocks, and, when the air is clear and the night still, they sing in soft and plaintive voices. If ever a traveller in the darkness accidentally breaks into one of the circles formed by these singers they disappear from sight, and his fate is then in their hands. But they never abuse their power when they have not been deliberately offended; at the very most they will play some harmless but mischievous trick on the innocent travellers.

The Island of Zeeland possesses elves who are much more formidable. They are the most mischievous and malicious sprites in all the north. The peasants have a magic tune which they call the Elf King's Air and which they are very careful never to play or sing. For scarcely have the first notes begun than all present, young or old, men, women and children and even inanimate objects, spring up and dance and dance without being able to stop, unless the imprudent musician is able to play the air backwards without a single false note, or unless a chance stranger comes in and cuts the violin strings.

The Scots see in their fairies, known by various names, dangerous enemies who poison the air of the place where they foregather to enjoy their nocturnal dances. The grass there withers at once and any imprudent passer-by who walks on this grass is seized by an irresistible drowsiness which ends in death. This grass is known as "fairy" or "quaking" grass; in England it is "briza" or "dawdle" grass. It grows up when fragments have not been left after a meal for the fairies. At the summit of Minchmuir passers-by must not fail to leave a "wad" or gift of cheese, the favourite food of the elves. Elves are particularly fond of tormenting horses; often in the early morning when one enters the stable these animals are found exhausted and panting, with bloodshot eyes and bristling mane;

obviously during the night they have been ridden almost to death by the elves of the neighborhood. In the cellars especially of rich people, bottles lie scattered, some empty, others filled with a liquid which is no longer wine. But the elves' chief passion is for hunting. One dark night a young sailor was journeying home in the Isle of Man. Suddenly he heard the sound of horses' hooves, voices, horns, barkings. Intrigued, he began to follow them in spite of himself. After running several leagues he at last leaped from the top of a high rock into a bog hidden in the darkness, in which he perished.

This supernatural luring to death is one of the commonest of themes in folk-tales everywhere in the west. The *Ellylldan*, or "luring elf-fires", inhabit caves and precipices. They have the habit of seizing passers-by and forcing them to choose between a voyage above the air or one on earth. If the wretch's choice is the former, he is wafted up into the clouds, whence he is allowed to fall without warning and dash himself to pieces. If he choose the latter, he is at once dragged over stones, rocks, thorns, marshes and cliffs, and perishes no less horribly. If his terror has prevented his making a choice and he remains silent, the *Ellylldan* merely spin him round and round until he is out of breath. Some of them live on farms. After having worked all day, when night falls and all is at rest they sit down by the fire, pull frogs out of their pockets, roast them and eat them. They look like old wrinkled men; they are never more than a foot tall and their garments are very poor. It is their nature to be helpful and not to do much harm; but sometimes they take pleasure in mischievous pranks. For example if a horseman loses his way in a mist, often an *Ellylldan* will climb up beside him on the saddle, seize the reins and lead the animal into a bog, then run away shrieking with merriment.[1]

Those spirits which are called in England elves are called *Duergar, Nokke, Droich, Kobbolds* and *Nixies* by the peoples of the extreme north of Europe. According to the customs of the country they inhabit, each species has different tastes, which nevertheless are very similar when compared, and this seems to prove sufficiently their common origin. The spirits generally inhabit solitary places where men can rarely venture. In Denmark, where they are called

---

[1] Compare, however, Wirt Sykes' *British Goblins* p. 18 seq., where the description differs from the foregoing considerably.—Ed. [The editor of "Paul Christian's" *The History and Practice of Magic* in 2 volumes was Ross Nichols, 1963.] See also Karen Louise Jolly's *Popular Religion in Late Saxon England: Elf Charms in Context* (1995).

Nokke, they live in the forests and the streams. They are great musicians, and are to be seen sitting in the middle of rivers playing on a golden harp which has the power to influence all nature. If one wishes to study music with them one must first of all seek an introduction to one of them with a black lamb and promise him that at the Last Judgment God will judge him like other men. It is said that once two children were playing in front of their father's house which stood beside a small stream, when a *Nokke* rose out of the water and began to play on his golden harp. "Dear Nokke," said one of the children to him, "what is the good of your beautiful music? You will never go to heaven!" At these words the *Nokke* burst into tears.

The children went into the house and told their parents what they had seen. The father was angry at the children for having behaved so badly and told them to go back to the stream and comfort the *Nokke*. The children did as they were told, they found him sitting in the same place, still weeping. "Dear *Nokke*," they said to him, "stop weeping, please, because our father has told us that you will have a place in heaven." Immediately the *Nokke* took up his golden harp again and played wonderful music for the rest of the day.

TOMTEN

A Famous Norwegian Poem about the *tomten* at Christmas, by Victor Rydberg:

> Midwinter's night is cold and hard,
> The stars twinkle and glimmer.
> Everyone on the lonesome farm is asleep,
> Fast asleep at the midnight hour.
> The moon wanders his silent way,
> The snow gleams on pine and spruce,
> The snow glistens white on the rooftops.
> Only the *tomten* is awake.
>
> He stands there so gray at the barn door,
> Gray against the pile of snow,
> Watching just as in previous winters,
> Looking up at the moon,

Watching the wood where firs and pines
Draw around the farm its shadowy rampart,
Philosophizing, though it doesn't help,
About a strange enigma.

He runs his hand through his beard and hair,
Shakes his head and its little hood,
"No, this mystery is too strange,
No, I cannot figure this out."
He chases away, as usual, after a while
These troublesome thoughts,
Goes back to his work and his arrangements,
Goes back to do his duties.

Translated by Ola J. Holten and Leonard R.N. Ashley

ELVES AND DWARFS

In the flesh of the Scandinavian personage Ymir maggots bred, and the gods in their wisdom decided to give these creatures superhuman intelligence. Thus came the fair and useful fairies and elves (who dwelt in *Alfheim*, Land of the Elves) and the malicious, black and treacherous dwarfs (whose abode was *Svart-alfa-heim*, The Black Elf Land). The fairies and elves were creatures of the air. The dwarfs (and also gnomes, trolls, kobolds and such) lived underground. Human beings were given *Midgard* or *Mann-heim* to live in. The first two humans came from blocks of wood or logs, one ash and one elm, and Odin gave them souls and life and thought and speech and endowed them with the power to love and hope and work. He also endowed them with life and death. In life they were going to have the help of the fairies and elves and the enmity of the undergrounders, the devils and demons of a minor sort in this mythology.

Elves were thought to be more malignant than pixies, but there were Light Elves (good) as well as Dark Elves (evil). Names such as *Alfred, Alvin, Avery, Auberon, Aubrey, Elfrida*, and so on, all come from the once-common belief in these small spirits.

BISHOP THOMAS PERCY ON DWARFS

The collector of the *Reliques of English Poetry* writes that "it is well known that our Saxon ancestors, long before they left their German forests, believed the existence of a kind of diminutive demons, or middle species between men and spirits, whom they called *Duergar* or dwarfs, and to whom they attributed many wonderful performances far exceeding human art."

Knowing, perhaps personifying, the powers and riches under the earth, the dwarfs were supernatural and yet resembled human beings, like fairies. They were said to be able to clap on their little red caps of invisibility and vanish on the instant and to hoard great wealth underground. If you could get hold of one before it could disappear, a dwarf would pay a huge ransom in gold, silver, or gems for its freedom. If you made an enemy of a dwarf, you were in for great trouble; they were very vengeful creatures. If their name is to be traced back to the Sanskrit *dhvaras*, they are deceitful and demoniacal.

METALLIC IMPS

The metals cobalt and nickel are named for little demons the Germans said inhabited the mines. Paracelsus said there were sylphs in the air, nymphs in the water, salamanders in fire, and *pygmæ* or gnomes in the earth, the four elements of Galen being inhabited by four kinds of spirits.

PIXIES

These are pucksy, pesky little piskies or pixies that bedevil people and make them pixilated. They dance by moonlight in fairy circles of the West of Britain, especially in Cornwall and other places where the Druids (whose ghosts they are sometimes said to be) were active in the days when huge stones were erected—not to be disturbed today without peril, it is believed—for religious purposes of some sort.

Gillian Edwards in *Hobgoblin and Sweet Puck* (1974), a study of "fairy names and natures," a book which contrives to make etymology fascinating, writes that

the pixies are on the whole confined to the one remaining Celtic part of England, Cornwall and Devon, [and] J. A. MacCulloch in the *Encyclopedia of Religion* has an interesting suggestion. 'The Celts of Gaul,' he says, 'worshiped Niksas and Peisgi, groups of water divinities, some of whom have personal names, and these are the nixies and perhaps the piskies of later belief.' But he offers no supporting evidence and the nixies, water spirits or elves, belong to German and Scandinavian [*nisse, pyske*] rather than Celtic folk-lore. They reached parts of Scotland, but never established themselves here [in England].

In spite of this Sir Walter Scott asserted that pixies as well as nixies were known in the Shetlands.

GOBELINUS

Oderic Vitalis wrote in the eleventh century that a goblin or demon named Gogelinus haunted the pagan temple of Diana near Evereux in France and that Saint Taurin exorcised him. However, the *goblin* (and *hobgoblin*) seem to be derived from the Greek *kobalos* (knave) and Latin *cobalus* and German *Kobbold* (from which our element cobalt, as above). Casaubon, in his *True and Faithful Relation*, writes: "But if it is so that all Sprites are either Divils or Angels, what shall we make of those that are found in mines, of which learned Agricola [Georg Bauer, a sixteenth-century German writer] hath written: of these that hath been time out of minde called *Kobaloi* (from whence probably...Gobelin in English is derived) who live in private Houses, about old Walls and stalks of Wood, harmless otherwise but very thievish."

In later writers, goblins are connected with ghouls and ghosts rather than with gnomes.

MINOR SUPERNATURAL CREATURES OF BRITAIN

Puck, Robin Goodfellow, Queen Mab, Tom Thumb, and many equally fanciful creatures who have not been given personal names, such as Kit with The Candlestick, Hop o'My Thumb, bugs, bogeymen, bull-beggars, fetches, sylens, firedrakes, pookas....

The pooka in Mary Chase's play *Harvey* is a six-foot rabbit invisible to everyone except Elwood P. Dowd, and a fine farce it makes.

Some of these creatures were considered malicious, some not. Your cattle, we have noted, could be "elf-shot." They would fall down dead and the hide would not be pierced, but near the dead cow you would find on or under the ground a small, triangular stone. It was the elf's arrowhead, of course. This was even worse than having your beasts "hag-ridden" by witches in the dead of night. To prevent this you hung up iron or stones with holes in them, "hag stones":

> Hang up Hooks, and Shears to scare
> Hence the Hag, that rides the Mare,
> Till they be all over wet
> With the mire and with the sweat.
> This observed, the Manes shall be
> Of your horses, all knot-free.

DOBBIES

With all the wicked fairies and mischievous imps and other creatures the British have to contend with, they also have some good spirits. One unknown to Americans is the dobbie. His name (like Robin Goodfellow's) comes from Robert, a name often associated with The Devil and occasionally with good spirits.

The dobbie is a family spirit who, in exchange for bowls of milk and oat cakes, provides protection and good luck to the home, but he can turn nasty (like the pixies) if he is not properly rewarded and respected. He is a sort of British version of the farm trolls of Norway and Sweden, generally a good spirit.

Unfortunately, modern Britons seem to have moved away from their dobbies, pixies, elves. "Fairies" doesn't mean what it used to. As Chaucer said, "Now can no man see none elves mo."

IDIOTIC ETYMOLOGY

The "learned" Dominican Sprenger, co-author of the *Malleus maleficarum*, when asked for the origin of the word *diabolus* suggested that it was from *dia* (two) and *bolus* (pill), indicating that The Devil could eat us up body and soul, two items, in one pill or mouthful.

INCUBI AND SUCCUBI

These are two words it is worth getting straight. That sex monsters might come at night (in dreams?) to bother both men and women is a belief that goes back well beyond the Judeo-Christian tradition. The Jews had a firm belief in monsters who visited the unwary in the night and stole semen from men, raped non-licentious women. The Christians came up with the *incubus* (stressing the weight lying on someone, a male sex fiend) and the *succubus* (that's the female form), but one demon could serve either sex if it wanted to. Basically, *incubi* attacked women and *succubi* attacked men. You can make that *succubæ* (female plural) if you like, but most people don't bother.

This was taken very seriously by the Roman Catholic Church. "It has come to our attention," wrote Innocent VIII in a papal bull of 1484, "and stricken to the heart we are to learn of it, that many persons of both sexes utterly putting their souls' salvation at risk are in the habit of having sex with evil spirits, both *incubi* and *succubi*." This seems to suggest that Catholics were welcoming these nocturnal visits rather than being the victims of pushy demons. Like angels, demons do not have bodies but can assume human form when required to appear among mankind. Why they also undertook to have real wings when wings are just a metaphor for their speed, no one has ever explained to my satisfaction. I do not believe in angels with real wings. I do not believe any human being has ever seen such a thing, whether the angel is good or bad. Nor do I see that *incubi* and *succubi* would make one feel guilty of enjoying oneself in unwarranted fashion if the *incubi* and *succubi* really came in such hideous forms as are illustrated in the old manuscripts and books.

It was church policy to admit that angels good and bad could appear to people. It was likewise church policy to encourage males not to have wet dreams and to feel guilty if they did. It may not be entirely unfair to say that the celibate church officials who made up and enforced the rules considered that women having enjoyable sex at all was greatly to be discouraged. The sex demons who appeared to women are often reported to turn out performances lasting many hours, which suggests still another way in which sex demons can make men feel inadequate. Women who were rumored to be *succubæ* are reported to have done a brisk business in Italy and Germany and elsewhere with paying customers, but essentially *incubi* and *succubæ* offered sex free.

Saint Augustine used to roll in nettles to take his mind off sex and is said to have prayed to be made pure—"but not yet." Hermits and anchorites and nuns from the earliest days of the church tried to desex themselves; they fought, perhaps not as spectacularly as Saint Anthony in the desert but certainly persistently and sincerely, against the sins of the flesh, horribly mutilating themselves, though the church frowned on self-castration in physical form. The early church fathers had no doubt sex demons terrorized the innocent and the lustful alike. Albertus Magnus (1193?–1280), the *Doctor Universalis* or medieval Mr. Know-It-All, was thought of in his time as a dangerous magician as well as a font of knowledge and a bishop (of Regensburg) of frightening efficiency, but came out wholly in support of the concept of *incubi* and *succubæ*. "We ourselves," he wrote, "know persons who have had actual experience of this," though the saint (he was later canonized) does not admit he ever had to struggle with this problem.

One consequence you don't have with *incubi* and *succubi* is pregnancy. In early theology, demons could breed with humans. They seem to have lost the knack. They are just DINKs: demonic *incubi*, no kids.

Minor devils, hobgoblins, etc., in a sixteenth-century illustration for a work by Olaus Magnus.

THE CHILDREN OF THE NIGHT

It is fashionable to make fun of the gullibility of Montague Summers, but it must be remembered that, whether his orders were in order or not, he held and boldly espoused the appropriate views for a Roman Catholic priest. Here he is on *incubi*:

> It must now be asked whether children can be born of the union of the witch [why just the witch?] and the incubus, and the general opinion of theologians and demonologists is that there have been and are such progeny. Sinistrati holds that it is undoubted by theologians and philosophers that carnal intercourse between mankind and the Demon sometimes gives birth to human beings. Thomas Malvenda, a famous Dominican writer (1566–1628), in his great work *Antichrist* [*De Antichristo: Libri undecim*] published at Rome in 1604, writes that "from a natural case, the children begotten by Incubi are tall [devils are traditionally tall], very hard and bloodily bold, arrogant beyond words, and desperately wicked." This description so exactly fits some of the prominent figures in the world today that it seems to me the real explanation of much appalling wickedness and of their infinite capacity for evil.

Neither Stalin nor Hitler was tall, nor the generals of the First World War such as Haig and Foch and Pershing. Charles De Gaulle was tall. This is foolishness.

Mere assertions that demonic spirits and humans can mate are insufficient. What proof is there? The history of theology is rife with assertions made with presumed authority for which no evidence whatever is adduced. I assume that the Roman Catholic Church no longer believes that Martin Luther was the son of a demon. I think of him as a good Catholic. He was a monk who married a nun. You can't get much more Catholic than that.

KERES

Spirits of the dead returned to plague the living, the Greeks call *keres*, but vampires are the commonest supernatural dangers of Greece.

SATURDAY'S CHILD

In Greece it is believed that people born on Saturday have special powers to see ghosts and vampires. A dubious gift.

BECOMING A VAMPIRE

If you died as a result of a vampire attack, you yourself would become "undead." You also might become a vampire if you had red hair (like Cain, like Judas Iscariot) or slept around too much. If you were a witch and slept with the Devil, your offspring would be a vampire. A vampire is a "devil"; Count Dracula in London assumes the alias of Count de Ville. To Renfield, Count Dracula gives the command to "fall down and worship me," as The Devil suggested to Christ in the desert.

THE *LOUP-GAROU* OF THE WEST INDIES

From Montague Summers, *The Vampire: His Kith and Kin:*

> The West Indian natives, and above all the black, Quashee as he is called, hold that loogaroos are human beings, especially old women, who have made a pact with the devil, by which the fiend bestows upon them certain magic powers on condition that every night they provide him with a quantity of rich warm blood. And so every night the loogaroos make their way to the occult silk-cotton-tree (*bombax ceiba*, often known as the Devil's tree or Jumbie tree), and there, having divested themselves of their skins, which are carefully folded up and concealed, in the form of a ball of sulphurous fire they speed abroad upon their horrid business. Even to-day [1928] visitors to Grenada have been called out of the house late at night by the servants to see the loogaroos, and their attention is directed to any solitary light which happens to flash through the darkness, perhaps the distant lantern of some watchman who is guarding a cocoa piece. Until dawn the loogaroos are at work, and any Quashee who feels tired and languid upon awaking will swear that the vampire has sucked his blood.

BURMESE HORROR

"Among the Karens of Burma we meet with the *Kephn*, a demon which under the form of a wizard's head and a stomach attached devours human souls."—Montague Summers, *The Vampire: His Kith and Kin.*

WEREWOLVES

In the Middle Ages various folk superstitions and theological dogmas combined to create the concept of lycanthropy: changing into wolves. The

Devil, it was said, could and did assume a werewolf shape. His demons appeared as wolves and as other were-animals on occasion, and those who lost their souls to The Devil became werewolves. In Normandy, for instance, there was considerable disagreement between those who were sure people became werewolves for three years and those who said it was seven years.

Typically, the "Rev." Montague Summers finds "support" for the were-wolf stores in the history of France. For example (*Witchcraft and Black Magic*, 1974 edition, p. 214):

> In 1521, at Poligny (Jura, Franche-Comte), three werewolf sor-
> cerers were executed, and their atrocities commemorated by pic-
> tures hung in the Dominican church to serve as a lesson and a
> solemn warning. Fifty years later the Parliament of Franche-
> Comte, appalled at the horrid increase of lycanthropy, issued spe-
> cial edicts regarding the punishment of witches who practised this
> inhuman foulness. Pierre de Lancre has left us a very full account
> of the werewolf of Bordeaux, Jean Grenier, a lad about fourteen
> years old....This wretched youth had bound himself to a demon,
> whom he worshiped as the Lord of the Forest....In 1925 there was
> a case of werewolfery at Uttenheim, near Strassburg. The lycan-
> thrope was a youth in his teens, and in some respects the history
> is not dissimilar to that of Jean Grenier....

Summers tells Jean Grenier's story at length, with many others, in his *The Werewolf* (1966).

The challenge to cinema technology to depict the transformation of the human into the werewolf was gladly accepted in Lon Chaney films, in the likes of *I Was a Teenage Werewolf*, *American Werewolf in London*, and other horror films. Predatory evil in werewolf and vampire and similar scare fare, however, seldom is stressed as coming from The Devil himself. It is treated in hospitals for the criminally insane these days.

GHOSTS

More people believe in ghosts than in God or The Devil, I suppose. Many Americans claim to have seen ghosts. Even if ghosts frighten or disturb us, they give comfortable assurance of one of mankind's most bizarre desires: what Tyrrell calls "the persistence of personality." Noël Taillepied has a full *Treatise of Ghosts*, which Montague Summers translated (1958).

Ghosts are sometimes devils and demons in disguise but even human ghosts can be particularly obnoxious if they have been:

Ulrich Molitor was the first to publish a picture of witches in flight on the way to the *Sabbat*.

unmarried
snuffed out in childbirth
left unburied
murdered
forgotten

Confronted with a ghost or a demon apparition, dispel it by asking it, "What do you want?" Occasionally the apparition will speak to inform you of some treasure that it buried that has been forgotten or some deed it needs accomplished and left undone. Generally it will vanish and never been seen again. A real ghost creates a cold atmosphere when it appears. Unless the temperature drops precipitously, you may be imagining things.

I have never quite figured out how characters such an Anne Boleyn can be said to haunt a number of places, not just one. She probably holds the record for the most places haunted. Another puzzler is Fulke Greville, Lord Brooke, said to haunt Warwick Castle. He was murdered by his valet, to whom he made the mistake of reading a will in which the valet was left nothing. However, he died and was buried elsewhere. What is he doing at Warwick Castle? Just trying to put the wind up tourist parties?

Sadly, there is no American place that can come anywhere near the convincing (to some) arguments for hauntings in Europe. Fake psychics in America (who are numerous, and egregious) may have scared most of our ghosts into retirement. Nonetheless, America boasts some haunted places.

HAUNTED HOUSES

Ghosts are not devils or demons, we presume, so we'll just note that here and pass on. No need to get into the spirits that some psychics or psychos say they have seen. In my old neighborhood in New York, for instance, there are rumors of a ghost who creates smells of fried onions or violets in a house on Gay Street. Violets sound good; a number of saints both before and after death are said to have filled rooms with the smell of violets, apparently an odor of sanctity. Fried onions, however, probably come from the neighbors. There are likewise stories—people love anything that suggests there is life after death—of Mark Twain and the ghosts of others who died after moving out of The Village but still seem to like hanging around it, and spooks even in such commercial establishments as Café Bizarre and the White Horse Tavern. Dylan Thomas died—elsewhere— after downing a record seventeen whiskies there and is said to haunt a table still. I hope not. I recall him as a repulsive drunk when alive there, and I don't think he will have been improved by death, though it was a good career move at the time. His poetry survives; the best of him.

The house I live in now, my psychic friends say, has lots of "energy" on the top floor. I am aware of no ghostly inhabitants. If I run into one, however, I know that to do. Do you?

A PRAYER FOR PROTECTION

From John Day (1574–1640?) quoted in *Hobgoblin and Sweet Puck*:

> Graunt that no Hobgoblins fright me,
> No hungry devils rise up and bite me;
> No Urchins, Elves or drunkards Ghoasts
> Shove me against walles or postes.
> O graunt that I may no black thing touch,
> Though many men love to meete such.

The Cauld Lad of Hilton

De lanijs et phitonicis mu-
licribus ad illustrissimum principem dominū Sigismūdum
archiducem austrie tractatus pulcherrimus

Familiars in the foreground, obscene familiarities in the background (the kissing of The Devil's rear) at the *Sabbat*.

7

Satanism in the Modern World

THE SATANIC PANIC

This study of how evil has been personified and even idolized over the centuries ends with a brief notice of its most dramatic, though probably not most significant, expression in the world today, Satanism.

Devil-worship is more a feature of primitive societies than the advanced societies such as our own. The prevalence of witches and devil-worshipers in the stranger parts of the world will be a feature of another book, *The Complete Book of the Devil's Disciples*, one that touches on the milestones of the history of witchcraft worldwide. That is too much to fit in here. Here we examine, for the most part, Satanism or alleged Satanism in modern America.

SATANISM ON THE CAMPUS

Bob Larson (*Satanism...*, 1989) and others, both in Christian ministries and educational administration, have noted that college undergraduates have moved from playing *Dungeons and Dragons* in some cases to dabbling in Satanism as well as getting involved in Hare Krishna, Scientology, "the Moonies," and other groups denounced as cults. An International Cult Education Program (Box 1232, Gracie Station, New York, New York 10028) offers publications, tapes, and more to students about how to "Say NO under Pressure." Marcia R. Rudin has edited an anthology including Satanic recruitment on campus, why college students are so vulnerable, and what counselors and clergy can do for students and their families. It is *Cults on Campus: Continuing Challenge* (1991). As a result of college student interest, it may not be too much to say that some sort of Satanic cult activity is more prevalent in the United States today than it has ever been before in our history. What the jargon calls "cult-impacted students" are badly in need of the advice of experts and educational resource organizations.

FOCUS ON SATANIC CRIME

As this book goes to press, a series of ten volumes to be edited by Alan H. Peterson is in the planning stage at American Focus Publications (USC-CCN International, Box 1185, Edison, New Jersey 08818). The prospective publishers, seeing the market (and splitting the infinitive) announce they are ready "to effectively address the grim reality of increasing crim-

OPHIEL

inal satanic and occult activity worldwide" with volumes on: (1) "the belief and the awareness of satanic and occult involvement and crime," (2) research on "witchcraft, satanism, santeria, ritual crime, demonic possession, cults and gangs," (3) "a startling and provocative look into the resurgence of occultism in America," (4) "numerous timely occult-related topics," (5) "secrets of the Illuminati" (which seems to be the same as Doc Marquis' book of that title from this publisher, 1994), etc. "Available and impending titles" are said to include: *Battling Satanic Elements*; *The Professional's Handbook on Occult Crimes*; *Teen Satanism*; *Hell Ranch*; *Occult Crime: Detection, Investigation and Verification*; and *Occult Crime Control: Investigation, Analysis and Prevention*. I have not been able to see any of these.

Satanic labels have often been put by the more irresponsible elements of the press on crimes ranging from teenage vandalism to serial murder. A 1995 film, *Copycat*, featured a neurotic serial killer expert who assured us that thirty-five serial killers are on the loose and active at all times these days right here in America. There is, of course, some actual attempt at Satanism, but I should think very little. Mostly, it is just adolescent rebellion and experimentation. The temptation to add the word *Satanism* is difficult to resist in a jaded world where even child abuse (perhaps the most common crime in the United States) has suffered inflation and is now often "Satanic abuse."

It is hard to be more victimized than other victims in our victim competitions. To be a dupe of Satanism trumps being drawn into Dianetics.

Also, there's a cult of Cult-Worry. *Halloween and Satanism, Demons in the Church, Selling Satan, The Darkness among Us, Satan's Underground, Out of Darkness, Breaking the Circle of Satanic Ritual Abuse,* and *Sexuality, Magic and Perversion* and many other pop books attest to that.

I understand that average American's horror at Satanists who are found to be bringing up their tots in that evil religion, but I am not at all happy either with children who have no choice in the matter being "brainwashed" by parents who are members of perfectly respectable religions. A toddler in a *yamulka* with curls at his temples makes me uneasy, too. Parents inevitably will, whatever you say, firmly hold to the belief that it is their right and their duty to bring up their children in the religion in which their own parents brought them up. Satanists will do this as well.

Where society's best interests and personal and religious freedoms intersect here is a matter for serious discussion. If Satanism can qualify as a religion—and I would hope it could not—then Satanists, like Jews, Catholics, Protestants, Mormons, Christian Scientists, Unitarians, followers of Islam or The Nation of Islam or whatever religious denomination (or cult) you choose to mention, can practice that religion and "recruit" and bring up their children in it. Always provided that no criminal laws are broken. If laws are broken, then we are talking about criminality, not cult activity. Blasphemy, though, is not a crime in the United States as it is in some other places (as Mr. Rushdie discovered). I hope it never becomes one in America. Will they censor blasphemy on the Internet?

Such Satanism as is practiced comes to public attention when its alleged victims, not its alleged practitioners, "out" it, usually with the idea of collecting damages as a result of court trials, not witchcraft trials. Psychics in the United States are more active in looking for criminals and missing persons than devils and demons. If they can fight crime, good.

No American has come along who has gained as much attention for prophecy as the long dead Frenchman Nostradamus, whose works continue to be published over and over in the United States, printed, out of print, and reissued with unflagging determination. No other American has quite surpassed the career of Edgar Cayce, even though his ramblings on The Lost Atlantis put him in the minds of many beyond the paie of respectability. Louise Huebner, who contrived on a slow news day to turn homemade astrology and a joke into the title of "Official Witch of Los Angeles County," did claim her cat Othello was a familiar, but was careful not to arouse officialdom by declaring she was dealing with devils and demons. For all I know, that might get you into jail in California, where a number of other outrages these days apparently will not.

If you or someone you know in the United States is actually dealing with devils and demons and is ready for scholarly inquiry and perhaps psychiatric and legal investigations as well, I'd like to hear from you. The so-called witches that call in when I "appear" on radio shows or drop in on TV shows have never confessed to drinking the blood of babes and raising The Devil. Not to me. Mostly I run into confused individuals who confuse astrology with science or coincidence with magical powers and who are not even sure they have a soul to sell to The Evil One or what they would take for it.

THE FIRST CHURCH OF SATAN

I was never sure whether LaVey (as in Sandor LaVey of San Francisco) was "Lévi" spelled sideways, but he was the one, in any case who reminded us all that "Evil is Live spelled backwards." It was Sandor LaVey who, when everyone else in San Francisco was trying to grab a little attention, found

BETHOR

that owning a pet lion was not enough. He announced that he was the High Priest of The First Church of Satan. This went well beyond the wild camp or his friend Kenneth Anger or the leather outfits of Monique van Cleef, who had once operated a sadist brothel in Newark.

LaVey published a *Satanic Bible* but he has not got in touch with devils and demons and probably doesn't want to. Real Satanists sacrifice human beings. His group spanks them. They seem to like it.

The Church of Satan run by LaVey in San Francisco lost some of its Satanic memorabilia when his common-law wife of many years sued in 1991 for half his possessions. I believe his church is a dead issue, or perhaps it has just lost its PR powers.

The law also presumably protects Satanic churches to some extent. In San Francisco, Lillian Rosoff accused Michael Aquino of harassing her after she left his Satanic congregation. He said she was never a member. The case was settled out of court in September 1994 and the terms of the settlement were not published. Nor were Ms. Rosoff's reasons for being in the congregation (if she ever was) in the first place.

Atlanta (GA) boasts a High Priestess—she calls herself Lady Sintana—but it is not reported whether she runs a church, a coven, or a *Kaffeeklatch*. Michigan's Upper Peninsula has a self-appointed young witch called Lisa. She is no more likely to be involved in a Satanic Church than are Christa

Heiden Landon was (or is) on Chicago's North Side and *wicca* followers in New York, Los Angeles, London, or Johannesburg, etc. The afore-mentioned Louis Huebler of Los Angeles gave all United States' witches a bad name by her silliness.

There will inevitably be some few persons who resemble the Cainites of old, who said that Cain was a hero, all pertaining to the Bible and the Bible's God was to be rejected, and The Adversary, not God, is to be rec-ognized and served. There will also be sociopaths eager to break all rules and be contrarian in everything. But it is highly unlikely that any Cainite-like religion or serious Satanic cult can be established in our society. In the United States, more than 90 percent of people believe in God, though only half that number attend religious services regularly.

TEN 1993 REFERENCES IN THE PERIODICALS TO SATANISM

B. Siano, "All the Babies You Can Eat," *The Humanist* 53 (March/April 1993), 40-41.

T. C. Morgan, "Bob [Larson] on the Block," *Christianity Today* 37 (17 May 1993), 74-75.

L. Wright, "Remembering Satan" [P. Ingram case, Olympia WA], *The New Yorker* 69, 17 May 1993 (60+) and 24 May 1993 (54+).

R. D. Perrin and L. Parrot, "Memories of Satanic Ritual Abuse," *Chris-tianity Today* 37 (June 1993), 18-23.

L. Bennetts, "Nightmares on Main Street," *Vanity Fair* 56 (June 1993), 42+.

E. Karlsberg, "Satanism: The Scary Truth," *Teen* 37 (June 1993), 24+.

P. Lambert, "Rites of Murder" [Misskelley, Echols and Baldwin case, West Memphis AK] *People* 39 (21 June 1993), 43-44.

S. O. Davis, "Sympathy for the Devil," *Los Angeles* 38 (July 1993), 48-55.

J. S. Victor, "Satanic Cults' Ritual Abuse of Children: Horror or Hoax?" *USA Today* 122 (November 1993), 58-60.

Wanda Draper, "Why Satanism Attracts Teenagers," *USA Today* 122 (December 1993), 14-15.

Since 1993 stories about Satanism, especially "ritual abuse" of children, have quieted down somewhat, but, as Z. Schiller in an article on Procter & Gamble's long battle against charges of Satanism says ("P & G Is Hav-ing a Devil of a Time," *Business Week*, 11 September 1995, 46), "rumors of Satanism persist." What *The Skeptical Inquirer*, which ran several arti-cles on it, called "The Satanic Panic" goes on, largely spurred by accusa-tions by children or former children, court cases (often in the South), and the need for sensational copy in sparse news periods. It is striking that Satanic practices which do not involve innocent youth are hardly noticed but "your child is in danger" or "innocence has been violated" are what the press calls hot buttons to press. Are not grownups endangered?

CULT

A "cult" appears to be any religion that is smaller than your own. Some cults, such as Hare Krishna, Scientology, and The Nation of Islam have considerable numbers of adherents and would object to the label. As for Satanic cults, their very nature means that serious ones are highly unlikely to be visible enough to gain notice in any handbook of cults in America or in the *Abingdon Dictionary of Living Religion*. Satanists lie low.

"GIRL TELLS OF SATANISM FIVE NIGHTS A WEEK"

A girl (10) from Epping Forest made the headlines when she testified in a British court in mid-November 1991 against fifty people, including her parents, alleging Satanic abuse. She said she was threatened with dire bodily harm if she spoke up, but she did so anyway. Satanic abuse cases have thrown legal experts on both sides of the Atlantic into a tizzy over the nature of admissible evidence and the testimony of children. Satanic abuse proceedings are making unusual case law in courts everywhere, and lawyers as well as others are concerned. The British have a history of children making accusations of witchcraft in the seventeenth and eighteenth centuries that frighten modern jurists.

A NOVEL ABOUT SATANIC ABUSE OF CHILDREN

Bob Larsen's novel *Dead Air* (1991) has been much debated. Is it fiction or fact, this story of Satanic abuse of a young girl?

"APPARENTLY MURDERED BY A CULT"

This comment aroused fear, and some police authorities allege may have spurred copycat killings, when Steven Baker (21), a student at the University of California, was found dead in June 1991. The extent to which cult murders or details of killings which might suggest cult murders should be reported is a matter much discussed in police and journalistic circles.

The public thrives on stories like that of the man who said he was the "Son of Sam"—Sam, his dog, was a demon who told him to kill, he says. There seems also to be a hunger for psychopaths, human heads in the refrigerator, exhumed corpses, dolls that turn homicidal, curses coming home to roost, and what *New York* 22 May 1995 called "a couple of white chicks in black pointy hats sitting around talking" about witchcraft. The public doesn't much care about the liability insurance involved in witches dancing in a public park for a World's Religions fest in Chicago in 1993, but it does thrill to human sacrifice and violent crime....

ITALY

Italy has more psychics than Satanists and they appear on television to be tested. Our *Skeptical Inquirer* reported on one such test in its Winter 1993 issue. The heart of Italian witchcraft is said to be not in Rome but in industrial Turin. There is supposed to be some energy in Turin which attracts the black magicians.

GREEK SATANIC CULT LEADERS

Two people, Asimakis Katsoulas and Manos Dimitrikalis, were sentenced in July 1995 for the ritual murder of a woman. In 1993 the book *Demons and the Devil* discussed the moral imagination in modern Greek culture but had no sensational revelations about Satanism in Greece.

TWENTY-FIVE BOOKS
ABOUT THE DEVIL AND SATANISM
IN THE MODERN WORLD

Balducci, C. *The Devil: Alive and Active in Our World* (1990).
Barton, Blanche. *The Church of Satan* (1990).
Bird, M., *The Witch's Handbook* (1984).
Blood, Linda. *The New Satanists* (1994).
Christensen, Evelyn. *Battling the Prince of Darkness* (1990).
Christiani, Leon. *Evidence of Satan in the Modern World* (1977).
Feldman, Gail C. *Lessons in Evil...Satanic Abuse and Spiritual Healing* (1993).
Freeman, Edith. *Satanic Beguilement* (1993).
Hicks, Robert D. *In Pursuit of Satan: The Police and the Occult* (1991).
Hoffman, Wendy. *Ascent from Evil: The Healing Journey out of Satanic Abuse* (1994).

Jacobs, L. *The Witch's Spell Book* (1985).
Joseph, Isya. *Devil Worship* (1972).
Larner, C. *Witchcraft and Religion* (1984).
Larson, Bob. *Satanism: The Seduction of America's Youth* (1989).
Lindsay, Hal. *Satan Is Alive and Well on Planet Earth* (1992).
Maury, Terry. *Satan in Modern America* (1989).
Newton, Michael. *Raising Hell* (1993).
Parker, John. *At the Heart of Darkness: Witchcraft, Black Magic and Satanism Today* (1993).
Richardson, James T. et al. *The Satanism Scare* (1991).
Sanders, J. Oswald. *Satan Is No Myth* (1983).
Schnoebelen, William. *Wicca: Satan's Little White Lie* (1990).
Spureon, Charles, *Satan: A Defeated Foe* (1993).
Thomas J. D. *The Omega Conspiracy...* (1990).
Unger, Merrill F. *Demons in the World Today* (1980).
Valiente, D. *An ABC of Witchcraft Past and Present* (1984).

In addition, see the catalogues of AMS and other reprint publishers, of TAN Books, Gordon Press, Whitaker House, various Christian ministries and tract publishers, etc.

SATANIC CULT PROGRAMMING AND MULTIPLE PERSONALITIES

There was a great deal of garbage following the publication of such books as *The Three Faces of Eve* and *Sybil*. Now there may be worse things happening in the field of Multiple Personality Disorder (MPD) treatment.

PHUL

Doctors are collecting millions from insurance companies for MPD cases allegedly connected with Satanic cults.

The FBI has investigated allegations of "organized Satanic conspiracies" and baby breeding for sacrifice, cannibalism, and other horrid crimes. It has officially concluded that "victims are alleging things that don't seem to have happened." It is not impossible that victims' therapists are putting these crazy ideas in the patients' minds.

On PBS, "The Search for Satan" (broadcast 24 October 1995), written by Ofra Bikel and Rachel Dretzin, told the horror stories of two women who cost insurance companies millions of dollars for treatments and hospitalizations and drugs over a period of years, women who had their families wrecked and their sanity almost destroyed. Mary S. and Pat B. are suing their doctors.

In the wake of books such as *Michelle Remembers* and Geraldo Rivera's sensational TV program on "The Devil Worshipers," some psychologists and psychiatrists have told patients that their own lives and those of persons close to them that they have been programmed by Satanic cults to destroy are in danger. The doctors have drugged them, confined them to psychiatric institutions, interrogated them, and—court cases will allege—filled their heads with lies they present as memories of Satanic abuse.

Doctors now involved in lawsuits include Bennett G. Braun, M.D. and Robert G. Sachs, Ph.D., of what is still the leading MPD teaching hospital in the U.S., Chicago's Rush Presbyterian, and Judith Petersen, Ph.D., whose private hospital in Houston was recently closed down.

Mary S. is recovering. She escaped Dr. Braun's care and found a psychiatrist who told her "you don't have to be multiple any more"—she had developed fifteen child alternate personalities and seven cult-related personalities, it was alleged. Pat B. says she "stopped following Dr. Braun's orders" after she and her children spent years in incredibly expensive treatment and did "goofy things" allegedly because of the doctor's suggestions.

These patients and others say they were told they came from generations of Satanic cult members and had been programed from their earliest years to murder and abort children, to lie, and generally to serve a god of evil and to bring up their children in the cult to do the same. Persons who don't believe in Satanic cult abuse, Dr. Peterson rejoined, "still live in the dark ages."

It may be that there are active and dangerous Satanic cults at work. It is possible that the "experts" such as Dr. Braun (award winner of the Institute for the Study of Multiple Personality and Dissociation, highly respected in some circles) and the likes of D. Corydon Hammond, Ph. D., of the University of Utah (another widely known expert on cult programming) are deluded and dangerous. If you accuse them of anything wrong, of course, you may be charged with defending Satanism and possibly being a cult member yourself. In any case, they and lesser lights in the psychiatric field have been for decades battling The Devil and his minions or cheating the devil out of pitiful, confused patients and their terrified families, or so they say.

I believe it is Dr. Hammond who has offered the explanation that Nazi doctors toyed with both MPD experiments and Satanic rituals and that a "Jewish collaborator," identified by Dr. Hammond as a man named Greenbaum who later came to the United States and became Green, are to blame for it all. Green is said to have earned an M.D. degree in New York and still to be "at the center of this business" of dedicating souls to Satan, mind-bending innocents with sexual and homicidal and deceptive and other awful brainwashing, and making huge amounts of money for self-appointed psychiatric guardians of the pace and sanity of us all.

In a nation where insurance fraud is soaring and where malpractice suits are multiplying (payouts are phenomenal), being a victim has become practically everybody's hobby and some people's livelihood. Additionally, families in the United States are breaking up fast enough and children's lives are being ruined often enough as is, without accusations of Satanism. This is perilous stuff. If Satan knows anything at all about it, he must be delighted.

Psychiatrists are the fathers confessor of modern and irreligious man. Psychiatry is the new faith. Those of us who are doctors but not M.D.s are "laymen." Wouldn't it be awful if the very people these priests of the

Roman Catholics foolishly assumed all Satanists had rituals blaspheming their own. Here is shown (*Compendium maleficarum*, 1608) an imagined baptism of a convert to the religion of The Devil.

talking cure (and increasingly "better life through chemistry") are supposed to help are being victimized, much as the ignorant layman was bamboozled by the credulous and crazy clerics of the real Dark Ages?

We are beginning to question the so-called experts in psychology and social work. Juries are now prone to exonerate the accused if a videotaped interview with a child is offered in evidence, and "summaries" of children's evidence are preferred by prosecutors. Improper interview techniques are now suspected of putting ideas in the child's mind, and Stephen Ceci and Maggie Bruck in *Jeopardy in the Courtroom* (1995) show how damage to the truth is done. Debbie Nathan and Michael Snedeker put the defense case in *Satan's Silence: Ritual; Abuse and the Making of a Modern American Witch Hunt* (1995). As jealousy and greed (who would get the witch's property?) and class warfare (according to Jules Michelet) sparked witchcraft persecutions in the past and led to changes in laws and trial procedures, so alleged Satanic child abuse is going to have increasing impact on jurisprudence today and in the future.

ALLEGED SATANISM IN PUBLIC SCHOOL

"It's unbelievable that we have to come here—in Bedford, the most educated community in America—and listen to this," said lawyer David Mencken to the meeting in Fox Lane High School in Bedford, New York. He may be insane to describe Bedford as "the most educated community in America," but he looked right in opposing Concerned Parents: Citizens and Professionals [I like the distinction] Against the Seduction of Children.

Mary Ann DiBari, another lawyer, founded Concerned Citizens (with a secretary, Ceil DiNozzi, who has four children in the local schools) and was objecting to "total immersion in paganism" in the affluent Bedford Central School District (which includes Mount Kisco and Pound Ridge) undertaken in the name of diversity. Concerned Citizens turned out 400 supporters in September 1995. Mr. Mencken and about a thousand others turned out for the November 1995 meeting on the subject. The school superintendent had discovered most of the attendees in September were not residents and called a second meeting, checking credentials at the door.

Ms. DiBari objected to Quetzalcoatl being mentioned in second-grade study of Mexico. "The Mexicans got over Quetzalcoatl," she argued. "Why not give us the Virgin of Guadelupe?"

Personally, I find the Virgin of Guadalupe even more redolent of superstition, harder to believe. The second grade was also accused of making

Hindu idols. A teacher held up a paper mask of the elephant god Ganesha to show what sort of an "idol" the kids were making.

The principal target of the defenders of Christian values represented at the meeting was not anything historical. It was card game called *Magic* played in school clubs. "It uses incantations to the devil, contact from below," asserted Ms. Di Bari. "There are 2,500 individual Magic cards," *The New York Times* quoted Adam Leeds (seventh grade) as saying. "It would be hard to find 20 that were objectionable. There are no chants, no sacrificing, no death and—definitely—no contact from below." In the card game kids pretend to cast spells on their opponents to win.

Bedford's "most manipulated public event I've seen in my twenty-seven years of public education" (according to Dr. Dennis, the school superintendent) is not untypical of the Christian Right's programs for cleansing the schools of "the occult" and even Darwin's theory of evolution. The fight is on all over America, and if one Jewish lady on Long Island can make the town take down all public Christian symbols put up at Christmas, and a school in California (as really was the case) can ban Halloween, if prayers in the public schools can come back whatever the Constitution says about the separation of church and state, brace yourself for ideological warfare.

"I think the amount of time and attention we have been giving to these two women," said the superintendent, "was adequate and sufficient, and now it's time to move on."

Don't count on moving on soon. The battle over Satanism or any other Judeo-Christian targets is not over.

TEENAGERS AND SATANISM

How best to rebel against Dad and Mom and all they stand for? In the sixties you became a Flower Child and turned to sex and drugs and rock and roll; you grew your hair long. In the nineties you may play at Satanism, listen to music with Satanist lyrics, wear a T-shirt with Satanist symbols on it (and form a Refuse & Resist group when the school authorities in Texas towns ban this). Bodies pile up as teenagers even try sacrifices. The ASPCA is leery about releasing black cats around Halloween, for fear they may be used in gory rites. In some school jurisdictions, Halloween is banned and the card game *Magic* and the spell game *Wizards* are decried. Some psychopaths are pleading Satanism instead of the usual insanity for butchering people The Christian Right is up in arms. Pat Buchanan is quoted in *Time* 6 November 1995 as deploring teenagers "literally hell-bent on sadism and suicide." When five teenagers who were friends die—

three by suicide and two in a high-speed car wreck at about the same time—
Satanism is strongly suspected. *Santeria* and voodoo are frequent topics of
feature stories. Exorcisms appear to be kept out of the press. The news in
the headline of the *San Francisco Chronicle* 12 June 1993, "Fear of Satanism
across the Nation" has since been frequently repeated. Los Angeles in 1992
revealed the existence of a Ritual Abuse Task Force in the police depart-
ment, and other investigative units followed in Snellville, Georgia, and all
over the United States. Nineteen ninety-two is the 300th anniversary of
the Salem witchcraft trials, and everywhere periodicals and books recall,
rehash, and reflect on the New England events of three centuries ago.

Minor "Satanist" incidents crop up in the newspapers and popular magazines (not to mention the theological, sociological, psychological, literary and other journals) all the time all over America. Here are a propitious
number of samples from the last five years or so:

November 1989: Residents suspect ritual sacrifice of disemboweled baby
in Rupert, Idaho. No one is convicted of Satanism.

January 1990: Rev. Joseph Brennan says New Orleans has some of an estimated 8,000 Satanic groups nationwide and tells the *Times-Picayune* that in
the previous five years he has counseled some 200 around the U.S. "involved
in Satanism." The Satanic cults I know in New Orleans are all fake.

March 1990: "Psychic Adventures" adult education class in Wyandotte,
Michigan, denounced by locals as Satanic recruitment by a teacher, and
worries about Satanism in elementary and secondary schools are exacer-
bated. In Five Forks Middle School (the *Atlanta Constitution* reports), the
PTA demands a total ban on "Satanic jewelry and clothing."

April 1990: Franklin, New Hampshire, adults debate Satanic abuse of children.

May 1990: Lowell Cohn in the *San Francisco Chronicle* probes the rumor
that Satan is the reason the San Francisco Giants play poorly.

July 1990: Site of murder and dismemberment becomes Warren, Michigan,
tourist attraction: Stephanie Dubay (15) has been skinned and beheaded.

September 1990: Los Angeles institutes $1,000 fine in hopes of stemming
animal sacrifices in Satanic rites. Animal rights and animal rites clash.

October 1990: Eric Zorn reports in the *Chicago Tribune* that Wanda Star-
czynski of Villa Park, Illinois, is campaigning against Halloween as leading children into Satanism (Zorn says she is "considered an idiot by many

258 The Complete Book of Devils and Demons

of her neighbors," but by no means all). In the *Los Angeles Times*, former mental patient Michael Robert Caewitz is convicted of murdering a three-year-old girl because "he thought she was Satan."

November 1990: Karen Phillips of Westwego, Louisiana, was one of many women drawn into Satanism to hold onto a boyfriend. Boyfriend David Mapes kills her and then himself in a North Carolina hotel room.

January 1991: Boy (four months old) may have been murdered by uncle as part of a Satanic ritual in Pueblo, Colorado, reports the *Denver Post*. In Montgomery County, Maryland, Jeffrey L. Eskew "avowed Satanist" is reindicted for "damaging Jewish school."

September 1991: Boy of seven testifies that Edenton, North Carolina, adults may have led prayers to Satan at The Little Rascals Day Care Center.

February 1992: John Taylor in *New York* writes on "The Demon Gap: America is Experiencing One of Its Periodic Paranoid Convulsions."

March 1992: More mutilated goat carcasses found and "Satanic worship has not been ruled out" by Harris County, Texas, authorities.

April 1992: Scott Edward May accused of attempting to murder a girl (aged sixteen) "to satisfy a cult requirement," reported in the *Houston Post*.

June 1992: "Only in America" could two witches in Concord, California, demand that schools ban "Hansel and Gretel" on the grounds of discrimination, says *Fortune*. Many other witches' rights protest nationally.

July 1992: Joel Homan of North Adams, Michigan, dead and *Detroit News* headlines: "3 Teens Charged with 'Satanic' Slaying of Friend."

July 1993: *Denver Post* reports that Mark Cloatre, convicted of murdering his girlfriend, "says he was a Satanist."

August 1993: Witchcraft supply store forced to close in Jonesboro, Arkansas. Others flourish in more cosmopolitan centers.

November 1993: Jackie Haskew, a school teacher, accused of bringing Satanist ideas into the classroom, reports the *Washington Post* (one of many hysterical reactions of worried parents).

January 1994: Kelly Wilson may have been ritually murdered in Gilmour, Texas.

February 1994: David Condry is arrested for ritually murdering Josephine Adolfino (aged eighty-nine) with a hatchet in Los Angeles.

March 1994: Michael Lester (found naked hiding in his closet, surrounded by Satanic and Nazi symbolism) after another teenager (Richard Rodriguez) who spent the night at Lester's home is discovered dead, stabbed nineteen times, in Spring, Texas.

June 1994: Three teenagers arrested for ritual murder of three boys (each eight years old), and *Los Angeles Times* reports: "According to one of the suspects, the murder was part of a Satanic cult ritual."

October 1994: Patrick Huyghe considers UFOs as war toys for Angels of the Dark in "UFO Update: The Devil's Design," *Omni*.

November 1994: Witchcraft in the schools: "Books, Ghosts 'n Goblins," Michael D. Simpson, *National Education Association Today*.

February 1995: Four teens charged with three incidents of animal sacrifice and arson in Marietta, Georgia.

May 1995: Witch suppliers in New York City: Gia Koulas' "Spellbound" in *New York Times*. Useful: Abyss Distributors, 48 Chester Road, Chester, Mass. 01011-9735.

June 1995: In *New York Times Magazine*, Ron Rosenbaum brings readers up-to-date on the nature of evil in feature: "Staring Into the Heart of Darkness."

July 1995: Satanic graffiti on Fairfax, Virginia, churches and one church set on fire. In *The Chronicle of Higher Education* on "Wrestling with the Idea of Satan."

August 1995: Satanic symbols beside Marietta, Georgia, corpse stabbed to death.

ALLEGED ABUSE OF CHILDREN BY SATANIC ADULTS

As we have seen, there has been a flood of accusations by children and former children that they were abused in Satanic rites. Parents sue schools and teachers and baby-sitters, Tennessee grandparents kidnap children from their parents in efforts to "save them," victims sue doctors and hospitals (at least one prominent California one was shut down as a result of complaints, newspapers report) and their own family members (one mother aged seventy-six was sued by her daughters in Orange County, California, for abuse many years earlier) and others. Psychiatrists, psychologists, therapists of all schools and none, social workers, the police and others are very active trying to discover if crimes have been committed or if crazies are "remembering" (or coaching into alleging) things that never happened. Reports by the FBI or *The New York Times* that no Satanic cults abusing children have been unearthed meet with disbelief and furious denial. Books such as Gail C. Feldman's *Lessons in Evil, Lessons from the Light* (1995) get poor reviews and excellent publicity.

Those found guilty of Satanic abuse of children receive harsh sentences, while there seems to be hardly any interest in prosecuting simple incest.

An old woodcut shows parents giving their child to the Devil.

Those found innocent of alleged Satanic abuse often continue to suffer for life: Three California teachers after one of the lengthiest trials in the history of American jurisprudence were completely exonerated and so sued for damages—and were awarded one dollar each. In California, also, Dale Aliki was jailed for two and a half years without bail, tried for kidnapping, torturing and Satanically abusing some children, was acquitted, and sued the church that had employed him, the expert witnesses, and the prosecutors. Whether he won or not, I can't find out in the welter of reports of new cases elsewhere. In Texas, two social workers (Debbie Minshaw and Ann Goar) were taken off cases when they "lost objectivity," according to authorities.

In Britain scandals erupted in a number of big cities, in "housing estates" and in the far-off Orkneys. Nothing like the rash of incidents reported in the United States, but Britain does have a number of sensational tabloids and this stuff was fodder for them. Typically, the charges were all over Page One and acquittals or dropped cases were regarded as boring details not suitable for "screamers" (headlines), just the occasional "leader" (editorial tut-tutting). The Manchester *Guardian* reported four couples charged, investigated for a long time, and eventually released—the journal asked: Why not sooner? The paper was faulted for this question. When the exonerated people sought huge damages, some people were outraged. When people are found innocent, many continue to believe the charges. We are losing faith in the jury system. Those who question the methods of investigation or the testimony of tots or of highly questionable experts are often said themselves to be in league with The Devil.

Patty Campbell has written in "The Sand in the Oyster" about books for young adults on Satanic molestation (*Horn Book*, January/February 1995). John Taylor in *Esquire* ("The Lost Daughter," March 1994) roused the public with "how one American family got caught up in today's witches' brew of sexual abuse, the Sybil syndrome [multiple personalities], and the perverse ministrations of the therapy police." The hysteria continues. Do not misunderstand me: I am as open as anyone to the possibility that Satanic rites are conducted and that children may be abused. As with all allegations, however, I insist upon open-minded and professional investigation and proof that will stand up to reasonable judicial scrutiny. I must say that the biggest victim in a number of recent cases in this matter, as in some other matters involving prejudice, often has been our faith in the helping professions and the legal system, including the verdicts of juries.

A PRISONER DEMANDS HIS RITES

Satanic rites, that is. Under the First Amendment, two convicted murderers and four other prisoners demanded the right to practice their religion while incarcerated, and Federal Judge Edward W. Nottingham in Colorado courageously made the unpopular ruling that they must be allowed to do so. So Robert James Howard and others can now legally demand that a robe, a gong, a bell, incense, candles, and a chalice be provided by jail authorities, along with a place (in their cells, presumably) in which to engage in devil worship. I can see the logic in letting them pray to Satan if they wish to, but I do not see why they have to be given the tools of the trade. Are Roman Catholics entitled to free rosaries or American Indians to free peyote in jail?

I wonder if the empty allegations by evangelicals and others that Masons and Mormons are practicing devil worship are protected under the Constitution or if people can go to court over that ?

VOODOO IN URBAN CENTERS

Those who expect to hear of voodoo in "The Big Easy" (where the stories of Marie Laveau still circulate and tourists seek out her grave in the

quaint cemetery) and in the Deep South where Zora Neale Hurston's "Mules and Men" is set may be surprised to learn that there is more trouble with voodoo in the hospitals of Detroit and Chicago and New York than in Charity Hospital or Tulane Medical Center in New Orleans. Many who have left the South still believe in hexes and hoodoos and are distrustful of traditional medical and psychiatric care. Many live animals are sold in Brooklyn, New York, for sacrificial use. Documentary films and periodical interviews have made "priestesses" here and others with "the gift" fairly well known to the general public, despite the fact that few outsiders would credit what is going on in Bizango or other secret societies and white people resist recognizing voodoo as a religion. They call it mere superstition. Voodoo, however, along with channeling and practices more aptly described as mere superstition, is proof that possession and necromancy are still very much alive in the modern world.

In 1982, a colloquium in Paris on the occult, magic and witchcraft in American culture concluded that the strong American pressure for conformity in society turns some people to extreme beliefs in the occult, to blood sacrifices of Africa and the Caribbean, and to magical-religious practices in general. Voodoo, *Santería* and other such religions may also, of course, owe much to the exclusion of people of color from the mainstream of American society and the reliance they place in their ethnic isolation on the pagan religions of Africa and also those influenced by them and still active in Cuba, Puerto Rico, and other places from which the United States has recently received immigrants.

I would call voodoo a religion, not devil worship, but many will expect to see something about it here in a discussion of Satanism. So be it. I omit *Santería*, which the public somehow does not associate as much with The Devil as it does voodoo and its walking dead (zombies).

THE DEVIL TO PAY IN COLORADO

I'm not sure what the locals in Telluride, Colorado, have to say to each other but I know that a third of the population is on-line with a computer system partly supported by government money. (Why?) That's been going on since 1993, and now censorship has had to be established. One resident was slandered as "evil" and is suing. Another in 1995 was banned from the system because he threatened on-line to kill anyone who did not show up at the local park for a Satanist rally.

EAST OR WEST, HOMEMADE IS BEST

"All religions," a Japanese proverb says, "start in Asia," but the United States has had a number of new religions spring up in the eastern United States, not the Far East. Among them are Mormonism, Spiritualism, and peculiar kinds of Ethical Culture and Unitarianism, if indeed these last two can be regarded not as substitutes for socially, or otherwise unacceptable religions but religions in themselves. Now some religions are coming out of western United States, especially New Age ones. Some of these amount to worship of The Devil, but none can be regarded as traditional Satanism in that they do not depend upon human sacrifice to The Evil One. There is a distinct difference between being damned and being damned silly.

The Far West still has the reputation for being Far Out, but the best candidate for a clearly established and growing religion dealing with evil powers is mostly centered in the Northeast. It is the religion of *Santería*. It combines elements of Christianity with devil worship and pagan, African elements. There are many books about it, some few reliable.

VOODOO AND THE DEVIL

Voodoo is practiced in the United States, though not as seriously or as widely as most people think. Most voodoo is no more serious than the fabled Marie Laveau of New Orleans, a black herbal-medicine and poison-potion practitioner of the nineteenth century who got a hold on a public who thought she lived well over a hundred years. In fact, she died and her daughter took over, pretending to be the mother mumbo-jumboing on in the service of casting and removing spells, getting black men out of jail, and generally fighting authority by magical means. Once people became afraid of such practitioners, the magic was potent.

Marie and her daughter seem to have known or cared little about the kind of voodoo that had some blacks turning to the dreaded Baron Saturday, a manifestation of The Devil, a powerful and demanding evil spirit who could raise the dead from the grave to serve as *zombies*. More likely the living were drugged into "walking-dead" states and put to work at hard labor for the benefit not of the underworld but of greedy masters. Whether the blood sacrifices (usually animal) to Baron Saturday were received and rewarded by an infernal power or not, those who sincerely were caught up in the cult were indeed devil worshipers. And their magic worked, just as a witch doctor pointing a bone at a believer in Africa can make the victim drop dead (of fear?) on the spot, just as priests and priestesses of *obeah* and other African religions can produce marvels for and in the credulous. It all works if you believe.

Some would say that Lourdes works on the same basis. There are few if any United States sites that have such a powerful attraction, however, and none with a great track record of miracle cures. Americans boast of being able to handle without damage to themselves both venomous snakes and violent devils. Our Bible-pounding preachers have always declared that they are willing to take on His Infernal Majesty hand to hand, and American pulpit oratory continues to owe much to the eighteenth-century's Jonathan Edwards and his terrifying sermon on *Sinners in the Hands of an Angry God*. The televangelist successors of the eighteenth-century enthusiasts may not be up to the old literary standard but they now far surpass any numbers that the great orators of the past swayed.

People lament that American sin has increased and that belief in God has diminished, but whatever you think of American morality today the numbers of the Born Again are ever increasing and, if belief in a personal God is weakening (though only 5 percent of Americans are out-and-out atheists), belief in The Devil is stronger here than it ever has been. Someone has said that we take refuge in the unknowable from the terrors of the unknown. Politically, AIDS can be more convincingly said to be used by The Devil than by government research gone wrong (or maliciously misapplied); demons can take blame one cannot put on Democrats.

To counter the "work of The Devil" among us, we have a typically American "War on Sin" waged by the high-profile clergymen of America's 1,600 religious denominations with tax-free churches which take in $57 billion a year. What Alexis de Tocqueville wrote in 1835 remains true today: "There is no country in the world where the Christian religion retains a greater influence over the souls of men." The traditional denominations have had a harder time lately, particularly those who unalterable positions on certain dogmas have clashed with lax American morality, but the charismatics and the evangelicals who offer painless solutions to problems are flourishing. Americans expect quick fixes and seek miracles, and a poll shows 37 percent believe they have witnessed one, 8 percent having had a visit from the Blessed Virgin or a saint in person, and a whopping 65 percent certain that a specific prayer or request has been answered. America has never been lacking in talented individuals famous for laying on of hands (and theatrics) and extracting money and demons from the possessed. For religious mania, religious cures. As Hippocrates said: "For extreme diseases, extreme remedies."

ANOTHER VOODOO VIEW

If you don't like *voodoo* being derived from the *Vaudois*, you can subscribe to the theory that the first part of the word comes from the Fon language of Africa, which today has 2.5 million speakers in Benin and Togo. But did American black slaves come from there?

AMULETS AND TALISMANS OF VOODOO

Devotees of voodoo use *ouangas* (amulets) and *bakas* (talismans) to protect themselves and to draw guardian spirits to themselves. *Bakas* can turn against the user if not properly employed and can be used for evil as well as good. The *baka* combines the *ba* (superior soul) with the *ka* (inferior soul). It is believed that, when the superior soul leaves the body at death, the *ka* remains with the corpse, and so some sorcerers go to graveyards to collect *ka* in jars to command such powers. The *ka*, it is said, can be laid by *froid* (cold) ceremonies in which *canaris* (jars) supposedly containing the spirits are broken. The pieces of the jars are to be disposed of at crossroads with appropriate rituals. Unlaid, the *ka* spirits are dangerous.

VÉVÉS

From Africa and later Santo Domingo come the elaborate *vévés* drawn with flour or other powder on the ground to accompany various voodoo ceremonies. Below is the vévé of Legba, Master of the Crossroads, one of the powers that enter voodoo worshipers during rituals and "ride" the individual, who may take on some of the characteristics of the spirit invoked such as the gait of an old man. This *vévé* illustrated is a symbol of the powers associated with this spirit Legba and shows the balance of stellar forces and representations of fish, Legba being connected with water. Milho Rigaud's essential work on the subject has been translated as *Secrets of Voodoo* (1985, and reprinted) and illustrates many *vévés*.

VOODOO

Bach, Marcus. *Strange Altars* (1952).
Deren, Maya. *Divine Horseman: Voodoo Gods of Haiti* (1953).
Haskins, James. *Voodoo and Hoodoo* (1978).
Melville, J. H. *Life in a Haitian Valley* (1937).
Métraux, Alfred. *Voodoo in Haiti* (1972).

Rigaud, Milo. *Secrets of Voodoo* (1970).

Tallant, Robert. *The Voodoo Queen* (1956).

———*Voodoo in New Orleans* (1946).

Williams, Joseph John. *Voodoos and Obeahs* (1932).

HAIL, COLUMBIA!

At the age of four, the Colombian woman now known both as Regina Betancourt de Liska and "Regina Eleven" had, or so she says, a vision in which she was assured that one day she would lead her nation. In 1992 she got as far as a seat in the Senate there. The *Washington Times* rather unkindly said "She Rode a Broom to Senate Seat in Columbia." She doesn't seem to me to be worse than an astronaut who parlayed a seat in a spacecraft into a seat in the United States Senate, or the Italian stripper who got into parliament

there with what we might call unusually "full disclosure" for a politician. My favorite is not a witch at all but a cocktail waitress from Las Vegas who changed her name to Dick Tracy-inspired "Sparkle Plenty" and ran on a campaign of "We All Need Plenty" in Nevada.

REVEREND KIRBY HENSLEY
SAYS HE WILL "CRUSH SATAN'S HEAD"

The Universal Life Church (send them a dollar and get all the privileges of clergy afforded by the IRS, etc.; send them twenty dollars and get a doctorate). *ULC News* (Spring, 1996) tells us that the Reverend Mr. Hensley regards Jesus Christ as the Antichrist and himself as sent to defeat Satan. *ULC News* (prose style their own):

> Hensley believes that the real head of the so-called church is the Snake! Hensley believes that the state was created by the Snake and run by the Snake....So you won't get confused, the Snake is spoken of as a serpent. It is spoken of as the devil. It is spoken of as the evil one. It is spoken of as the destroyer but is also spoken of as a savior, life-giver. The next time you walk by a doctor's office, look what's out front, you will find a snake wrapped around a cross [the caduceus of Mercury is intended here]. Hensley believes that Eve, in the garden, actually had sex with the snake, this is where the snake seed got into the bloodline.
>
> According to all scriptures you will find the snake was going to rule for 6,000 years and then a man will come who will crush Satan's head. I still believe that I am that man! This man is going to convince the people, church and state that they have been following an Anti-Christ....Jesus was and is the Anti-Christ!

Universal Life Church headquarters is at 601 Third Street, Modesto, California 95351. You may wish to join for tax purposes or just to be one of their clergymen and thus able to regard as buddies Jerry Lewis, Hugh Hefner of *Playboy*, the late President Lyndon Johnson, the late actor James Stewart, and others.

TAKING SATAN'S NAME IN VAIN

A film about a deadly virus was called *The Satan Bug* and a program named SATAN was noted in both *Time* and *US News & World Report* on 17 April 1995 in connection with "viruses" in the Internet.

"THE PRACTICE OF HELPLESS WITCHCRAFT"

Englishman Raban's "American Voyage" down the Mississippi, as reported in *Old Glory* (1981), left him highly critical of many United States mores. In St. Louis, Missouri, he read the *Evening Whirl*, "full of advertisements for clairvoyants and wizards. HAS SOMEONE PUT A HEX, A SPELL, A VOODOO ON YOU? CONSULT: THE MAN WHO KNOWS." He was "tempted to believe that the awfulness of the place could be accounted for only in terms of hexes and spells."

In every large city of the United States one can see the ads and the handbills for faith healers similar to St. Louis' Reverend Mother Taylor ("Got bad luck, voodoo?"), evidence of "a society so bad that only magic could explain it." Superstition and desperation are rampant.

"What kind of a city was this," asked Raban "where people had been reduced to the practice of helpless witchcraft?"

THE DEVIL IN LITERATURE, AND STILL IN PRINT

There will be much on this in *The Complete Book of the Devil's Disciples*, but:

Radwin, Maximillian. *The Devil in Legend and Literature* (1931, reprinted).
Russell, Jeffrey B. *The Devil: Perceptions of Evil from Antiquity to Primitive Christianity* (1977).
———*Lucifer: The Devil in the Middle Ages* (1984).
———*Mephistopheles: The Devil in the Modern World* (1990).
———*Prince of Darkness* (1988).
———*Satan: The Early Christian Tradition* (1988).
Woodhull, Marianne. *Epic of Paradise Lost* (1907).

THE DEVIL: SELECTED BOOKS IN PRINT IN 1995

Anshen, Ruth N. *The Anatomy of Evil* (1985 reprint of *The Reality of the Devil*).
Ashton, J. *The Devil in Britain and America* (1972).
Baskin, Wade. *Satanism...* (1988).
Chrysosotom, St. John. *The Devil* (1987).
Gokey, Francis X. *The Terminology for The Devil and Evil Spirits in the Apostolic Fathers* (1961, reprinted).
Gravers, Kersey. *The Biography of Satan* (1993).
Ling, Trevor. *The Significance of Satan...* (1961, reprinted).

ARATRON

A LITTLE LIBRARY OF BASIC BOOKS ON
THE DEVIL, DEMONOLOGY, AND WITCHCRAFT

Ahmed, Rollo. *The Black Art* (1968).
Ashley, Leonard R. N. *The Complete Book of Magic and Witchcraft* (1995).
Ashton, John. *The Devil in Britain and America* (1896).
Baroja, Julio Caro. *The World of the Witches* (1964).
Barrett, Francis. *The Magus* (reprinted 1967).
Bernanos, Georges. *The Star of Satan* (trans. V. Lucas, 1927).
Black, George F. *List of Works in the New York Public Library Relating to Witchcraft in the United States* (1908) and *in Europe* (1911).
Bruyn, Lucy de. *Women and The Devil in Sixteenth Century Literature* (1979).
"Carus, Paul," *History of the Devil and the Idea of Evil* (reprint 1969).
Cohn, Norman. *Europe's Inner Demons* (1975).
Conway, Moncure Daniel. *Demonology and Devil Lore* (1879).
Davies, Reginald Trevor. *Four Centuries of Witch Beliefs* (1947).
Del Rio, Martin. *Disquisitionum magicarum (1599).*
Douglas, Mary, ed. *Witchcraft Confessions and Accusations* (1970).
Ewen, C. L'Estrange. *Witchcraft and Demonianism* (1933).

Flint, Valeria I.J. *The Rise of Magic in Early Modern Europe* (1991).

Godwin, William. *Lives of the Necromancers* (1835).

Graf, Arturo. *The Story of The Devil* (trans. Edward Noble Stone, 1931).

Grillot de Givry, Émil. *Witchcraft, Magic and Alchemy* (trans. J. C. Locke, 1954).

Guiley, Rosemary Ellen. *Encyclopedia of Witches and Witchcraft* (1989).

———*Encyclopedia of Ghosts and Spirits* (1992).

Hole, Christina. *Witchcraft in England* (1947).

Hopkins, Matthews. *The Discovery of Witches* (ed. M. Summers, 1928).

Hufford, David J. *The Terror that Comes in the Night* (1982).

Huxley, Aldous. *The Devils of Loudun* (1952).

James I and VI. *Demonology* (ed. G.B. Harrison, 1924).

Johnson F.R. *Witches and Demons in History and Folklore* (1978).

Klaits, Joseph. *Servants of Satan: The Age of the Witch Hunts* (1985).

Langton, Edward. *Satan, A Portrait* (1949).

Lavater, Ludwig. *Of Ghosts and Spirits Walking by Night* (ed. John Dover Wilson, 1929).

Lea, Henry Charles. *Materials toward a History of Witchcraft* (1957).

Leland, Charles Godfrey. *Arcadia, or The Gospel of the Witches* (1899).

Lindsay, Gordon. *Satan, Fallen Angels and Demons* (3 vols., n.d.).

Logan, Daniel. *America Bewitched* (1974).

Mackay, Charles. *Memoirs of Extraordinary Popular Delusions* (reprint 1932).

Malinowski, Bronislaw. *Magic, Science and Religion* (1954).

Martino, Ernesto de. *The World of Magic* 91972).

Marwick, Max, ed. *Witchcraft and Sorcery* (1982).

Michelet, Jules. *Satanism and Witchcraft* (trans. A.R. Allinson, 1949).

Molitor, Ulrich. *De Lamiis et phitonicis mulieribus* (1489).

Morey, Robert. *Satan's Devices: Recognizing the Enemy...* (1993).

Morrison, Sarah Lyndon. *The Witch's Spellbook, I and II.*

Murray, Margaret. *The God of the Witches* (1931).

———*The Witch Cult in Western Europe* (1921).

Newell, Venetia. *Encyclopedia of Witchcraft and Magic* (1974).

O'Keefe, Daniel L. *Stolen Lightning: The Social History of Magic* (1982).

Papini, Giovanni. *The Devil: Notes for a Future Diabology* (1955).

Philpott, Kent. *Manual of Demonology and the Occult* (1973).

Pratt, Sister Antoinette Marie. *Attitude of the Catholic Church to Witchcraft* (1915).

Rémy, Nicholas. *Demonolatry* (trans. M. Summers, 1930).

Rhodes, H. T. F. *The Satanic Mass* (1954).

Robbins, Rossell Hope. *Encyclopedia of Witchcraft and Demonology* (1959).

Rudwin, Maximillian. *The Devil in Legend and Literature* (1973).

Russell, Jeffrey Burton. *Witchcraft in the Middle Ages* (1972).

Rydberg, Viktor. *The Magic of the Middle Ages* (1897).

Sanders, Andrew. *Without a Name....* (1995).

Scot, Reginald. *The Discovery of Witchcraft* (ed. M. Summers, 1930).

Scott, Sir Walter. *Letters on Demonology and Witchcraft* (1830).

Seligmann, K. *The History of Magic* (1948).

Sergeant, Philip W. *Witches and Warlocks* (1936).

Seth, Ronald. *In the Name of the Devil* (1970).

Spalding, Thomas Alfred. *Elizabethan Demonology* (1880).

Spence, Lewis. *An Encyclopedia of Occultism* (n.d.).

Sprenger, Jakob and Heinrich Kramer. *Malleus Maleficarum* (trans. M. Summers 1928, 1948).

Summers, Montague. *The History of Witchcraft and Demonology* (1926).

Thomas, Keith. *Religion and the Decline of Magic* (1971).

Thompson, Reginald. *The Devils and Evil Spirits of Babylonia* (1904).

Thompson, R. Lowe. *The History of the Devil, the Horned God of the West* (1929).

Thorndyke, Lynn. *A History of Magic and Experimental Science* (1923).

Trevor Roper, Hugh R. (Lord Dacre). *The European Witch-Craze of the 16th and 17th Centuries* (1969).

Verner, Gerald, ed. *Prince of Darkness* (1946).

Wedeck, A. *A Treasury of Witchcraft* (1961).

Wheatley, Dennis. *The Devil and All His Works* (1972).

Woods, William Howard. *History of the Devil* (1974).

Zachias, Gerhard. *The Satanic Cult* (1980).

SUPERSTITION

Ashley, Leonard R. N. *The Complete Book of Superstition, Prophecy and Luck* (1995).

Hole, Christina. *Encyclopedia of Superstitions* (1961).

Krantz, Grover. *Big Footprints: A Scientific Inquiry into the Reality of Sasquatch* (1992).

Potter, Carole. *Knock on Wood: An Encyclopedia of Talismans, Charms, Superstitions and Symbols* (1983).

Puckett, Newbell N. *Superstitions: A Compendium of American Folklore.* 3 vols. (1981).

Williams, Howard. *Superstitions of Witchcraft* (1865).

WITCHCRAFT NOW

Bellah, Robert N. *Beyond Belief* (1970).
Brese, David. *Satan's Ten Most Believable Lies* (1987).
Crowley, Aleister. *Magick in Theory and Practice* (n.d.).
Eliade, Mircea. *Occultism, Witchcraft and Cultural Fashions* (1976).
Gardner, Gerald B. *Witchcraft Today* (1974).
Hughes, Pennethorne. *Witchcraft* (1967).
LaVey, Anton S. *The Satanic Bible* (1969).
Luckmann, Thomas. *The Invisible Religion* (1970).
Seabrook, William. *Witchcraft, Its Power in the World Today* (1970).
Smyth, Frank. *Modern Witchcraft* (1970).
Stivers, Richard. *Evil in Modern Myth and Ritual* (1982).
Valiente, Doreen. *Witchcraft for Tomorrow* (1980).

ROBERT BURTON ON SUPERSTITION

Anthony à Wood in his *Athenæ Oxoniensis* praised Robert Burton as "a curious Calculator of Nativities" (horoscopes) and tells how he foretold years in advance the day of his own death in 1640, "which being exact, several of the *Students* did not forebear to whisper among themselves, that rather than there should be a mistake in the calculation, he sent up his soul to heaven by a slip about his neck."

Whether Burton hanged himself or not is unclear, but his *Anatomy of Melancholy* was (as Lord Byron said) "a mine of knowledge." On superstition he wrote:

> If *Democritus* were alive now, and should but see the superstition of our age, our religious madnesse...so many professed Christians, yet so few imitators of *Christ*, so much talk of religion, so much science, so little conscience, so much knowledge, so many preachers, so little practice....

That is not a bad description of America as the second millenium approaches, a country which seems to have launched an international vogue for anything dealing with angels—mostly the good angels—and which has translated both good and bad supernatural forces into aliens, cyborgs, extraterrestrials of all kinds. The Devil suits the New Age, too, and, while Generation X continues to regard God as ever more vaguely conceived and ever more distant, at the same time it appears to regard The Devil as a real and present danger.

BE OF GOOD CHEER

I do not wish to end this examination of evil on a note of pessimism, even though I recall that, when Voltaire said of superstition that we must root it out, his practical friend Frederick the Great answered that it would be a good idea were it not incapable of execution.

Here are some more optimistic words of wisdom, four hundred years old and very much forgotten today but worthy of remembrance. They are from Justus Lipsius as translated by John Stradling in *Two Books of Constancie* (1594):

You say, this age is the unhappiest that ever was. This has been an old lay, long ago used. I know your grandfather said so, and likewise your father. I know also that your children and children's children will sing the same note. It is a thing naturally given unto men to cast their eyes narrowly upon all things that are grievous, but to wink at such as are pleasant. As flies and such-like vile creatures do never rest long upon smooth and fine polished places, but do stick fast to rough and filthy corners, so the murmuring mind does lightly pass over the consideration of all good fortune, but never forgets the adverse or evil. It handles and pries into that, yet, and oftentimes augments it with great wit. Like as lovers do always behold something in their mistress whereby they think her to excel all others, even so do men that mourn, in their miseries. Yea, moreover we imagine things that are false, and bewail not only things present, but also such as are to come. And what gain we by this fore-reaching wit of ours? Surely nothing else, but that as some spying afar off the dust raised by an army, do thereupon forsake their tents for fear; so the vain shadow of future danger casts us down into the pit of desperation....

The horrors of superstition and of witch hunts I sincerely hope may lead us to try to avoid the errors of the past and approach that time which, as E. M. Forster has his character say at the end of *The Machine Stops*, "Humanity has learned its lesson."

NUNC DIMITIS

From Baxter's *The Certainty of the World of Spirits* (1691) an encouraging story for the modern world in which there is no such certainty. Mr. Samuel Clarke used to tell this story which he had from the hero of it himself, a

Mr. White of Dorchester, assessor to the Westminster Assembly at Lambeth in the seventeenth century. Confronted with The Devil himself, Mr. White retained what we now could call his cool:

> The Devil, in a light night, stood by his bedside: he looked a while whether he would say or do anything, and then said, "If thou hast nothing else to do, I have": and so he turned himself to sleep.

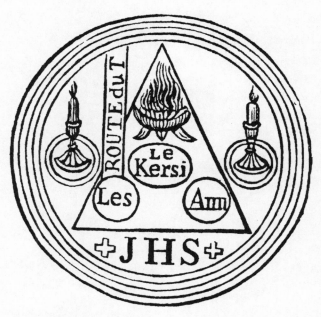

The *Kersi* (magician) stands in a circle before burning offerings (willow-wood charcoal, brandy, camphor, incense) with two assistants also in circles and the "route of the T" will lead him to Satanic treasure. This is the triangle of the pacts in *Le Dragon rouge* (1822).

Index